MW01064085

"MY SON- THE ENGINEER"

...MOM

Eugene V. Dotter

B.S., M.S., Ph. D., Litt. D.

with special thanks to
FREDERICK JACOB BRIGGS
missionary with Oriental Missionary Society,
JAPAN, CHINA, KOREA

Any money received for this book
will be given to missionary endeavors.

Bloomington, IN

Milton Keynes, UK

AuthorHouse™
1663 Liberty Drive, Suite 200
Bloomington, IN 47403
www.authorhouse.com
Phone: 1-800-839-8640

AuthorHouse™ UK Ltd.
500 Avebury Boulevard
Central Milton Keynes, MK9 2BE
www.authorhouse.co.uk
Phone: 08001974150

First published by AuthorHouse 11/16/2006

ISBN: 978-1-4259-4109-3 (sc)
ISBN: 978-1-4259-4108-6 (hc)

Library of Congress Control Number: 2006905825

Printed in the United States of America
Bloomington, Indiana

This book is printed on acid-free paper.

Additional copies of this book are available by mail:

Eugene V. Dotter
2801 Turban Court
Fort Myers, FL 33908
(239) 454-3921

This is a well-executed
life story of an engineer
telling how his secular
experiences were combined
with his spiritual journey
by the Lord Jesus Christ

The Sermon on the Mount was like a guiding light that illuminated Gene's pathway. He understood in general that Jesus Christ is the Light of the World, but here we find some particulars enunciated by Christ in the book of Matthew:

Be generous
Avoid hypocrisy
Show meekness
Seek righteousness
Be merciful
Act as a peacemaker
Rejoice always
Judge not others

Do not commit adultery
Love your enemy
Help the poor
Pray in your closet
Fast when instructed
Serve God
Take no thought of
what is not eternal

Gene's mother always
introduced him as
"My son, the engineer."
It did not matter if he was
a brilliant engineer or not.
Her introduction came from
a heart filled with a mother's love.

ACKNOWLEDGMENTS

This book is gratefully dedicated to

my wonderful mother, Katherine Wiereshausen Dotter,

and to

my dear wife, Elizabeth Wood Dotter,

who has been a true helpmeet and inspiration

during our fifty-five years of life together

and to

my friend, Mildred Harrod Smith,

who has had a true Christian testimony

and has been a great blessing to the Dotters.

Table of Contents

PREFACE

It seems unbelievable that I have reached this point in my life. As a young man, it appeared to be an impossible dream that I would ever be eighty years of age during the year 2000. Yet God has allowed me to experience a full spectrum of secular opportunities as well as spiritual blessings as His servant. At the times of these experiences I wondered if I had really deserved His blessing, but I always felt that I had done my best.

In the forty-seventh chapter of Genesis it tells of Joseph's relationship with Pharaoh in Egypt. The famine had affected Canaan as well as Egypt but Joseph had stored food in Egypt for the people. So he requested that his father, Jacob, and his brothers and their flocks and their herds and all that they possessed come to live in Egypt during the famine. When they arrived, Joseph brought in his father Jacob and set them before Pharaoh; and Jacob blessed Pharaoh. Then Pharaoh said to Jacob, "How old are you?" And Jacob said to Pharaoh, "The days of the years of my pilgrimage are one hundred and thirty years, few and evil have been the days of the years of my life, and they have not attained to the days of the years of the life of my fathers in the days of their pilgrimage." So Jacob blessed Pharaoh and went out from before Pharaoh.

No doubt all of us feel that there have been times when we have acted unwisely. We wish that we could have time to do it over again. But the days, weeks, months, years slip by so rapidly and we do not go back. In fact, we can never go back to the same circumstances--what is done, is done. Balak, king of the Moabites, was fearful that the children of Israel would overrun his land. He sent for Balaam to come at once to curse this people. He promised Balaam much honor and riches. Balaam prayed about this matter and God answered, "You shall not go with them; you shall not curse the people for they are blessed." Nevertheless, eventually Balaam did saddle his donkey and go with the princes of Moab. On the way the angel of the Lord caused Balaam to see that he had been wrong. So Balaam offered to go back. But--the angel of the Lord did not allow Balaam to return. He had to go onward, and do what God wanted him to do. We must persevere, in spite of mistakes made.

After Hurricane Andrew did much damage in Homestead, Florida, a Christian organization called "MASTERSERVE" came to rebuild the destroyed churches and homes. Their motto was, "SERVING GOD, HELPING MAN," which motto should represent the desire of all Christians, particularly those of us in the general field of the design and construction of buildings. As a consulting engineer for architects, I was able to witness for Christ while offering technical expertise. Even when monetary remuneration is not given, we can rest in knowing that God sees and understands our efforts.

It is impossible to recollect all the events of a lifetime. Even many memories of good friends and associates have faded; however, some experiences are still clear and my remembrances may be helpful to others. They have been to me as I continue this journey through life. So I write this book to satisfy my acquaintances and to be an inspiration and blessing to others.

I. PART ONE

Formative years, 1920-1941

1. BACK GROUND

If a person were to stand on the eastern shore of the Hudson River, somewhere about the midpoint of Manhattan borough of New York City, and look across the river to the west, he would see the Palisades along the eastern shore of New Jersey.

In the year of 1920, that was about all most of the people of New York City knew of New Jersey. That forbidden hill of stone represented the "wild west" to them. But to the people of New Jersey it was an entirely different matter.

Along the top of the Palisades was a continuous stretch of city life starting from Jersey City down on the New York Bay and proceeding northward through Hoboken, Union City, Weehawken, West New York, Guttenberg, North Bergen, Fairview, Cliffside Park, Edgewater, and Fort Lee. And a person standing on the Palisades in Guttenberg, where Gene was born on September 25, 1920, could see the entire length of Manhattan Borough of New York City. From the Statue of Liberty at the south end in New York Bay to the George Washington Bridge across the Hudson River at the north end was about twenty miles of continuously changing skyline.

What a beautiful sight with its breathtaking expanse of lofty skyscrapers such as the Chrysler Building and the Empire State Building as well as thousands of additional and impressive buildings.

The Hudson River was about a mile wide at this point so it could accommodate the docking of ocean-going vessels of truly majestic size and appearance, such as the Queen Elizabeth from England, the Normandie from France, and the hundreds of others from all parts of the world. Each day there was a constant stream of industrial ships which carried fruit, fuel, and other supplies. There were ferry boats, pleasure craft, tugboats, and every kind that one could imagine.

But if the scene by day was inspirational to all--and especially to architects and engineers--the scene at night was even more beautiful with the millions of lights from the windows of buildings and on the streets and from vehicles scurrying in endless profusion. If a person desired a closer look at this awesome sight, he could go to the ferryboat at Forty-second Street in Union City and pay four cents for a ride across to Forty-second Street in New York City or pay six cents to go across to the southern tip of Manhattan at Battery Park. Just a short walk from the ferry slip was Times Square and the glitter of Broadway theatres, or at the southern end the financial section surrounding Wall Street.

All this beauty was free to be observed by the residents of Guttenberg. All that was necessary in this town, four blocks wide by ten blocks long, was to walk to the Palisades and stand in the garbage dump where the primary amusement of the children was to throw rocks at the rats feasting on the refuse. This area also provided an access down the steep slopes and cliffs to the Hudson River. The dock laborers could be observed wending their way down the tortuous trails for an exhausting day of shoveling coal or linseed.

During the summer young boys ran down the same trails to the road where they gleefully slipped out of their clothes and plunged into the river without benefit of bathing suits. Many times they had to push aside a dead rat or even human excrement in order to get out to the rotting hulks of tugboats or barges. In fact, often a dive into the water meant coming to the surface with coal dust slime streaming from hair and face. The truth was that the Hudson River was badly polluted. Man had created a beautiful panorama of inspiring buildings, roads, and bridges but had destroyed the environment in doing so; in fact, even in New York City where a person could ride the elevated trains and subways all day and all over New York City for only five cents, the elevated trains crossed above streets in ghettos where crime and prostitution flourished.

But there were nobler sights to be observed. Every two years the U. S. Navy anchored in the Hudson River. Stretched out from the George

Washington Bridge down to New York Bay was a continuous line of battleships, aircraft carriers, cruisers, destroyers, and numerous support ships. It was possible to visit some of these ships without charge. Gene's favorite was the aircraft carrier, "SARATOGA' which still remains a hallowed vessel in the history of the U. S. Navy.

New York City attracted many visits of dignitaries from foreign lands and famous people such as Charles A. Lindberg who was the first man to fly solo across the Atlantic Ocean. But the most memorable sight was to see the Graf Zeppelin fly majestically above the Hudson River and land a short distance inland at Lakehurst, New Jersey, after crossing the Atlantic Ocean. Several years later, the Hindenburg did the same thing. You can imagine the horror that was experienced when the Hindenburg exploded into a huge ball of fire as it was landing. All the passengers and crew members perished. Also many of the ground crew under the descending zeppelin could not escape the huge burning monster that fell upon them in a matter of seconds. This terrible accident probably had much to do with the decision of the government to cease using these lighter-than-air dirigibles in the armed forces. Although it must be pointed out that one of the U. S. dirigibles, the SHENANDOAH, had crashed during a violent storm. The gas used to inflate the craft was susceptible to explosion from lightning strikes.

Many immigrants were arriving from Europe. They entered the U.S. at Ellis Island in New York Bay. Many went to live in the New York City area or the nearby New Jersey area here on the Palisades. Guttenberg received many who were Italian, Hungarian, and Czechoslovakian. These people were uneducated and could obtain only menial laboring jobs.

Guttenberg was known as the slum area and it lived up to its reputation. Robbery and violence were commonplace. It was a difficult place to live. Gene's grandparents were of German and English descent. His father's parents settled in Guttenberg at 25 Polk Street and shortly thereafter his mother's parents located in an adjacent house.

His father was one of five children while his mother was one of eight. Education was not a priority. Children were soon absorbed into the working force. He often heard his mother laughingly remark that she was better educated than his father was. She had finished the fifth grade while he had finished only the fourth. Soon his mother was busy in an embroidery shop while his father left home to work as a deckhand on the barges up and down the Hudson River. He wanted to see more of the country so he eventually worked on the barges on the Allegheny and Ohio Rivers near Pittsburgh, Pennsylvania. In spite of this rough beginning, his father loved to read and he appreciated a formal education for his children. It became one of Gene's goals when his father stopped him on the street to give him some advice. He pointed to some laborers digging a ditch for a sewer line with pick and shovel and told Gene in no uncertain terms that he should never waste his life digging ditches. Get an education, finish high school, go to college if you can. He promised to help Gene but he recognized that his resources were inadequate, so Gene's progress would depend upon his own desire to achieve.

This was good advice but it remained only a subconscious thought buried in Gene's mind. As a boy, he became part of a gang of immigrant kids who were often in trouble. His father and mother had been married at a young age and had begun this new life in an old tenement house in one of the worse sections of Guttenberg. When Gene was born, they had two daughters: Margaret, age 4, and Ruth, age 2.

2. MY SON--THE BOY

Gene's father was ambitious. He wished to better himself and his family. In spite of his poor education, he was an intelligent thinker. And he was a hard worker. So, at the same time that he was the janitor of a rather dilapidated apartment house, he worked as an automobile mechanic, bus driver, taxi driver, etc. He probably loved his children but subscribed to the admonition, "Spare the rod, and spoil the child."

An example demonstrating this occurred when Gene was about two years old. Mr. Dotter had bought his prize possession, a pocket watch probably costing the fabulous sum of fifty cents. Gene was intrigued by this ticking object. He carefully set the watch on top of a low wall and dropped down on the watch the largest rock he could lift. He gleefully told his sister that he had found out where that ticking noise came from. But he was not so gleeful when his father saw the smashed watch. Retribution was swift and painful.

Another time when Gene was about four years old he and his mother went to eat dinner at Aunt Hannah's house. He was sort of bored with life in general, without any other children around. One of Aunt Hannah's friends, Caroline, thought that he was so handsome that she bent down and gave him a big kiss. Unfortunately, Gene was not the kissing type and he emitted a loud scream and ran away from her. She apologized profusely but he kept running around the room, crying loudly. Finally his mother stopped him but promised that his father would hear about this. Sure enough, his father was informed of his behavior. "The board of education was applied to the seat of knowledge" or something to that effect. Actually, it was not a board but a big, heavy hand that was applied to his "darling" boy.

Gene always looked like a little angel. Most people were fooled by his pretty, innocent face; however, in his mind and heart, he was always considering how he could get into some mischief without getting caught and punished. As the Holy Bible points out, we were born in sin, and Gene was a good example. But, already, his life was being shaped by his

Grandmother Wiereshausen

Grandfather Wiereshausen

Gene

young companions. Even at the age of five, these kids roamed on the streets with no supervision. All the families were very poor, although the fathers usually were hard working men. They were absent from home all day. In the evening, they ate and drank heavily, then fell asleep. No time for father to associate and give good counsel. As Proverbs 1:8 says, "My son, hear the instruction of thy father, and forsake not the law of thy mother." Unfortunately, the fathers were asleep or drinking at the saloon, and there were plenty of saloons to attract thirsty men!

Life slipped by in those early years without any good guidance from adults. Just get out of the apartment and roam the streets and tenement houses without yards or playgrounds. When a child feels like going to the bathroom, which seemed like a long way off, it could be taken care of in a field wedged between two old apartment houses. Gene's problem was that he came home with his pants on backwards. That may have contributed to his discomfort with his private parts. In any event, his father felt that it was a problem to be solved by a Rabbi and circumcision. For quite a few years, Gene thought of himself as a Jewish boy.

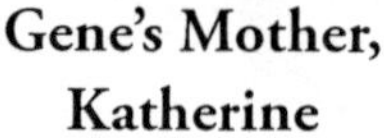

Gene's Mother, Katherine

Gene's Father, Bertram

Gene's first real remembrance of girls was not his sisters but a girl in the kindergarten. She was the homeliest girl in the class--and she adored Gene. Whenever she saw her Prince Charming, she would make a beeline for him. When he saw this girl with her missing teeth, big nose, and stringy black hair, he would shout, "Here comes Jenny Gavechi," and run as fast as he could (like a football player making an end run) and head for the other side of the room. He would leave this admirer standing in adoration with wide eyes, saying, "Come back, come back. I only want to kiss you!"

Family

3. MY SON--THE STUDENT

Grade School

At the ripe old age of five years, Gene entered Guttenberg Grade School No. 1. Actually it was the only school in the town but it provided a good education--to those who wanted it. The others left school after a few years, or put up with the inconvenience. Gene was one of the latter, but fortunately he was a quick learner and managed to get passing grades. Run home from school, say hello to Mom, then out on the street. The street was a rough place with many fights and minor thefts. The news stands were the easy source of a few coins that had been left by people picking up the newspaper. Quite often Gene felt hungry so he begged for food, using the bakery stores as his target. The procedure was to look as pathetic as possible and ask plaintively of the store owner, "Do you have any staleys?" The women could not resist this poor little boy and always gave him something to eat. One day a sales person had no stale items so she gave him a whole lemon meringue pie that really was not stale. He was almost overcome by her generosity but he managed to grab the pie and dash out the door. He hurried a block or so away, sat on the street curb, and ate the whole pie himself. No fork or spoon, of course!

He liked to watch others get into fights. Especially his companion, "Shorty," a little Italian kid who tried to beat up every boy that crossed his path. This excited Gene and he craved action. One time he participated in a minor theft where he and another boy would jump on a boy delivering newspapers, knock him down, and run away with the money that he had collected. The two culprits had not estimated their target's size and they were knocked down and forced to run for their lives.

The idol of Gene was a professional boxer, James J. Braddock, who lived nearby. Gene was introduced to Braddock by Mr. Dotter, who had become acquainted with him when providing taxi service. He was, according to Mr. Dotter, "a big, dumb Irishman who would soon be in a fog from beatings in the ring." Braddock picked Gene up by his arms and held him high in the air while asserting that this good-looking kid would make a great fighter some day like he was! Most people thought that he was batty already, but he fooled them. The Heavy Weight Boxing Champion of the World at that time was Max Baer who was a good fighter but a real clown. He was fighting a series of contenders for the title. One of these has-beens dropped out of the match only a few weeks before fight time. The fight promoter frantically sought a decent substitute. And he decided to use James J. Braddock, feeling that he was no real threat to Max Baer. During the fight Max Baer thought Braddock was a stumblebum who would fall down near the end of the fight. So he clowned around, talking to people at the ringside while Braddock peppered him with lefts and rights. Unfortunately for Baer, James J. did not know when to fall down and the referee awarded the decision to the contender. He was the new Champion of the World but lasted only a year or so. He had to face a great fighter, Joe Louis, who knocked him silly in a few rounds.

Another friend of Gene was "Booby" who often went down to the 5-and-10-cent store with Gene to steal any items that they could slip into their pockets. Then they would go to the U. S. Highway No. 1 where they would get a thrilling ride for four or five miles at a high speed by sitting on the back bumper of a car or hanging on the back of the interstate busses that zipped along this important highway. The traffic signal lights situated one or two miles apart gave Gene the perfect opportunity to slip off his vehicle and use another going in the opposite direction. Booby often was left behind. He was a big, lumbering boy who lived with his uncle at the only horse stable in Hudson County. Booby was actually a kindhearted kid but, unfortunately, with not much in the "upper story."

At this time Gene had another source of amusement. Any boy standing on the Palisades and observing the splendor of New York City with its tremendous accumulation of buildings and ocean-going vessels, would desire to go there and view this at close range. So he would leave in the morning (playing "hooky" from school), hang on the back of a trolley car going to the ferry, slip on the boat unobserved, walk across Manhattan on Forty-second Street, descend to the subway, and duck under the turnstile. Then he had the luxury of riding the subway train, which often became an elevated train, up north to the Bronx Zoo or down south to Coney Island, a distance of over twenty miles. Some days, back and forth for several times. Steal some fruit when hungry, then back home by late afternoon.

Some of Gene's escapades were financed by stealing coins from his father. At night, when all were sound asleep, he would slip out to the kitchen in the dark and very, very quietly extract some coins and some cigarettes from his father's clothes which were hanging from a nail on the wall of the kitchen. One night, to his surprise (and delight), he took out a loaded revolver and began to play "cops and robbers" or "cowboys and Indians." It is a wonder that he did not kill himself with that lethal weapon. The next day, he wanted to find out why his father had this handgun but he was smart enough to know that any reference by him to the gun would lead to his being asked how he had any knowledge of the gun. Later he found out the reason. It seemed that his father had started his own taxi business. To obtain the necessary capital to purchase three taxis and the necessary supplies he had invited three men to become his partners in this endeavor. They were: a brother-in-law, Fred; another brother-in-law, George; and the boxer, James J. Braddock. Each contributed one thousand dollars. George and James J. looked at this as a financial investment, but Fred become more involved. He was a tough, mean, troublemaker who hung out with the hoodlums of Hudson County. One day, he demanded more of the income than his rightful share. When refused, he knocked Bertram (Gene's father) to the floor and threatened to kill him. Bert had one of his friends challenge Fred and beat him to a bloody mess. He disappeared from Hudson County for a year or so, but Bert purchased the revolver for self defense. Fortunately for him, Fred had gone to New York City and joined a gang of robbers. But he tried his strong-arm tactics too often and one day the police pulled his dead body from the Hudson River.

It was not that Gene hated school; in fact, he thought that it was fun. But he felt that he had better things to do. He paid little attention to what was going on in the classroom. This led one of his teachers to blurt out in front of the class, "Gene Dotter, you are the laziest, most stupid individual in this class. You will never amount to anything worthwhile." This was the feeling of some of the other teachers, too, They criticized him in sarcastic tones or just ignored him. What they did not know was that Gene had very poor eyesight and never was able to see the writing on the blackboard. Even playing games like basketball in the school gymnasium was difficult. He played more by instinct that sight. His parents never realized this so he never had eye glasses and had to depend on his buddies to keep him informed on important things like where the ball was. Surprisingly, he was quite good in sports--playing baseball, basketball, football, etc. Sometimes he was in trouble for, example, being hit in the chest with the baseball before he saw it coming.

But Gene also tried some of the more legitimate amusements. One of his friends told him about the Boy Scouts of America. He was always willing to try anything once. His mother thought that this would be a good thing to keep him out of trouble. She scraped together enough money to buy part of a uniform. Unfortunately, Gene was not old enough to join the Boy Scouts. When he appeared at the school building one evening where the meetings were held, he was told that he was allowed to join only the Cub Scouts. It was all right with Gene but not with the other boys. He was a troublemaker and especially with these "little kids." So before the meeting was over, he had slipped out and gone home. He never returned.

Gene, the Boy Scout

One place in Guttenberg to be avoided was 70th Street. It was particularly dilapidated--a collection of saloons, small shops, and small houses crammed together like the homes left behind in Europe by these immigrants. One place in particular was the center of criminal activity. It was the bowling alley where tough young men met at night. Here, after a day of manual work, they could play a few games; drink some beer, whiskey, etc.; get into a fight; and pick up a prostitute for some sexual activity. There was constant activity here and it appealed to Gene. He would head for this place after supper after telling his mother that he could earn a little money setting up pins for bowling. It was necessary to be very cautious though, for the kids living on 70th Street regarded this as their territory, and they fought to hold it. If he was setting up pins and a gang of them approached, he would quickly allow them to take over and he would fade into the background. He could recognize them by their belligerent attitude and dirty, ragged appearance.

Often he headed for 71st Street where the boys had more discipline. They could play some ball games under the streetlights or some running games. Gene liked the running games best as he did not have to be able to see well. The rules were that one group of boys were allowed five minutes to disappear. They could run within a ten-block-square area. They could hide on roofs, in trees or backyards, etc., but not in buildings. Some nights, kids ran for one or two hours with hardly ever a rest. Actually, this was good exercise and training for later life--if they did not fall off a roof and break a leg.

A very traumatic experience entered Gene's life during this period of his life. In 1928, the Great Depression occurred. Many people lost heart when they realized that all of their worldly possessions had disappeared. They could not face the future so they committed suicide. Gene's father had a fair-sized taxi service and an interest in a large garage for car repair and storage. In a short time, he was wiped out completely. He became a bitter, discouraged man, and it was felt keenly by his wife and children. At age eight, in the third grade, it meant little to Gene. His sisters were confused by the change in lifestyle but at ages ten and twelve they really did not comprehend fully what had happened. But Gene's mother, Katherine, was unable to stand the abject poverty and her husband's constant vituperation. She finally had enough so one night she packed her few belongings and slipped away. It seemed so desolate without Mom so the three children pled with their Pa to find Ma and bring her home. He had no idea where she was so, for several days, there was no success. Then one of the aunts told him that Kate had a job in a bakery over on Park Avenue. The next day Pa took the three children and visited several bakery shops. The third was a winner. There was Ma resplendent in a clean, white uniform selling baked goods. She was enjoying her new freedom so it took some persuasion to convince her to return. She was finally convinced that she should return home--more for the children's sake than anything else.

Then another calamity descended on the family. Gene's sister, Margaret, age 12, began to experience a problem with her heart. The doctor did not seem to understand the extent of her sickness. Gene's parent were beside themselves, feeling absolutely frustrated with their inability to handle the deteriorating situation. No funds for medical treatments were available; in fact, day after day, dinner was a bowl of soup and one slice of bread. Holes in their clothing were carefully replaced with patches of any cloth available. Shoes worn out were repaired with stiff cardboard inside the shoe until the luxury of a rubber sole could be glued to the bottom. Gene was rarely at home, usually on the street. So he did not notice that Margaret's condition worsened each month. She was a good patient and never complained to her mother. At first she carefully walked around the small apartment but then found it necessary to remain in bed night and day. They were without a nurse so her parents did their best to satisfy her needs. Finally, after several years, Margaret died. Her Aunt Hannah had told her about the necessity of knowing Jesus as her Savior. Margaret made this decision and Jesus was very real to her. It helped her through the long hours of pain and suffering. When at last she knew that it was time to go, she assured her parents that she was ready; and she passed away with a wonderful glow on her face and singing softly some of the hymns that she had just learned. She whispered to her mother, "Don't worry about me, Jesus is here to take me to heaven."

Grade School Graduation

Gene graduated from Guttenberg Public School No. 1 at the early age of twelve years. He had been "double-promoted" twice because the classes were too large. It never bothered him until later in life when he often said, "I never knew much about South America because it was studied in a class that I skipped." He was a disappointment to some because his two sisters had graduated from this school before him with honors. But at least one person had faith in him. The principal, Mrs. Anna L. Kline, was an elderly woman with much experience. She sent a beautiful note to Gene's mother saying that Gene had great promise for the future and someday he would utilize his latent ability and she would be proud of him. Later, when Gene graduated from college. Mrs. Kline wrote another note to his mother. She said that she was proud of him and that he would go on to excel in life.

High School

Guttenberg did not have a high school. Their students attended Hoboken High School about five miles away. Transportation was provided by Guttenberg's issuing to each student free tickets for the trolley. Also they paid a fee to Hoboken for each student. It always surprised Gene that Guttenberg did this. The adjacent township, West New York, had a beautiful high school only one mile away. He decided that West New York would not allow this--probably did not want the riffraff from Guttenberg to soil their new high school.

In any event, it did not make much difference to Gene. He resumed his carefree life. Poverty did not bother him--everybody he knew was poor. And he continued to steal whatever he could eat or squander on himself. Hoboken was a tough place with many rough kids and many street fights. Gene made friends with this undesirable element. One reason for his acceptance was that he learned quickly in class and did not mind helping his buddies with the answers to the questions on the exams. One day, in the History class, the teacher gave a test with fifty true and false statements. Gene had three roughnecks sitting in front of him in his row. The next day the teacher announced the results by giving the name and number correct, row by row around the room. The numbers ranged from 25 to 35. But in Gene's row, the marks were 43, 44, 45, and 47 with Gene as the highest in the class. The teacher was amazed but the students thought it was funny and burst into loud laughter.

Gene muddled his way through the freshman year. Quite often he was absent from class having "more important things to do." But his life was about to change drastically. First, an event took place in a Geometry class during his sophomore year. While lounging in his seat, dreaming of what he would do that afternoon and evening, he suddenly was jolted back to life when he heard his name shouted out by the woman teacher. Vaguely he surmised that she wanted him to come to the blackboard. He thought, "What does this ____ want from me?" Then he heard her say, "Dotter, recite the entire Theorem No. 1 to the class!" Now he was in a quandary. He had not done any homework and he had no idea what a theorem was. But Gene was adept at finding an excuse for his behavior when confronted by the impossible. So he quickly put his most angelic smile on his face and said, "Mrs. Hartman, I really am unable to do that. You will have to ask some other student. You see, I have very poor eyesight and I cannot see anything on the blackboard." Mrs. Hartman was a middle-aged, tough cookie. She said, "Don't try to kid me, get to work!" Gene replied, "No, it is the truth. Just ask all the students in the class." And the entire class rose and defended him. She grudgingly gave in and asked another student to proceed. But she glared at Gene and said, "I want to see you after the class."

She was not to be deterred. After the class, they went down to see the principal of the high school. She told the principal, "This is absurd. Send a note home to his parents that this boy needs eyeglasses. I want him to be able to see normally when he comes to the next Geometry class." Gene really had poor vision. The optician stated that he was on the border of being classified as blind. Somehow Gene was given the necessary eyeglasses and he was ready for Mrs. Hartman when he attended the next Geometry class.

This was a turning point in his life, but an even greater change occurred in his life a few months later. Two of his older cousins, George and Raymond, attended a Sunday school class at the Assembly of God church about two miles away. His grandmother had talked them into going but could not interest Gene. Once in a while Gene did go with them. Then one day they told him that they were going to the Sunday evening service. He decided to tag along, especially because he could get a sandwich and ice cream at their house after church. To his surprise, his two cousins responded to the invitation and went forward to the altar.

Gene wondered what his response should be. Then he decided that he should follow them and see what this was all about. He made no real confession of faith and mimicked the testimonies of his two cousins. But somehow this encounter with Christ had penetrated deeper into his heart than he realized. For the next three years Gene gave halfhearted attention to the church; in fact, he was often playing football or some other sport on Sunday morning.

But the Holy Spirit convicted him about his personal life. He was an inveterate thief so that had to be changed. Also, he realized that his life was not pleasing to God. It was a difficult decision--he had no Christian in his family to guide him at that time. He hardly ever read the Bible but somehow be became convinced that wasting his life was a sin and an affront to God. After all, God had created him and deserved a better use of it by Gene. No more stealing or lying. Speak the truth!

The pastor of the church, Rev. Jacob Kistler, realized that Gene needed some training to solidify his Christian beliefs. The summer vacation between his sophomore and junior years at the high school was at hand. He arranged for Gene to work on the grounds at the Maranatha Bible Retreat Center in Green Lane, Pennsylvania. It was an excellent move, for Gene enjoyed the two months of July and August, drinking in the beauty of the country setting, eating three good meals every day, and listening to great preaching in the auditorium every evening. Also, he profited by his association with his peers, Christian young men and women. He slept in a "pup" tent, on a blanket on the grass. It was very small so he was surprised one day when Rev. Kistler came to the campgrounds with a middle-aged man and asked if this man, Brother Brusoe, could stay with Gene in the tent for one week. Gene wondered how he could get along with this "old guy" but he agreed. The night went by with no untoward incidents. There was no light available. Early in the morning as the sun began to rise over the horizon, he felt a stir in the tent. When he shook the sleep from his eyes, he found Brother Brusoe praying on his knees in the grass. When it was light enough, Brother Brusoe began to read his Bible and continued until the afternoon preaching service. For the next week, the schedule for

Brother Brusoe was the same: prayer and reading the Bible, afternoon preaching service, prayer and reading the Bible, evening preaching service, prayer, then into the tent for sleep.

One day Gene asked him why he did not eat. His reply has remained with Gene ever since. He said, "For two reasons. First, I have no money and, second, I came here to become better acquainted with God and the Lord Jesus Christ, and I mean to spend every possible moment in prayer and meditation." Later, Gene asked him quietly why he had waited so long in life before seeking God so seriously. He told Gene that he had spent over forty years in a ghetto in New York City. He had led a terrible life and had spent the last fifteen or more years as a gangster--in robbery, assault, even murder. One day he found a dirty, old Bible that someone had thrown away. He read some of it and realized his lost condition. When the opportunity came, he slipped into a small church where he found the pastor "waiting for him." He repented of his sins, accepted Jesus Christ as his Saviour, and determined to live for Christ. He left the ghetto and his criminal companions and went to New Jersey to a place where he would never be recognized. Now, only a few months later, he spent all of his time saturating his mind with the things of God. Brother Brusoe spent the rest of his life as an associate pastor of the Assembly of God church in North Bergen, New Jersey, visiting people in need physically and spiritually. Several years later he was a help to Gene's mother. She accepted the Lord but she was a very weak Christian. She would always bow to her husband's demands even though she understood that he hated any Christian beliefs. Brother Brusoe would quietly pray with her and give her sound Christian advice.

Gene's life changed drastically at Hoboken High School. He still enjoyed life and loved to see a fight between the rougher element of the student body, but he knew that he would not develop as a Christian if he did not change the type of friends that he associated with. So gradually they disappeared and he substituted more time for his studies. Even his best friend, Roy Leenig, who lived near him in Guttenberg noticed the change. Once in exasperation he blurted out, "Gene, what has happened to you? You seem so different and you are always whistling songs that I have never heard!" Unfortunately, Roy would not wait for the answer. His life was absorbed in basketball at West New York High School. He became a member of the varsity squad and made friends in the basketball crowd. Actually, after high school, he went to Columbia (University) Preparatory School where he was chosen as a member of the National Prep School basketball team. Then he became assistant basketball coach at St. Peter's High School (Catholic), later coach at St. Peter's, and then coach of the basketball team at Holy Cross University, a Catholic school in northeast U.S.A. Gene was dropped like a "hot potato," especially after Roy found out that Gene had tried out for the Hoboken High School basketball team and had been cut at an early stage. He did not know that Gene had broken his eyeglasses and had tried to play without them. The coach started two teams of five with Gene on one of them. Soon, in the game, the ball came to Gene who took a short dribble and scored a basket for two points. The coach wasn't very pleased because Gene had made a basket for the opposing team!

Hoboken High School had few sports facilities. It could not field a track, football, baseball, swimming, or wrestling team. Gene would have tried out for all the teams, even football, although he only weighed about 120 pounds. In a way, it was for the best. He could spend more time with academic pursuits. And Gene advanced through the last two years, going from a dropout (average at F) to having the highest average grade in all the Mathematics studies and the Science studies.

Having achieved top place in these two academic fields brought him to the attention of the principal of Hoboken High School, Mr. Harry Stover. Mr. Stover was not liked by the tough student body, but he always tried to help every student to best achieve his potential in life. One day Gene was called to his office. He asked him if he had considered going to college. Gene had never given it any thought. All he could consider was his family life in poverty in Guttenberg. It was obvious that he would be nonplussed by the question and quickly answered negatively. But Mr. Stover would not be deterred. He inquired about

Gene's plans for the future. The answer again was negative. Gene had never really given it a thought. Finances were discussed with Mr. Stover assuring Gene that a college like Columbia University in New York City would accept Gene as a student and provide at least a partial academic scholarship. The conversation opened a new train of thought in Gene's mind. No one had ever broached the idea of going to college but certainly a prestigious place like Columbia University could not even be a possibility. Gene had been working in a local butcher shop on Saturdays where the owner had promised him a full-time job when he graduated from high school. The meat market seemed the logical place for him, although he knew that the proprietor of the shop was a conniver who had to be watched carefully.

Then Mr. Stover mentioned something that would change Gene's life forever. He told Gene that an examination would be given to all worthy students who could compete for four academic scholarships given by two engineering schools. Three partial scholarships would go to the top three students and one full scholarship to the fourth student. The first school was Stevens Institute of Technology in Hoboken, a school rated highly in the nation and desired by all students interested in the engineering field, a real prize attracting many applicants. The other school was the Newark College of Engineering in Newark, New Jersey. This was a school funded by the state of New Jersey and shortly thereafter received large grants of money and was renamed the New Jersey Institute of Technology.

Gene was excited at the prospect of this competition. Three subjects would be included in the examination--English, Sciences, and Mathematics. He was confident that he could make an excellent showing so he assured Mr. Stover that he would compete. He would give extra attention to these subjects for the next several months. Not only that, he also made some research as to his competition. He found that the most formidable were three classmates: James Forgiets, Louis Cassini, and Edward Israel. They were very bright students and were always seen together exchanging ideas and information. It would be difficult but he felt confident that he would overcome all competition.

The day of the examination arrived. The air was charged with electricity and the tension showed on the faces of all the competitors. None of his teachers, friends, or family had even discussed the examination with him. Gene was on his own! He knew that he was equal to the task so he plunged into the lengthy examination, completed it in good time, and submitted it, feeling that he had done his best and excelled.

Several days later the results were announced. Gene was shocked to see that he was only fourth--behind Forgiets, Cassini, and Israel. It could not be possible! He mulled it over for a day, than decided to approach the teachers for information. Perhaps a mistake had been made by them. Even though this would be frowned upon by the school, he doggedly went ahead. The Science teacher gladly told him that he had been first in that portion of the examination. The English teacher first gave him a scolding for doing this against school protocol, then she reluctantly told him that he had been first in that portion of the examination. When he approached the Mathematics teacher, Mrs. Houseman, she refused to listen to him and complained about his "insolent attitude." Gene was crushed. Over the past few months he had come to the point where he felt that this examination was the most important thing in his life. He had failed in his quest to enter Stevens Institute of Technology. He could attend the Newark College of Engineering but it seemed to be no consolation to him.

Perhaps it would be wise to interject some further light upon this traumatic event in Gene's life. Forty years later, Gene was a consulting structural engineer with an office in Pittsburgh, Pennsylvania. They had completed the structural design of a large building in New Jersey. As the "Responsible Engineer," Gene was required to bring his design plans to the New Jersey Director of Building Inspection for review and the qualifying signature. To his surprise, the director was Edward Israel, a graduate of Stevens Institute of Technology, and one of the competitors for the scholarships awarded many years before. Gene told the receptionist that he had been a high school classmate of Mr. Israel. She passed the information on and in a few minutes Gene was ushered into Ed Israel's office. Here he was greeted effusively by Israel. With a very apprehensive look on his face, Edward told him the following story.

> I have just returned from several months leave of absence, recuperating from a serious heart attack. It is a coincidence that I returned on the only day that I will ever have the opportunity to speak with you. I want you to know what happened forty years ago when we competed for the scholarships. Please forgive me but I cheated you. The three of us knew that you would be the favorite to win top place. We were certain that we could not match you in English or Sciences. So we decided to cheat in the Mathematics exam. We found out that Mrs. Houseman would compose the exam so we took several review classes with her. She was in her seventies and should have retired long before. To our delight, she allowed us to attend a review class where we three were the only students. Slowly we manipulated her thinking and her lectures until in a few weeks she began to explain to us the problems on the Mathematics exam. We had almost perfect papers--after all, we knew what each problem would be. Our perfect grades in Math gave us the ability to overcome your lead in the other two exams. Gene, I am sorry for what I did.

Without hesitation, Gene assured Ed that he no longer had any bad feelings about the whole affair. He told Ed (a Jew) that he was a Christian and Jesus Christ was his Lord and Saviour; in fact, Gene used this opportunity to explain to Ed that God had control of his life and that it was God's will for Gene to be fourth and to attend the Newark College of Engineering, and eventually establish an office in Pittsburgh where he was blessed by God in his personal life and secular work.

High School Graduation

For the next few months after the exam Gene was depressed. He went to work at the New York Life Insurance Company in New York City. His supervisor was Mr. Ralph Brinkerhoff, a gruff, elderly disciplinarian who constantly berated this young man for his appearance, his work, his talk, etc. It did not bother Gene for he was discouraged with life in general anyway. Soon Gene was faced with the decision that he had to make. To accept the academic scholarship to Newark College of Engineering or to stay at the insurance company and make this his life's work. It was not an easy decision but Gene decided to attend college. Perhaps, he felt, anything must be better than having the cantankerous Mr. Brinkerhoff around him all day. Really, though, it was Mr. Brinkerhoff who was sorry to see Gene leave.

College

College life had many drawbacks. It was at least twenty miles from Guttenberg to the school. This had to be traveled each day back and forth through city traffic on public transportation. There was no money at home so Gene had to work in the evenings and on Saturdays. He complained that the courses offered merely reviewed high school subjects and were not interesting. He had little understanding of the various fields of engineering. The only sport offered was basketball and it was too sophisticated for Gene who was accustomed to sand lot games and had not played on the team in high school. Doubts began to arise in his mind. Perhaps he had made a mistake when he chose college instead of his job at the life insurance company. He was always hungry and never seemed to have enough time to really accomplish anything. One thing that he missed was the fellowship of the Christian young people at church. He prayed about his decision and it came to him that God told him to at least finish out the freshman year.

In the second semester of his freshman year, Gene felt more at ease with the situation. He learned more about the engineering fields offered at this time (1937). Chemical and electrical engineering were eliminated from consideration. Mechanical and civil engineering remained but Gene could not make a definite choice. Finally, the choice had to be made, and it was civil engineering. He reluctantly notified the civil engineering department of his decision. The department head had to know so that he could schedule the necessary classes and the teachers. He had little knowledge of the size of the class at that time. There were many dropouts after the freshman year. Gene knew this because of a personal incident. A young man of German descent,

Fritz, was attending the North Bergen Assembly of God church. He fell in love with Muriel, a pretty girl about his age. But somehow he thought that Muriel was paying more attention to Gene than to him. Fritz's father enrolled him at N.C.E. in the year of 1937 when Gene was there. During the year Fritz figured that this was a good time to demonstrate his masculine superiority so he suggested a boxing match. Gene surmised that Fritz had more in mind than a friendly bout. Sure enough, Fritz charged ahead with fists flying. Gene managed to hold his own for five minutes or so, then he came to the conclusion that this had to end before one of them (Gene) would get hurt. He noticed that Fritz had a bad habit. He would pause for a few seconds to renew his wind, then hop up and down several times and then charge into the fray again without really looking carefully. Gene watched for Fritz to hop up and down and then Gene struck out with his left fist. Poor Fritz never saw it coming, he ran smack into the left. He stood there just swaying groggily, dizzy from the blow. Gene was happy that Fritz did not fall to the floor; but one thing was certain, Fritz had lost all desire to fight. Gene put his arm around the shoulders of Fritz and explained why Fritz had lost the fight. But Fritz probably did not hear what was said. As the saying goes, he was "out on his feet." Later, Gene told him that he was not serious about Muriel and that Fritz should and could pursue her without competition from Gene. He was happy to hear this.

One day near the end of the freshman year, Gene asked Fritz what field of engineering he would register for. He was surprised when Fritz told him that he would not be back. His father upholstered furniture and he had decided that Fritz should follow in his footsteps without any further formal education. Gene found out that the freshman class of 350 had fallen to 250 in the sophomore year and then to 200 in the junior and senior years. The graduating class of 200 was composed of 25 in civil engineering, 50 in chemical engineering, 50 in electrical engineering, and 75 in mechanical engineering. The largest number of M.E. was probably due to Newark's being known as an industrial community and the prospect of a better future for those graduates. The Depression was still a potent force in the nation.

The president of the college was Allen Cullimore. He had only one arm but he managed to present a very impressive figure to the student body. His words of wisdom at the assembly times, usually twice per month, remained in Gene's mind for many years. The college grew in size greatly under his leadership and achieved a fine reputation among the schools in the metropolitan New York City area, such as Columbia University, New York University, Fordham, etc. Another outstanding administrator was the treasurer, Peter Kerman. He had a sort of father-son relationship with Gene. At one time (junior year) he hired Gene to do some surveying and paid him the magnificent sum of twenty-five dollars. Nevertheless, he told Gene that he owed the school seventy-five dollars when he was about to graduate and that he would not receive his degree of B.S. in C.E. unless he paid before graduation. Gene pled absolute poverty but to no avail. Later, when Mr. Kerman heard from the Civil Engineering Department that Gene was to receive two prestigious awards along with his degree, he realized that it certainly would look bad to the audience at the graduation convocation when this outstanding student was not allowed to be in attendance.

Gene saw an advertisement on a bulletin board at the college sent by the U. S. Department of Agriculture. It stated that the department was accepting applications for summer work. Those who were hired had to appear on July 1 at the town of Newburg in New York State. They were to report with heavy work clothes and, above all, high-top work shoes laced up to just below the knee. The work was to walk in groups of men spread out through the woods of the Catskill Mountains. They were to find all the Dutch elm trees and check them for any evidence of Dutch Elm Tree Disease. They were to climb the tree that looked suspicious because of patches of yellow leaves. The sample would be sent to the headquarters. If it was afflicted with the disease, it would be cut down and burned immediately as the disease was spreading rapidly.

The pay for this "fun" job was good. It attracted many students from colleges all over the East including Gene; however, he did not have high-top work shoes and no money to purchase them. So he asked a friend of his who was in the U. S. Army for a pair of "puttees" used by the soldiers. Puttees were made of heavy cloth about four inches wide and long enough to be wrapped around and around the leg from the ankle up to the knee. Unfortunately, when Gene reported for work, he was refused because the puttees were not acceptable. Again Gene had to plead extreme poverty. Finally he was allowed to work if he would use part of his first week's pay to purchase the regulation type of shoes. He agreed and spent a wonderful two months hiking in the Catskill Mountains. After each day, these young men could eat a lusty supper, then drink a couple of 12-ounce cans of Coca Cola, and eat a quart of ice cream without a stop. Some of these fellows wanted to drive to California and back before beginning the next year at school. They invited Gene to join them but he begged off. He needed all the money he could accumulate for the next year at school and he wanted to spend the remaining week or two at home.

The sophomore year was a great improvement over the freshman year. The subjects were interesting and Gene knew that they would be a valuable part of his professional life. The professors were excellent teachers and also gave personal advice freely. Professor Cummings was the head of the Civil Engineering Department. He was rather quiet but was a good thinker and always well prepared. He taught Highway Design and Soil Mechanics (mostly foundations of buildings). One day he decided that he should give Gene a man-to-man talk. The gist of his conversation was that Gene should give up his religious beliefs--they were old-fashioned and erroneous. To succeed in the field of civil engineering, a person must socialize often and let his inhibitions drop off. Gene told him that the Bible was the Word of God and taught us how to live. It contains the TRUTH and that is what he needed, more than his social standing.

Professor James Robbins taught Surveying and Sanitation. He had a great deal of experience but was handicapped because of a speech impediment. When he began to speak to the class, in a lecture or on a personal basis, he would give four or five sounds like "tuch, tuch, tuch." Everybody thought it was funny although it would have been exceedingly unwise to laugh or say anything about it. His father taught

Surveying at the Massachusetts Institute of Technology and had written an outstanding surveying textbook. No doubt Professor Robbins would have been teaching at M.I.T. if he had not been handicapped with the speech impediment. All the students, including Gene, liked him very much. Although Gene wondered why he was so sarcastic when he referred to his assistant, an instructor, sometimes laughing at him in front of the whole class.

The surveying class in the field was especially interesting to Gene. It was conducted in a large wooded area about ten miles southwest of the school. Professor Robbins knew the area well. He lived near the place and he knew how to get permission for his class to use the open places as well as the woods; in fact, the streams were large enough to afford excellent means of teaching stream gaging, finding the depth, the velocity, and quantity of the water flow. The students had to wear rubber pants reaching from the chest down to enclose their feet. Some of the class would venture too far into the stream. Water would pour over the top of the pants and the person would hurry back to shore in a pool of water--much to the amusement of his fellow students.

Surveying class in the field

Professor William LaLonde taught Structures. He excelled as a teacher but he was also the professional link to the various societies such as the American Society of Civil Engineers. He was quite often in New York City and served on many committees. During the summer he often worked at a large structural consulting office at N.Y.C. He had ties to M.I.T. also, like Professor Robbins, and it was natural that he would follow Professor Cummings as the head of the Civil Engineering Department. He was not as well liked by the students as was Professor Robbins.

It was a new world to Gene. It was during this time that he developed a love for Structural Engineering. It was to be a enduring passion in his life. The thought of actually knowing how to design the supporting structure of a building or a bridge caused him to tremble with desire to get started in this new endeavor. His classes at college were starting him in the right direction but he craved more. About this time he read a small book titled, How to Become a Millionaire.

The central theme of the book was easy to understand and Gene reasoned that his own ideas were similar to those in the book. Of course, he did not aspire to become a millionaire. The church he attended was composed of a group of strict, conservative people who believed the Bible to be God's Word and contained all the directives for a person to lead to a close walk with God. They did not object to each person working hard in his field of endeavor and becoming rich--after all, the Bible said that a person was worthy of his hire; that is, work hard and receive an honest pay for your time. They were careful though to assert that your finances belonged to God and should be used according to the Lord's will. Just as Jesus said to the rich young man, "Sell all that you have, give this to the poor, and follow me." They tried to follow the teaching very closely. Perhaps too strictly, as, for example, when Gene was once walking through the sanctuary whistling a hymn, the senior elder stopped him and said, "Singing, but no whistling!" This did not deter Gene in any fashion in his religious beliefs or in his secular aspirations either. Just be truthful in following God's Word.

The book had advised the reader to carefully choose the type of work that he could give the utmost attention to, read all he could about this field, study the entire subject in school or at home, observe others working in this field, gain experience in all aspects of the actual application, and let nothing interfere with his disciplined efforts. Do not worry about the pay as you are gaining a foothold in the profession--the money will come when you are established. Gene thought that this was excellent advice. He would follow it closely; in fact, he did so but as the years slipped by, he changed these broad concepts to suit his own personal journey through life. One thing that did interfere with what he gleaned from the book was Gene's love of sports. He sought a place on the basketball team but was soon cut from the roster. There were no facilities for football, track, baseball, tennis, or golf. Wrestling or boxing were out of the question because of his light weight and poor eyesight. One day he saw a notice that N.C.E. was having a track meet against the Brooklyn Polytechnic Institute on the next Saturday morning. He arrived late but nobody expected him anyway. One adult was there acting as the coach, Professor George Entwistle, the physics teacher at N.C.E. Gene asked him if he could run. The coach asked him what event he had some experience with. The coach was surprised when Gene told him that he had never run before and that he did not know one distance from another. The coach was a kind old man so he told Gene that the next event was the 880 yards (one-half mile) and he could run in this event if he wanted to. Then he was surprised again when Gene took off his jacket and exchanged his shoes for a pair of sneakers and announced that he was ready to go! Professor Entwistle was not a real coach but he quickly gave Gene some instructions about starting, running twice around the track, and how to pace himself during the race. Gene had no training at all but he managed to stay up with the leader until he reached the last 100 feet, then he could hardly move his legs. He dragged himself over to Professor Entwistle to apologize; but now, to his surprise, the coach said, "Get track shoes and a track uniform--you are on the team! How did you learn to run so well?!" Gene answered, "Playing games with my buddies and running away from the cops!" So began Gene's career on the track team.

Another professor, Norman Tully, was now appointed as coach of the track team. He had been on the track team in his college days so he was able to offer good running instructions to the team. Again Gene was asked about his distance specialty. He thought for a few minutes, then told this new coach, "The 100-yard dash is too fast, the 220-yard run has two good team members, the 440-yard race is over too quick, but I may not be able to last for one mile or two miles. I guess the only thing left is the 880-yard event." Gene participated in four or five track meets. He did pretty well with some firsts, seconds, and thirds. Gene was not pleased with his showing so he decided that somehow he would have to practice if he wanted to win more regularly. He formulated his plan for practice. When he was home for supper, three or four times during the week, he would study from 7 P.M. to 11 P.M., then he would run to Woodcliff Park about one mile away. He was afraid of being mugged so he would run down the middle of the street. He felt that there were no cars on that street at that hour and if some guy tried to jump him, he would see him in time and run away. At the park there were some tennis courts with a high chain-link fence around the group of courts. It appeared that the gravel path around the outside was about 440 yards so it would mean two times around to equal his event, the 880-yard run. After that, he went around once rather slowly, then once around as fast as he could. All this in pitch black darkness. Fortunately, the path was smooth with no holes. Gene often thought that he was lucky that he never broke a leg running in the dark. Then run home one mile away but at least with some streetlights to illuminate the pavement.

The season ended with the college participating in the prestigious Penn Relays in Philadelphia, Pennsylvania. N.C.E. had only one event, the mile relay. This means that N.C.E. had to have four one-quarter-mile runners. The coach decided to use Gene even though he usually ran only the 880-yard event. He placed Gene as the third runner because he knew that all of the other coaches put their worst 440 runner in the third position. There were ten teams in the event. The first two runners for N.C.E. steadily lost ground until N.C.E. was in the last place. Gene was not discouraged because he thought of all the quarter miles he had run in the dark. He figured that it was easier to run in the sunshine than in the darkness. Responding to the cheers of the tremendous crowd of spectators, he steadily gained ground, going from tenth place to the second place as he entered the final straightaway. He gave it all he had as he desperately wanted the coveted first place but to no avail. He passed the baton to the final runner still in second place. This man lost ground until N.C.E. finished in fourth place. Gene was sad about this loss but the coach was ecstatic as he thought that fourth place for N.C.E. among the top teams was a victory for N.C.E.

The junior year at N.C.E. was crammed with activity. This was the time when the students who had survived the first two years of college were given the full schedule of advanced subjects in their professional fields. Gene was exhilarated by the depth of learning in each course. It was difficult to remain abreast of the flow of knowledge but he did his best. He had never tried to represent himself as a straight A student. Instead he considered himself to be a B+ student or, at best an A- student. Some other members of the student body thought otherwise. The student members of the Tau Beta Pi, the honorary fraternity of N.C.E. with branches in every engineering college in the United States, elected Gene as one of the members of this outstanding group of students. It was truly a great honor. He was the only one in the Civil Engineering class to be invited to join Tau Beta Pi.

Even the student chapter of the American Society of Civil Engineers honored him. The teacher who represented the college at the A.S.C.E., and the student members elected him as president of the N.C.E. chapter. Upon graduation later, he joined the A.S.C.E. as a member and years later was honored again as a "life member."

In spite of the heavy demands on his time because of the academic studies, Gene still loved to compete in sports. They were usually intramural basketball and softball; however, his greatest enjoyment was at the track meets. Because of his outstanding exhibition at the Penn Relays the coach had him run in both the 440-yard race and the 880-yard race. And even had Gene run in the two-mile race. Actually he excelled in this long distance event and probably should have competed in this event at every meet. The coach was afraid that three races would have been too taxing on Gene's physical condition; but his early life, even during the Depression, had given him great stamina. As the coach once explained to Gene, "You are physically made to be an excellent runner. God gave you a good height, six feet tall; thin body,about 140 pounds; long, muscular legs, size 30; and a large, strong chest, size 42. And up to this point,

Gene, captain of track team

the Depression and constant participation in running games and sports have kept you in a fit condition for the track team." And Gene could have added, "I love to run. It is pure joy when I let myself go down the back stretch with the finish line ahead. I feel like I have wings."

A highlight in Gene's running career came when the members of the track team elected him captain of the team. He was surprised by this demonstration of approval. There was more than running events at the track meets, such as the pole vault, high jump, broad jump, shot put, and the javelin throw. No doubt the members of the team respected his dedication to the team. He was always present at the meets and offering encouragement to all who participated.

He had heard of a young man who was in the freshman class who had been an outstanding high school runner in the 440-yard and the 880-yard races. Gene talked with him and managed to entice him out to the next track meet. The new runner participated in both events and won both. Gene was happy to have him there. He felt that now N.C.E. could have 1-2 finishers in both events. It did not matter to him who won first place, just so the team received the points. Unfortunately, some personal happenings occurred in the life of the new team member which caused him to drop all sports; in fact, he probably dropped out of college at the end of the freshman year. He may have been recruited by another college with some "inducements."

Gene had an incident like this occur a few months later. The New Jersey College Track Championships took place. The coach entered only a few of the team members. The problem was that Seton Hall had entered at least three of their members in every event. They were known as the "power house" among the U.S.A. national colleges. And rightly so, for they dominated every track meet that they entered. Gene was one of the N.C.E. track men entered. He ran only one event, the 880-yard race. Sure enough, there were three Seton Hall runners among the group at the starting line. The three quickly shot to the front of the race and remained there during the entire race. As the runners reached the final stretch of the track, Gene was in fourth place behind the three Seton Hall runners. They sensed that he could be a formidable challenger so they "boxed" him in; that is, two ran abreast of each other ahead of Gene, and one dropped back with Gene but stayed on his right, thus hemming him in against the inside edge of the track. He could not add speed and spurt forward ahead of the three and he could not pass on the right side because of the presence of the third Seton Hall runner. He was completely frustrated and wanted to charge right into the two runners ahead of him. He knew, however, that he would be disqualified if he touched them. Shortly before the end of the race, the three opponents suddenly speeded up and finished 1-2-3, almost in a tie. Gene finished fourth.

A few minutes after the race he was picking up some track materials when a stranger came over to speak with him. He remarked that he liked the way Gene had run. He asked about his experience and training. Then he was amazed when Gene said that he had no training and had only run for one year-plus at Newark College of Engineering. The man then introduced himself as the head coach at Seton Hall College for track and field events. His next question stunned Gene. He asked if Gene would leave N.C.E. at the end of his junior year, in a few months, and come to Seton Hall. Gene stammered an answer somewhat to the effect that he could not leave as he had an academic scholarship. Also that he was too poor to come to an affluent college like Seton Hall which ranked on the par with the best in the country. The man laughed and said that Gene did not understand. He explained, "We take good care of our recruits!" He quickly added, "What I tell you is absolutely confidential. We will give a sports scholarship to cover room, meals, and tuition. Then a cash stipend of $50 per week which is more than you would earn as an engineer." Gene was beginning to think that this was a very attractive offer. So he asked, "How long would this last." To his surprise, the answer came without hesitation.

"We want you to run for us in the 1948 Olympics. That is about eight years away. Let's say that will be eight years--four years at Seton Hall Prep School and four years at Seton Hall College. You are now about 19 years old so you will be about 27 years old--at your peak performance year. Your personal affairs are your own business. The three fellows that you ran against today are married. They are getting ready for the 1944 Olympics. How does that sound to you? All you have to do is to come to my office and put your name on the dotted line."

That was a different story! Gene had in mind a transfer to Seton Hall but for only two or three years running for this coach before graduating with a B.S. in C.E. This proposition did not seem absolutely honest and the thought of running all day, every day, for eight years for this tough disciplinarian coach was not what he desired. He told the coach, "I'm a Christian. My life is in God's hands. I don't think that God wants me to be running for the next eight years. I'm afraid that I must turn down your kind offer." This startled the coach so he tried a little more persuasion, but the issue had been settled in Gene's mind.

This just about ended Gene's career as a runner. A month or two later he borrowed a pair of ice skates from a friend. He was a poor skater. As he made a wobbly path across the ice on the lake at Woodcliff Park, he fell to the ice and sprained his ankle badly. Later the coach from Seton Hall caught sight of him warming up for a running session and invited him to join his group. When he saw Gene's top speed was only about three-quarters of what he had anticipated, he quickly said good-bye.

The school year at N.C.E. was nearing the end of the junior year. Gene was chosen by Professor Cummings to be an usher at the graduation convocation. He quickly accepted this honor. A few days later he found out that he would have to be dressed in a tuxedo. Gene had never had a tuxedo and was without funds even to rent one. He had one suit. It had been a gift from an uncle when he had graduated from high school. Now it was worn out; in fact, his elbows were showing because the sleeves were worn through. Even the pants had holes at the knees and the typical shiny places in the rear. Gene wondered how he could continue to use this suit through the senior year. He was about to confess to Professor Cummings that he could not serve as usher when he confided to a friend his predicament. The friend was the star of the basketball team, Raymond Hall, a very friendly young man. One evening he borrowed his father's car, went to Gene's home, and took him to his home. He explained to his mother that Gene needed a tuxedo and he was going to lend his to Gene. She pointed out that her son, Ray, was six feet four inches tall while Gene was only six feet. Also Ray weighed about 180 pounds while Gene weighed 140 pounds. Ray did not give up. He suggested that his mother do some quick renovation of the tuxedo. She agreed and shortened the sleeves and the pants about three or four inches each by tucking the ends back and using a few stitches to keep the ends in place. When Gene appeared at the convocation, his white shirt was two or three sizes too large, his coat reached almost to his knees, and both the coat and the pants looked like Gene had just stepped into some large potato packs. Gene felt absolutely stupid but Ray insisted that he looked great.

It had been a good year for Gene, and his grades for all courses were high. One day Professor Robbins asked him if he wanted to do some graduate studies at the Massachusetts Institute of Technology during the summer. The summer school for civil engineering students was near East Machias, Maine--at the northernmost tip of the state. Gene agreed, worked for a few weeks at a summer job, then headed for the school in Maine. It took an overnight trip by bus (with numerous "pit" stops) to get from New York City to East Machias. In the early morning the bus stopped along a narrow two-lane country road and the driver said to Gene that he was to get off. It was in the middle of the woods but the driver assured him that someone would pick him up shortly. Sure enough, a van arrived and took Gene to the school buildings about ten miles into the woods along a dirt road. It was situated on a large lake and, to Gene's inexperienced eye, it was absolutely beautiful. The school term lasted two months and Gene enjoyed every minute of it. Even when Gene went for a walk along the dirt road at the lake. Suddenly he stopped short. Only 25 or 30 feet away at the side of the road was a monster with antlers at least six feet wide. This creature glared at Gene for a minute, then slowly ambled away through the dense woods. Gene was told later that it was a fully grown moose and that he was very fortunate that the moose had not charged him and impaled him on his antlers.

Gene was allowed to study two courses for graduate credit. One was Geodetic Surveying (long-distance transit sighting with theodolite instruments) and the other was Limnology (the study of places for water supply). The courses were exceedingly interesting and useful later, specially the surveying course.

Gene had never seen such wonderful scenes in nature. He often rowed out on the lake and spent some time just watching the sun drop below the horizon. He marveled at the beautiful shades of color in the sky.

He returned to school for the senior year. He determined to take part in every sport that he could and still carry a full schedule of courses. His reputation as the "number one" center fielder for his intramural softball team was established when an opposing player hit a sharp liner between center and right field. It was certainly a home run, when Gene sprinted over and leaped high into the air to catch the ball and prevented a home run. Then without stopping, he threw the ball to first base to catch the man who had been at first base. But the full study schedule kept him from practice times for running at the track meetings, much to his sorrow.

The school year was difficult but Gene knew that he was equal to the task. Graduation was a tangible objective now. He began to speculate on his goal of becoming a consulting structural engineer. He realized that he needed a job in structural engineering so he began to investigate some of the sources to begin the search. One place was a directory published by the American Society of Civil Engineers listing the members and their places of employment. One listing caught his attention. Russell Chew was the head of the steel fabrication design department of the Bethlehem Steel Company in Pittsburgh, Pennsylvania. This was about four hundred miles to the west of Guttenberg and it suited Gene exactly. He had read a joke about the newlyweds that advised them to locate their first home at least 400 miles away from any of their parents. Gene was not a newlywed or even had any desire to be, but he was determined to get away from home. His father was constantly complaining about the government, about church, and just about everything. His father and mother had long arguments that disturbed Gene and he felt that it was imperative that he get away. He contacted Mr. Chew about a job. To his delight, Mr. Chew told him to come out to Pittsburgh after graduation and he could start work immediately. In a way, it was a hard decision to make. He really did not want to leave his mother. The dingy apartment and his father's negative vituperation, however, firmed his resolve and he felt that the Lord was showing him that he should go.

The day of graduation finally arrived. Gene received three invitations for members of the family. His mother and father had first choice, of course--the third was given to his Grandfather Dotter. That evening Gene's father ate his supper as usual and drank a quart of beer. When it was time to leave, he was tired and half drunk. He refused to change his work clothes for a better-looking outfit. It did not bother Gene's mother as she was accustomed to this behavior. As far as Gene was concerned, he just wished it was over with. He was more worried about a car accident with a partially drunk man at the wheel. He prayed that all would go smoothly, and God answered his prayer.

Portrait of Gene for N.C.E. Graduation

By the time the program started and the speeches were finished, Gene's father was asleep. Then the awards were distributed and the degrees given to the graduating class. The first award went to Gene for being part of a select group of students known as the "Honors Option." Later he received the award for being the outstanding Civil Engineer with the best standing academically and in general, such as sports, activities, etc. Then he received an award from the American Society of Civil Engineers for being the Civil Engineering student with the most promise for a successful professional life in engineering. Then the final event of the evening was the distribution of the 200 degrees, and Gene was the recipient of a B.S. in C.E. (Bachelor Science in Civil Engineering with a major field of Structural Engineering). He received many congratulations from both the teachers and his fellow students. To his surprise, his father had a word of congratulation. His father had never commended Gene for anything that he had done. That night he turned to Grandfather Dotter and said, "Gene was the best of all. He got three prizes and that is more than anyone else."

N.C.E. required all graduates to get a portrait so it could be included in the class book. Gene did not like to have his picture taken. His experience was that his fellow students usually laughed and made some humorous remark like the favorite remark of Howard Broadman who would say, "Well shaped head!" But it had to be done. He went to one of the major department stores in Newark. The lady taking the portrait was amused when Gene asked if it would make his friends laugh. She replied, "You are no moving picture star, but you will do."

A young lady had entered Gene's life. She was Muriel, the girl that Gene's friend, Fritz, had fallen in love with. But she had rejected Fritz's advances and he had faded out of her life. The Civil Engineering students had arranged a graduation party at a hotel. He had to take a girl so he asked Muriel to go. To his surprise, she gladly accepted. When they appeared at the party, she was the cynosure of all eyes. She was very attractive and possessed a great personality; in fact, some of his fellow students remarked, "How in the world did a backward guy like you ever find a stunning girl like this?"

It looked as if Gene was going to have some close feminine fellowship in his life. But Gene was not ready for this. He could not handle this type of experience. So a few days later, he said good-bye to only his parents and sister, boarded a bus for Pittsburgh, and left the girl and everyone else there at home, to wonder where he had gone.

* * *

So the question, "What is truth?" remains in doubt. At this phase of his life, Gene had little time to cogitate about serious religious or philosophical questions. He had experienced major changes in the formative years of his life. The history of his years as a boy and as a student had made a deep impression on his thinking. He would never be the same again.

In the scripture of John 18:38, there is this question of "What is truth?" asked by Pontius Pilate, the Roman governor. "Pilate therefore said unto Jesus, Art thou a king then? Jesus answered, Thou sayest that I am a king. To this end was I born, and for this cause came I into the world, that I should bear witness unto the truth. Everyone that is of truth heareth my voice."

"Pilate saith unto him, What is truth? And when he had said this, he went out again unto the Jews, and saith unto them, I find in him no fault at all."

Pilate sensed that something was wrong when the Jews brought Jesus into the Judgment Hall. He tried to avoid the issue. He told the Jews to judge Jesus themselves; in fact, Pilate would like to help Jesus. He was puzzled at this point and he did not realize that Jesus was pleading with him. Jesus told him that an essential of His kingdom was truth.

Pilate was a cynic. He stood in the presence of the Lord Jesus who was and is the Way, the Truth, and the Life. Later in the Bible, the Apostle John said that he had written about Jesus so that we might believe that Jesus is the Christ, the Son of God.

Gene had asked himself, "What is truth?" Then he had faced reality in Jesus. Now he had repented and accepted Jesus as his personal Saviour and had determined to live for Him. But there was much in his life to be changed and he needed the presence of the Holy Spirit in his life to be sure of God's will in the future.

II. PART TWO

World War II Experiences

1. MY SON--THE EMBRYO ENGINEER

War clouds were looming on the horizon. The President of the United States, Franklin Delano Roosevelt, had said that it was only a matter of time before we were involved in the war with Germany, Italy, and Japan. No one knew when this would happen but Gene reckoned that it would be a year or more away; therefore, he was ready to plan for beginning his engineering career. He started with three categories:

a. Fabrication of steel members for buildings and bridges.
b. Structural engineer design of buildings and bridges.
c. Construction of buildings and bridges.

Bethlehem Steel Company, Pittsburgh, Pennsylvania

Gene reached Pittsburgh late Saturday afternoon. He registered at the YMCA (Young Men's Christian Association) at North Side, Pittsburgh, after eating. Then to bed for a good night's sleep. In the morning, Sunday, he attended the North Side Assembly of God Church where he made some new friends. That afternoon he was walking in the park adjacent to the YMCA when he met a middle-aged, nicely dressed man with a pleasant manner. They conversed for a time, then the man invited him to his apartment for "a good time." Gene had experiences with homosexuals in Guttenberg so he refused the invitation and hurried back to the YMCA. The desk clerk informed him that the North Side was filled with vagrants, alcoholics, homosexuals, and the lowest of human beings. He advised Gene to switch to the Downtown Pittsburgh YMCA where the area was much nicer.

Gene met Mr. Russell Chew, the department head, where Gene was to work at Bethlehem Steel. The department under Mr. Chew was now engaged in preparing steel fabrication drawings for a massive bridge across the Mississippi River. It was exhilarating to see how the bridge went together and how the hundred or more men working there worked so well together. Practically everything was new to Gene. College had not delved into the details like this; in fact, the squad boss (in charge of a small group of five or six men) who liked Gene once said to him, "Didn't that college that you attended ever teach you anything?" But Mr. Chew knew that it took time to develop an experienced steel detailer and he recognized good potential here.

Mr. Chew lived in Wilkinsburg, Pennsylvania, near the Bethlehem Fabricating Company and he suggested that Gene find a place to live in Wilkinsburg. One reason was that this area was a nice residential area and many recent college graduates were living there. Also Mr. Chew helped Gene to attend engineering seminars and technical meetings like the American Society of Civil Engineers.

Gene found a place to live in Wilkinsburg. It was convenient to his place of work, and his landlady (Mrs. Peachee) invited him to attend her church just a few blocks away. It was an old Presbyterian church which had lost members until it now had only fifty or sixty members and the church was now nondenominational. Gene had a high regard for these Christian people and hated to leave them when he decided to move on to the next place of employment.

He had noticed the name of the company that had done the engineering design of the bridge. They were in Long Island City, New York. Gene had worked for Bethlehem Steel for nearly eight months. He liked the work but he thought about the future, talked with Mr. Chew, and decided to leave Bethlehem. He told Mr. Chew that he had never expected to remain a structural steel detailer all of his life. He wanted to gain experience as an engineer. Mr. Chew agreed and urged him to make the move.

Madigan-Hyland Consulting Engineers,

Long Island City, New York

Gene returned to Guttenberg, New Jersey, where he lived with his parents. It was convenient to commute to his new job. He did not mind the poverty there as he usually stayed in New York City after work.

To him, it was a wonderful place. He was beginning to appreciate music and soon he began to take advantage of the Metropolitan Opera House, New York Philharmonic Orchestra, and many other places such as libraries, bookstores, colleges, etc. He found that he could get reduced price tickets; in fact, he attended many opera performances for an admittance fee of only one dollar. Of course, he had to sacrifice some comfort. He came early to the performance and stood in line at a side entrance. The people who entered there had to stand during the performance. Then during the intermissions, they could sit where people had left for the lobby.

One day to his surprise, while standing in line, he was asked if he would take part in the performance of the opera, "Aieda." He agreed and was ushered into the dressing room where he removed his clothes and slipped into a loin cloth. Then his whole body was covered with a dark brown solution. He was to be a Nubian warrior. At the proper time he dashed across the stage, picked up a slave girl (small), carried her up a flight of stairs to an altar, and sacrificed her to some deity with his wooden sword. After the performance, he covered himself with cold cream and removed his dark brown color. For this "outstanding" opera performance, he received the magnificent sum of one dollar.

But he was in New York City to work as an engineer. He soon found that the firm of Madigan-Hyland had a good reputation with the city. It received many city projects, often leading to work outside the city, and even outside the U.S.A. The work that they performed was top level engineering design, and Gene enjoyed every minute of it. Some of the projects were for example, the West Side Elevated Highway and the Bronx-Whitestone Bridge. To his great satisfaction, the company had buildings to design also. One project was the Guantanamo Bay Naval Station in Cuba.

The structural engineers working with Gene were very helpful, often offering engineering advice, and sometimes personal advice. At this time, all drafting was done manually (1942). The chief draftsman soon found out that Gene was a very fine draftsman so he took advantage of the situation. Whenever it was possible, he had Gene do the drafting. Gene was happy to oblige, but one day the engineer at the desk behind him asked if he could talk to him privately. At a convenient time they met and this experienced engineer surprised Gene by saying abruptly, "Gene, don't be so careful with your drafting work! If you continue to turn out such fine drawings, the chief draftsman will use you more and more as a draftsman. And pretty soon that will be all that you do! You are young and you came here to gain experience as an engineer and not as a draftsman! Make a few mistakes or do some shoddy work. Don't worry, we engineers will correct it when we check your work."

That was difficult advice to follow. Gene was accustomed to always doing his best and that is what he decided to do. But as he thought about this, he was reminded that World War II was getting closer and closer. Pearl Harbor had been bombed by the Japanese and the nation had been aroused. Gene knew that he should move on to the next job. If he did not, he might be drafted and lose the opportunity. It had been only a six-month stay at Madigan-Hyland. The chief engineer dismissed him with a wave of his hand. Engineers were moving to other firms at the "drop of a hat" or, rather, at the promise of a higher salary. The chief draftsman tried to get Gene to change his mind. He liked Gene and he recognized his capability as a draftsman. But Gene reluctantly quit his job.

E. I. DuPont de Nemours, Wilmington, Delaware

Gene had read in an engineering magazine that DuPont had the need of civil engineering graduates. The company was known as an outstanding producer of chemical products. Gene wondered why they would need civil engineers but he decided to write a letter of application anyway. In a few days, he received a reply. Come to Wilmington as soon as possible--all expenses paid!

During the interview he learned that DuPont had a contract with the U. S. Government to produce smokeless powder for ammunition for the armed forces. The first plant was in Terra Haute, Indiana. It was underway but there was a great need for more workers, all types, laborers, carpenters, masons, engineers, typists, etc.; in fact, the work force was planned to be ten thousand persons when construction was at its peak. Gene was thrilled at the prospect of working in construction. That was what he had planned for and he was sure that the Lord had supplied this job. So he accepted the offer without even considering his pay, and off he went to Indiana.

Gene had never been so far west in his life. When the train chugged through the farmlands, he marveled at the tremendous size of the farms. Back in Guttenberg, the joke was often told that a typical New Yorker had never in his whole life crossed the Hudson River. To them, New Jersey was the "Wild West"!

The first position that Gene had was as a safety engineer. He did not care for the work. All of the construction people thought that it was a waste of time and money. They were willing to take their chances on having an accident. Gene had to endure their jibes for a month or so. Then he had enough! He told his boss that he was quitting. This man did not want to lose Gene so he asked the head of the surveyors if he would use Gene. This man was not known for his intellect. When he looked at Gene's application, he saw that Gene had attended Newark College of Engineering. He congratulated him for graduating from a college in England.

In another month or two, the project was about one half finished. The government had poured tens of millions of dollars into the construction. Then some administrator in Washington, D.C., decided that smokeless powder was not a priority. In three days, the entire ten thousand work force had been dismissed and had received their back pay. No one seemed to be upset about losing his job. Texas, California, New York--let us go to the next place. There was plenty of work and many considered that they would be in the armed forces soon anyway. So off they went. Gene took the bus to Pittsburgh where he decided to stay for a few months. The first place he went was to his familiar rooming house. Then he stopped at a hospital nearby, looking for a job. Anything would do. He was offered a choice. Either he could run the elevator or fire the furnace. He chose to fire the furnace during the night shift. It worked well although he fell asleep a few times. The absence of steam caused the generator to slow down and the lights to dim and many other bad results. The incessant telephone ringing woke him up quickly.

Fortunately a friend told him that Westinghouse Electric Manufacturing Company needed employees. He had taken one course in electrical engineering which he felt qualified him to work as a machine test inspector. The voltage for testing was 440 volts and he soon knew what that felt like. Several times he touched the open wires and it knocked him to the floor. Some of the machines were motor-generator sets designed for submarine use. This made him feel that he was helping the war effort. The pay was good. The company offered many courses in electrical theory. Basically, he was satisfied but deep within he knew that this was not what he was preparing for as his life's work. In a surprising move though, he decided to be patriotic and join the army. Professor LaLonde at N.C.E. had offered to take Gene to the naval recruiting station during his senior year. Gene had turned him down. Now it was different though. He had some experience in three branches of structural engineering in the last year and a half since graduation, and when he saw his friends leaving for the armed forces, he knew that it was time to go even though he possessed an occupational deferment. Even one of the girls at the church had left for service in the Navy and he was afraid that he would be called a "slacker."

One evening he went to the main Pittsburgh Post Office and carefully thought this over. Then he decided to go ahead. He went to the U. S. Army recruiting station and told the sergeant that he wanted to volunteer for service. The sergeant took all the necessary information, then spent quite a long time discussing Gene's qualifications. At that point Gene had received a B.S. in C.E. from the Newark College of Engineering, completed two courses of graduate work for an M.S. in C.E. from the Massachusetts Institute of Technology, and his experiences included work in structural engineering in three outstanding companies.

The sergeant was really impressed. Without hesitation, he told Gene that he would write a letter stating that Gene should be sent to the U. S. Army Corps of Engineering headquarters in Columbus, Ohio, where he should be accepted as a commissioned officer at the rank of first lieutenant or captain. Meanwhile Gene should leave Westinghouse and go back to his Selective Service Board in New Jersey where he was registered in the draft and change his classification to voluntary inductee. The letter would be at the Distribution Center on Long Island when Gene arrived.

At the Selective Service Board Gene was asked if he had any objection to killing a human being. His answer was definite: if a person was a murderer, he or she had to be punished. He had no objection to capital punishment. His answer was acceptable to the Board and his classification was changed to voluntary inductee. He was then scheduled to leave for the Distribution Center on Long Island with the next group of draftees. A few days later his mother and sister stood in Grand Central Station in New York City watching him board a train for the Center. They waved good-bye, wondering if they would ever see him again.

2. MY SON--THE SOLDIER

The train carrying the new recruits left New York City and proceeded about eighty miles out on Long Island to the Reception (Distribution) Center. The train entered a siding where it stopped in the middle of a large number of barracks. The men stepped off the train and lined up for instructions. Then they were divided into smaller groups and taken to the proper barrack which was to be their home for the next few weeks. Quickly, they dropped their belongings and were marched to the Infirmary for the first of many physical examinations--mostly to detect any venereal disease. Then they were marched between barracks filled with men who didn't seem to have anything to do but shout obscenities at the new recruits. The most prevalent cry from these "experienced soldiers" was "Watch out for the hook." It seems that the new recruits were headed for their shots, injections, and they were being warned that the needle had a hooked end. Certainly it really meant nothing but it was surprising how much apprehension it caused. When the new recruits approached the nurse with her array of hypodermic needles, it was a common sight to see a husky young man slump to the floor in a dead faint.

The recruits were then herded into a large assembly building where they were sworn in as members of the U. S. Army. Next they received the regulation army clothing (hopefully near the right size), then back to their barracks to remove their civilian clothing and pack it for return to the homes they had left behind. Unfortunately, Gene was now "chosen" for K.P. (kitchen patrol). For the next three weeks, every day from 4 A.M. to 7 P.M., he cleaned dishes, pots and pans, swept the floors, cleaned tables, helped the cooks, etc. By this time, Gene was quite upset. Here he was practically a captain in the U. S. Army Corp of Engineers and all he did was K.P. duty. As soon as he had some free time he hurried to the Administration Building to inquire about the delay in the receipt of his orders to go to Columbus, Ohio. Gene did not realize it, but he was about to enter a period in his life that he facetiously referred to as "The Ten Great Disappointments."

First Great Disappointment

Gene was received at the Administration Building without any untoward incident. He was directed to an inner office where the records were kept. The sergeant in charge listened to him without any remarks. Then he went to a huge bank of files and extracted the records of Eugene V. Dotter. He quickly found the letter from the recruiting officer at the Post Office in Pittsburgh, Pennsylvania. It was exactly as he had promised. Send this man to Columbus, Ohio. He has been chosen because of his education and experience to receive a commission as lieutenant or captain and will serve there for the remainder of his time in the U. S. Army.

Gene was nonplussed. He asked the sergeant why he had not been sent there in accordance with the directions in the letter. The answer stunned Gene. The sergeant said, "You will never be able to serve as a commissioned officer." Then he showed Gene that the letter had stamped across it in large black letters, "LIMITED SERVICE ONLY."

Gene exclaimed, "But I passed the physical examination without a problem." The sergeant replied, "No, this report shows that you did not pass the vision test. I guess that the doctor did not tell you. A commissioned officer must have eye vision of 20/20 with eyeglasses and at least 20/100 without eyeglasses. Your record shows that you have eye vision of 20/20 with eyeglasses but only 20/400 without eyeglasses. That is on the borderline of being classified as blind. You will never be accepted as a commissioned officer."

"What can I do now?" Gene asked.

The sergeant then told him that he had two options. They were: (1) Resign because of eye problems, go home to your Selective Service Board and apply for your former status, get a new job, and forget the whole thing. (2) Stay in the Army as Limited Service. You will be given some kind of a safe job.

Gene could not accept option 1. How could he face his friends when they asked why he was not in the army? He would feel like a slacker by having a good job while his friends were serving their country. So he told the sergeant to put the letter back in the file. He would do his best where he would be sent even though he was greatly disappointed.

After two more weeks of K.P., he was notified to pack his things and be ready in the morning to ship out. He and a trainload of recruits left for an unknown destination. They traveled all day, trying to figure out where they were going by observing signs or places that looked familiar. They could not do so; in fact, it became very confusing when they halted momentarily at a number of railroad signs. Finally the train reached their destination. It was a wooded area in Virginia at Fort Belvoir about twenty miles south of Washington, D.C.

Second Great Disappointment

Fort Belvoir was the training camp for soldiers who were chosen to become combat engineers. It was very large and had many permanent brick buildings as well as many temporary wooden barracks for lodging the trainees. Four companies of 250 men formed a battalion of 1,000 men. And each company consisted of five platoons of 50 men each. Life in the barracks was difficult. The men came from all walks of life with all kinds of backgrounds. Many of the men were vehemently opposed to army service. They complained bitterly because they thought that they had been drafted unfairly. A surprisingly large number tried to get a discharge so that they could go home. In the army there was a discharge called a "Section Eight." First a man seeking a discharge would try a physical disability like bad feet or a broken arm, or a chronic sickness. If that failed, and it usually did, for the army was "no piece of cake," then they would try the "Section Eight" or a mental disability. There were some men who had really mastered the art of looking crazy. However, very few succeeded in getting a discharge.

Some of the men were just plain evil. They had lived outside the law before the army and the army did not make any change in their attitude. One young man was always getting into trouble. He gambled, drank excessively, and borrowed money constantly. One day he asked for a loan of two dollars from Gene. That night he accosted one of the young ladies who worked at Fort Belvoir. He couldn't control himself so he tried to rape the girl. Fortunately, an M.P. (military police) heard her cries and interfered. The soldier was immediately taken to the stockade and a court martial was arranged for later. They never saw that soldier again.

Gene soon found out that, although poor eyesight could prevent him from becoming a commissioned officer, it did not prevent him from learning to kill. He entered a basic training period of seventeen weeks. At first it was geared to making a recruit physically fit. All kinds of exercises, marching, and running. One tough training routine was for a soldier to march twenty miles in the hot sun with a full field pack (75 pounds) along with his rifle and helmet. Then he learned how to use a pistol, a knife, a carbine (small rifle), a regulation rifle, the machine gun, and even the bayonet in hand-to-hand combat. He had to go through obstacle courses often. It meant climbing over walls, through barbed-wire entanglements, crawling on his stomach under live machine-gun fire, and always under the most rigid of discipline. He was taught to do everything that his superior officer ordered him to do. He was not to hesitate or think--"just to do or die"; in fact, he was told that if he questioned the command, the officer could and would shoot him. This absolute total discipline taught him to follow implicitly but it also caused him to hate some of the company officers--commissioned and noncommissioned. He felt that they went too far; for example, grabbing a recruit by the throat and shaking him violently in order to get absolute obedience.

After enduring five weeks of this "torture," Gene was surprised when he was ordered to report to the administration building immediately. He worried about what was ahead but he reasoned that it could not be worse than basic training. He met four other men when entering the building. They were directed to an office where an officer spoke to them. He wasted no time. He told them that they were the only five to be selected from their battalion of one thousand men. Their education and experience qualified them for commissions to be given through a program known as the "President's Commissions." In a few days they would be transferred from their battalion to this next assignment. Suffice to say that Gene was very pleased and he very graciously accepted the congratulations of this officer.

One week flew by. Gene hardly noticed the tough training. He would be away from all this in a few days. He was certain of this when he was notified to report to the administration building. Again the five soldiers were ushered into the office where they had been previously. This was different though. The officer sadly informed them that the program of the "President's Commissions" had been halted. No more commissions were to be made available. The five men were to return to the basic training program. It was another great disappointment for Gene. His army career seemed to be taking a decidedly negative direction. Gene wondered if this was actually the Lord's will for his life. Perhaps he had not made the right decision when he decided not to go back to civilian life. But he brushed aside his questioning of God's place in his life and devoted himself to getting through the remaining eleven weeks.

He had never fired a gun in his life. After some training, he was asked to go to the firing range. It was a very competitive part of his training. The men with the higher scores were considered as a step above the others. Here he was, he hardly knew which end of the rifle was the place the bullets came out. Then he decided that it wasn't too important and he settled down. Unknown to him, this was what was needed--a steady hand and arm. Many of the other soldiers were nervous and scored low. Out of his company of 250, Gene was in the top three. He was known as a "sharpshooter," but he never fired a regulation rifle again. He carried a carbine.

Third Great Disappointment

One thing about basic training was that the food was abundant. Gene's weight went from 140 pounds to 180 pounds. His friends labeled him as "a growing boy." But it required a little ingenuity on his part. When mess call sounded (time to come to the dining hall to eat), he was always ready and managed to get at the front of the line going into the hall. He did not "waste time" talking. He found that he could finish the meal before all of the line had entered the building so he would hurry out and get back at the end of the line and eat a second meal. The food was not particularly tasty but it was enough to satisfy a hungry young man.

Also, Fort Belvoir was near Washington, D.C. The recruits often received evening passes, and there were many attractions such as the government buildings and great musical events; in fact, Gene was able to get several weekend passes during the seventeen weeks. The train from Washington, D.C., to New York City was very fast. The distance of about 250 miles could be covered in several hours. If money was scarce (pay for a private in the army at that time was only $30 per month and Gene sent home part of it), they could use the bus which was much cheaper but took about twice the time. Gene did not drink or smoke or seek the company of women so he managed to go on a trip when he received a pass.

The officers liked Gene. He was well educated and physically fit. He was a friend to all and tried to live as a good Christian. The chaplain of this training section of Fort Belvoir was a good preacher so Gene always attended the Sunday morning church service. He was not a good singer but he joined the choir because he loved the old hymns of the church. One Sunday the chaplain announced that any recruit who would join the choir and practice with the choir every Wednesday could go out on a Saturday evening to visit a local church where the chaplain had arranged for a social night. The army choir would sing, then the church would provide refreshments. Finally the choir and the church members (girls especially) would have a chance to socialize. It worked very nicely for five or six weeks, then one Sunday morning the chaplain told the congregation that the program had been canceled. The men of the choir did not want to practice and the singing of the choir was so poor that the chaplain was embarrassed. The choir wanted the refreshments and the socializing but would not make any effort to present a decent performance.

After the grueling basic training, the recruits now began to feel like a finely tuned group of soldiers, ready to see some action. Their group pictures showed them to present a camaraderie that comes when men have been tested together and have survived the ordeal. (See page 65 for Gene's army company picture.)

But the army was not concerned about recruits remaining together. After basic training some of the men were sent immediately into combat as combat engineers while others were transferred to the infantry and sent into action. For Gene, it seemed unusual for a man to go through seventeen weeks of basic training and then go into action as an infantry soldier; however, many things happened in the army that were unusual. A friend of his told him about his brother-in-law. He was 34 years old when drafted (the limit at that time was 35 years of age). He was married with a wife and five children. He received only five weeks of basic training, and it amazed his brother-in-law that he was able to complete his training. He was awkward and absolutely uncoordinated. He was sent into action immediately with the infantry. In two weeks he was dead.

A few days before the end of the seventeen weeks of basic training, a group of forty recruits were ordered to report at the administration building. Gene was included in this group. They were told that they had been chosen to be part of the A.S.T.P. (Army Specialized Training Program). At the end of basic training, this group boarded a train and went to the University of Pennsylvania in Philadelphia. They were billeted at one of the dormitories at the university which was quite different from Fort Belvoir. A captain, leader of this class, explained to them their schedule. They were to spend two weeks reviewing engineering knowledge, then go through three months of training as sanitary engineers. If they completed the course satisfactorily, they would be commissioned as first or second lieutenants, depending upon their background and type of service.

The first task for the group was to take a test designated as "Prior Knowledge Examination." It was difficult for many of the soldiers because

ERTC
6A
4TH PLATOON

they were only about eighteen years of age and had been drafted shortly after graduating from high school; in fact, a surprisingly large number had enlisted before graduating from high school. In any event, they had no college training and many of the questions on this examination were taken from the standard college engineering courses. It suited Gene very well, however, and he scored 168 on the examination. The captain was amazed as he had never recorded this high a grade. He assured Gene that he would be granted the high commission of first lieutenant. He would be assigned to inspect the sanitary facilities at the training camps in the U.S.A. and Hawaii and even in other countries like England, Philippines, etc. Gene would rather have been in structural engineering in Columbus, Ohio. Meanwhile, he would be content to spend the next three months at the University of Pennsylvania studying the Sanitation Courses that were offered in Civil Engineering.

The first two weeks went by rapidly. Gene enjoyed the academic atmosphere. The review of engineering basics was exciting to him, and he looked forward to the three months of sanitation courses. Then the captain dropped a virtual bombshell. He said to the class, "Fellows, I hate to tell you that the A.S.T.P. has been terminated! You will be assigned to some other duties. As far as I know at this time, the class will be sent to Camp Claiborne in Louisiana to go through another basic training period of twelve weeks." What a shock to these young men! And a great disappointment to Gene. He had looked forward to the college training and to receiving the commission of first lieutenant. Now he had neither of them. Also, he detested the hot weather basic training for twelve weeks in the future.

Fourth Great Disappointment

The schedule was very confused. The orders did not come through for another week. The men lived in limbo, hoping against hope that the information from the captain had not been correct. Their hope was in vain. The official orders came through and it was packing their belongings in the duffle bag and "hitting the road," or rather "hitting the railroad." It was a long trip to the "deep South." The seats were hard wood without cushions or upholstery. The train moved slowly and it seemed that they would never get to Camp Claiborne. Most of the time was spent gambling--cards or dice. After a while, sleeping on the hard wooden floor--or trying to--seemed better than bouncing along on the train rails while sitting on the uncomfortable seats. But finally the "torture" ended. Camp Claiborne at last. Even the cots in the barracks were better than the train--a real luxury.

The basic training here at Camp Claiborne was worse than that at Fort Belvoir. The weather was hot and the mosquitoes and bugs were worse. There was a constant irritation from a bug called a chigger. It had a knack for getting inside the stockings and even in a tight place like under the belt holding up the pants. Instead of just biting, it would burrow into the skin. It was difficult to get it out. Scratching was dangerous. Dirty hands and skin would cause the skin to fester and even cause blood poisoning. The standard treatment was to examine the skin where the itching occurred, then smear nail polish where the chiggers were. This would cut off the air from the chigger which would soon die. The body then discharged the dead bug--eventually.

Another problem could be classified as "good" or "bad." By this time some fighting had taken place. The soldiers needed to rest from combat duty. Often they were sent home and used as noncommissioned officers at the basic training camps. They were rough with recruits that they thought were having an easy life. Gene's group came to be considered in this category. In their way of thinking, these recruits had been through seventeen weeks of training as well as A.S.T.P. and here they were in another basic training when they should have been sent overseas. They were mean and nasty and often drunk. Of course, this situation could have been to the advantage of the recruit, for they could have profited by the experiences of the former combat troops. Instead it was too difficult and the recruits came "to hate their guts."

Gene tried to maintain a positive attitude but twelve weeks of constant grinding "torture" began to get him down. He had thought that the fact that he and his group of recruits had gone through a complete basic training at Fort Belvoir would have meant an easier life here at Camp Claiborne. But it was not so. There was not even a decent church service to attend on Sunday morning. And no passes for relaxation off the base. This was a great disappointment to him.

Another problem for Gene was his constant appointment to K.P. duty. It was tough because of the hot weather and the long hours. His buddy often had to serve with him. One day he convinced Gene that they should receive something extra in the way of food that they liked. The cooks did not approve of this. His buddy had a plan, however, and he begged Gene to help him. Gene's early life in Guttenberg had left more of an impression on him that he thought, so he agreed. Gene and his buddy were to wait until it was time to clean up. Gene would sweep the floor in front of the "walk-in" refrigerator and his buddy would don a cook's cloak and step into the refrigerator, leaving the door slightly ajar. If a cook approached, Gene would drop his broom to the floor to make a noise to warn his buddy. The buddy would quickly cut some large pieces of baloney and cheese and slip them into his shirt. Gene would ask the cook for a short "break" period--ten minutes or so. They would hurry to their barracks where they already had some bread and pickles and enjoy a "Dagwood" sandwich. Gene never regarded this as stealing. He felt that he was being paid for his extra work. And he kind of thought of this as a "fun" thing.

Fifth Great Disappointment

The days rolled into weeks and weeks into months. Finally the basic training was over. The camp had a "graduation" ceremony. The whole battalion assembled on the parade grounds. Complete with an army band and flag bearers, the battalion marched around the grounds. Each time they passed the reviewing stand, all soldiers saluted the flag and the reviewing officers.

It was a constant question in a soldier's mind: Where will I be assigned next? Gene did not have to wait long to find out. The next morning his company lined up for inspection. Then the company commander had them count off in groups of six. Gene's number was three and he and all the threes were sent to a school. Gene expected to be assigned to some engineering school. Instead his group was sent to the Cooks and Bakers School! Gene had never had any desire to cook and certainly not in the army. When he thought of months in a school cooking and then cooking for perhaps years during the rest of his service, he was greatly disappointed. That the army would choose where he would serve by counting off numbers was preposterous!

But he had to march with the others to the school building. When the officer started his talk about the school rules and regulations, he paused after a few minutes. Gene quickly asked if he could say a few words. Permission was granted so Gene told the officer that the army had made a mistake. He said that he would not make a good cook and, besides, he was an engineer. The officer tried to change his mind by telling him that it was easy, he would have plenty to eat, and he would not have to worry about his safety when in combat. Then Gene told him about his education and experience in Civil Engineering. The officer was impressed by his credentials. He told him that he understood his predicament and he would give Gene permission to speak to the major who was in charge of the schools; but, be prepared for some trouble, the major was not an easy man to convince or even to talk with.

Gene was not to be denied. He entered the administration building and proceeded to a large open room where the major had his desk along with twenty typists and support people. The major hardly raised his head and shouted, "What the ... do you want?"

Gene answered, "I've been assigned to the Cooks and Bakers School. I'm an experienced civil engineer and I think that I should be transferred to another school where my engineering ability can be better utilized by the army." The major shouted in a louder voice so that everybody in the room could stop work and listen to this conversation. His face was as red as a beet. Gene was afraid that this old man (about 45 years old) was going to have a heart attack. The major bellowed, "Who do you think you are? You are just a stupid private to me! And I hate stupid people! You are insubordinate and I am going to have you court-martialed. Get out of here and go to your company commander and tell him that I said you are under arrest and confined to your barracks!" Gene figured that "court-martial" didn't mean much. He was only a private so they couldn't demote him. He tried to reason with the major but all he got was a flow of nasty language adding up to the advice that some men in the infantry were dying in the mud and filth while this crazy private couldn't even realize what a good life he would have as a cook. He ended by saying, "Get out of here before I call the M.P.s. I am going to have you reassigned to the infantry. What do you think of that, you dumb jerk!" Gene realized that it was time to hurry out. This major looked like he could pull out his pistol and shoot Gene "deader than a doornail."

Gene checked in with the company commander, then went to sleep on his cot. A few hours later he was informed that he had been "court-martialed." Actually, it just meant that he received company punishment--two weeks of extra work around the company quarters. He did all sorts of tasks--like cleaning latrines, scrubbing floors, washing windows, painting walls--from early morning until late at night. He worked so hard that the captain found it difficult to find enough work to keep him busy. The captain and Gene became good friends before Gene had finished his "company punishment"; in fact, the captain gave him some evening passes that he could use later. The trouble was that Gene did not know where to go. Besides, he had no money to finance any trips anyway.

Sixth Great Disappointment

A few days after the company punishment was finished, the captain told Gene that somehow his talk with the major had caused him to relent. Now Gene had been reassigned to an engineering school. He packed his duffel bag and the next day joined a group of soldiers headed for the engineering school. To his delight he learned that they were going to Fort Belvoir, Virginia. But he wondered what kind of college was located there--he had never seen anything like an engineering school while there. But hope springs eternal and it sounded like a step in the right direction.

After a long, dirty, bumpy train ride, Gene arrived at the school. To his dismay, it consisted of one room. The course was to be "Engineering Drafting." He would gladly have returned to Camp Claiborne but he was stuck here for ten weeks. The course was absolutely elementary and Gene felt that this was a great disappointment and was a waste of his time.

The first lesson was to teach the students what their instruments were: a T square, a 30° triangle, a 60° triangle, an architect's scale, an engineer's scale, pencils, and various hardnesses of lead for the pencils. Then they were given a sheet of drawing paper. The second lesson was to learn to draw a straight line. And to draw lines of various widths. The third lesson was how to add fractions, using the least common denominator method (probably learned in the third or fourth grade). The fourth lesson was to learn the various kinds of lines, such as center lines, hidden lines, etc. And so it went, lesson by lesson, with the final lesson being to copy a large number of engineering drawings. Your grade in the course was based on how many drawings, not on how much you "understood" about the drawings.

Two of the students became very friendly with Gene. Both were nineteen years old and had finished only one year of engineering college. Gene was twenty-two years old and had finished college as well as worked at three engineering companies. So they regarded him as an elder brother or perhaps a father! One of them was Warren Houghten who had been a student at Massachusetts Institute of Technology. He had lived in a suburb of Boston and was a devout Catholic. Gene often invited Warren to go to the Protestant church at the base but he adamantly refused. Finally he compromised by agreeing to go with Gene one Sunday to the Protestant church if Gene would go with him to the Catholic church on the next Sunday. Gene quickly agreed but that was the only time Warren ever went to the Protestant church. Warren was a happy, friendly young man so he was a nice companion. He had high morals and never used filthy language.

The other young man was Charles Koch. He lived in Newark, New Jersey, and had finished one year at the Newark College of Engineering. He was absolutely opposed to anything religious. Gene had to be careful how he treated Charlie but he found out one day that he was the only child of his German parents. They were a very close family and all their conversation at home was in the German language. Perhaps the fact that the U.S.A. was at war with their homeland made them to shy away from gaining any friends. Also, Charlie had some odd characteristics. He had no other friends and did some unusual things. For instance, he never ate anything after supper. He explained this by saying that he had already cleaned his teeth. He thought that his mess kit was too bulky. He threw away his knife and fork, sharpened one side of his spoon and used it instead of all three. He threw away the lid of his mess kit. He never drank coffee, tea, or soft drinks and never went to the movies. If he had a weekend pass, he never considered going home. He would spend all of his time riding back and forth on the trolley cars. He knew all the specifications of practically all the trolley cars in the U.S.A. He often debated with Gene about future local transportation. Gene's position was that small airplanes or helicopters would fly from homes to landing areas on roofs, etc., but Charlie was certain that they would never displace cars, busses, or trolleys. Charlie thought that all sports were a waste of time. He never went to a sports event and never participated in the usual things like volleyball or basketball.

Seventh Great Disappointment

The Engineering Drafting Class was over. Charlie Koch had spent every bit of his time doing extra work so he was at the top of the class. No one cared except him. He was ecstatic because he had surpassed his idol, Gene. But Gene congratulated him and wondered if Charlie realized how much he had lost by not availing himself of all the wonderful opportunities found in Washington, D.C. Now they were on the way back to Camp Claiborne and Charlie would never again see Washington, D. C.

The group arrived at Camp Claiborne and dispersed to their own barracks. Gene had been transferred to another company but it was the same thing day after day. For almost a month he was busy with K.P. One day, after lunch, he took a little break by sitting in front of the mess hall, basking in the sun. Along came a second lieutenant carrying a transit on a tripod. He paused, then sat on the bench next to Gene. "Sure is a hot day," he said, mopping his face with an extra large handkerchief. After a minute or two, Gene ventured a comment. "What are you doing with the transit?" The officer was surprised. He answered, "How did you know that this is a transit?" Gene was amused and replied, "I should know. I took three semesters of Surveying during the four years of college studying for my B.S. degree, and then I took a graduate course in Geodetic Surveying." The lieutenant was astounded. "What is Geodetic Surveying? Wow, I could use you in the Surveying School." Gene explained what Geodetic Surveying was. The lieutenant then invited him to come to his office the next day. Gene declined. Then he expressed his great disappointment with army life. He had gone to basic training and Engineering Drafting and now he had served a month already on permanent K.P. and that appeared to be his future. "No," the lieutenant said, "I am going into this mess hall and order the cook to let you off from K.P. tomorrow for a few hours in the morning." Then he said something that Gene would hear many times, "Then I will make like a hoop and roll away."

Eighth Great Disappointment

The next day Gene visited the lieutenant in his office. He had noticed that there were forty students who were listening to one of the three instructors explain the parts of a transit. Later Gene learned that this instructor knew nothing about surveying. He had taught himself how to take apart the transit and a level, clean them, and check them for accuracy. That was his job. The other two instructors did not know much more; in fact, the lieutenant was the only one with much experience in surveying and his knowledge came from working with a company of surveyors and reading some books on surveying.

The lieutenant asked many questions about Gene's experience at college and about his work in Indiana with E. I. Dupont. Then, of course, about Geodetic Surveying. The lieutenant asked Gene if he would come to the Surveying School as an instructor for the class and then in the evenings after dinner as a teacher for the instructors. If Gene also would teach the instructors (and the lieutenant) about Geodetic Surveying, everybody would be very happy. As an incentive for Gene to come, he promised an immediate noncommissioned officer rating for Gene. Then when he, a second lieutenant, was promoted in the near future to the rank of first lieutenant, he would have Gene commissioned as second lieutenant. Gene accepted the offer, although with his experience in the army, he was dubious that it would ever happen.

The soldiers in the class were eager to learn about surveying. It was something of value to them all of their lives. Gene responded to them with good teaching. Also, he added a practical application to the lectures by using some examples from the work that he had done. Fortunately, he had brought two surveying textbooks with him. For his class, he had Surveying by Davis and Foote. It was an exceptionally complete textbook, so much so that he had to use only a small part of the text in order to finish within the eight weeks allotted to the class. For the instructors and the lieutenant, he had Practical Astronomy by Hosmer. This textbook had a portion of The American Ephemeris and Nautical Almanac incorporated in it, which listed the position of the sun and certain stars for each day of the year.

Geodetic Surveying is the survey of long distances, like the establishment of boundaries between states or countries. It means that sights had to be several miles and needed the use of a high-powered transit called the theodolite. Obviously, this surveying class at Camp Claiborne did not have a theodolite and Gene taught in the night anyway so he taught some things related to long distance surveying. Those were how to use a transit for sighting the stars and using this information with the ephemeris to determine the latitude and longitude where the transit was situated. Also, it could be used to determine the exact time of the sighting.

Because the transits are never perfectly accurate, the error had to be eliminated. This was done by taking eight readings on the star, then reversing the transit and taking eight more readings on the star. Finally, all sixteen readings were averaged in order to arrive at an accurate value. The person taking the readings was known as the transit man. And there was a certain feeling of having achieved a higher standing in the surveying field if the transit man could be fast and accurate. The lieutenant, as the head of Surveying School, was anxious to show that he was fast and accurate. To do this, he would have to compete against Gene and do better. So after a few weeks of instruction by Gene on the subject of Geodetic Surveying, the lieutenant arranged a competition at a night session. Gene would go through the procedure first, then the lieutenant would perform. The lieutenant was delighted when he was able to finish a few seconds faster than Gene.

Gene enjoyed teaching Surveying. The men all seemed contented with the class, except for one group. It was composed of blacks (American Negroes) who showed absolutely no desire to learn. One day Gene asked the leader of this group to tell him why these men were so disinterested. The answer was blunt: "Because we know that we will never be surveyors. We are here because our commanding officer did not know what else to do with us. Everybody knows that we will be truck drivers when we get out of this school!" Gene tried to reason with him but he would not listen.

Then Gene had his own problems to worry about. After two months as a teacher, he realized that he was still a private. He had received no promotion as the lieutenant had promised. When he spoke to the lieutenant, he was told that nobody had been promoted. Gene was greatly disappointed but comforted himself with the thought that at least it was better teaching then doing K.P.

Ninth Great Disappointment

When this class was completed, Gene looked forward to the next group of students. Instead, he was told to report to Major Graves at the 1524th Engineering Construction Group. The major asked if Gene would like to join this new group. In a joking way, Gene said, "I'm only a private. You are a major. I thought that I was supposed to do what you decided!" The major replied, "Yes, but I like all of the men in this group to be satisfied." "In that case," Gene said, "I am satisfied teaching at the Surveying School. So I will choose to remain there." The major was stunned by this answer. All he could say was, "Take a few days to think it over." But the next day the major sent a lieutenant over to tell Gene to pack up and get over to the 1524th E.C.G. immediately. They had to start the overseas preparations right away. That meant a review of basic training and the added load of fitting into the permanent duty that was the assignment. Gene was actually in charge of the engineering construction duty of the group. The commissioned officers running the 1524th E.C.G. were as follows:

Colonel Williams, administrative head officer

Lieutenant Colonel Masters, Assistant head officer

Major Graves, head of the construction work

Captain Fields, company commander

Second Lieutenant Levinson, architectural design

Here were five officers chosen to lead a company of ninety men whose very name, "Engineering Construction," signified that they were to be experts in engineering design and construction. Not one of them could handle engineering design and its relationship to construction work. The core of the 1524th E.C.G. consisted of Gene leading 25 men who were architects, engineers, surveyors, and experienced construction workers. The rest of the personnel, about sixty men, were only support people.

Basic training was the usual marching, weapons, infiltration, etc. Some of the days and nights were spent on the hills away from Camp Claiborne. It was often cold at night after the sun went down; in fact, one early morning Gene scrambled out of his pup tent and found that the water in his canteen had frozen solid. But the worst problem was the chiggers. One day Gene was bitten under his sock on his left leg. He scratched the place where the insect had burrowed under the skin. It became infected but Gene was ready to leave for his final "overseas" travel pass for home in Guttenberg so he paid no attention to it. When he arrived home three days later his leg was swollen. He went over to the Recruiting Station at the main Post Office in New York City where an army doctor had an ambulance take him to the army hospital on Governor's Island. His leg was swollen from blood poisoning. The doctor had never heard of a chigger. Four days with antibiotics cleared up the problem and he was allowed to go home for a three-day rest. Unfortunately, the doctor did not write out a report of this serious medical problem. When he returned to Camp Claiborne the M.P.s (military police) were ready for him and were about to put him in the stockade (prison) as he was three days late and he was listed as AWOL (Away Without Official Leave). It was serious to the M.P.s as the 1524th E.C.G. was now almost ready to be shipped overseas. The only official transaction was to be given in a few days when the general of Camp Claiborne made a last inspection of the 1524th E.C.G. Their final project was the engineering design and construction of a large wharf suitable for ocean-going ships. In a few days Gene did practically all the design and drawings for the wharf. When the general came through the drafting room, he stopped to see what Gene was doing. He was entranced by these complicated drawings and asked Gene for an explanation. For thirty minutes Gene kept the general spellbound. Then the general straightened up from leaning over the table and said loudly, "This man is a top-notch engineer. I need him in my office. I want him to help me run this camp!" He looked at the colonel and ordered him to send Gene over immediately.

The colonel knew that the overseas orders had already been given. In a day or so they would be on their way to the Point of Embarkation, which was to be Camp Dix near Trenton, New Jersey. He appealed to the officer in charge of overseas movements and was told to disregard the general. Overseas orders took precedence. By then Gene had received a promotion and now was a noncommissioned officer, a sergeant. He was greatly disappointed that the general was a day or two late and he had again missed the opportunity to get the commission that he was entitled to.

Tenth Great Disappointment

Among Gene's papers in his records folder was the original letter from the Pittsburgh Recruiting Station that ordered him to report to the U. S. Army Corps of Engineers in Columbus, Ohio.

Imprinted on it were the words, "Limited Service." He had learned that this had been stamped on the letter because his vision without eyeglasses did not conform to the requirements for commissioned officers. He knew that all soldiers going overseas had to pass one final physical examination. This included a vision test without eyeglasses. He knew that the requirements were the same as those for commissioned officers. It looked as if Gene would fail the exam and be sent back to Camp Claiborne, perhaps to the general's office or at least to the Surveying School. He did not feel unpatriotic for wishing that this would happen. He felt that he had suffered much grief unfairly and this was the opportunity to have some "pay-back" time.

Everything was done in secrecy. No information at all was to be given anywhere. The Germany Navy was wrecking havoc on the Allies' shipping with their U-boat submarine. They constantly looked for information regarding shipping days especially the movement of soldiers in the U.S.A. and across the Atlantic and Pacific Oceans. So they, the 1524 E.C.G. traveled by train up to Camp Dix, moving mostly under cover of darkness. Here they received their final orders and equipment. Then a short trip at night to Hoboken, New Jersey, for the overseas physical examination and to board the troop ship. Gene passed everything easily as he was in excellent physical condition.

Finally, he reached the eyesight exam. He read the letters on the chart with his eye-glasses on. When asked to remove the eyeglasses and read the chart, he told the examiner that he could not read anything. The officer was incredulous and asked, "How did you get into the army?" "Well," Gene replied, "I am classified as Limited Service with a reading of 20/400 without eyeglasses." "In that case," the examiner stated in a very determined tone, "I must refuse you and send you back to Camp Claiborne." Gene was overjoyed, but just then the E.C.G. Company commander, Captain Fields, came into the room. He motioned to the exit door and quietly said only one word, "Pass." The examiner turned to Gene and repeated, "Passed." Gene was now on his way overseas even though he was greatly disappointed that the army had once more changed the situation for their advantage and had totally ignored Gene's education and experience.

Schedule of Events

N.C.E. graduation		June 13, 1941
Bethlehem Steel Co.	8 months	February 23, 1942
Madigan-Hyland Co.	6 months	August 8, 1942
E. E. DuPont de Nemours	2 months	October 10, 1942
Westinghouse Electric Co.	3 months	January 14, 1943
Long Island, New York	1 month	February 15, 1943
Fort Belvoir, Virginia	4 months	May 25, 1943
University of Pennsylvania	1 month	June 10, 1943
Camp Claiborne, Louisiana	2 months	August 9, 1943
Fort Belvoir, Virginia	2 months	October 10, 1943
Camp Claiborne, Louisiana	3 months	January 12, 1944
1524 ECG (training)	1 month	February 15, 1944
1524 ECG (France)	16 months	June 21, 1945
1524 ECG (Germany)	6 months	December 8, 1945
Ship (Philippines)	1 month	January 12, 1946
Batangas, Philippines	6 months	June 14, 1946
Ship (USA)	1 month	July 20, 1946
Vacation	2 months	September 8, 1946

Massachusetts Institute of Technology 11 months

M.I.T. graduation June 13, 1947

European Theater - Phase 1

The troopship slowly made its way through the New York City bay and met a number of other troopships. Gene's ship was a converted Cunard Line ship named "The President." It had been a luxury liner before the war, but now was stripped down to bare walls. Each stateroom was jammed with bunk beds at least three tiers high. Gene was in the fifth level down in the ship. To get out to the deck, he had to climb a ladder through a small hole in each level. When orders were given to go to the deck, he had to wait until all the levels above him were evacuated before he could climb up the ladder. It often occurred to him that if the ship was about to sink, he would probably go down with the ship before he had a chance to get out. So he was glad to learn that the troopships were ringed with destroyers. That afforded some measure of protection from the German submarines.

The convoy made its way across the Atlantic Ocean. The ocean was rough and the waves were very high. It was wintertime so it was cold. The soldiers never went on deck. Usually they stayed in their bunks reading or playing cards. It would take at least a week to get to their destination although no one knew where they were going. The first day everyone was active and the dining rooms were crowded. Then the ship tossed and rolled with the angry waves. Soon about 99 percent of the soldiers were seasick. Gene fared better than the majority and found that the dining rooms were virtually deserted. But by the time the voyage was over, Gene had been seasick also.

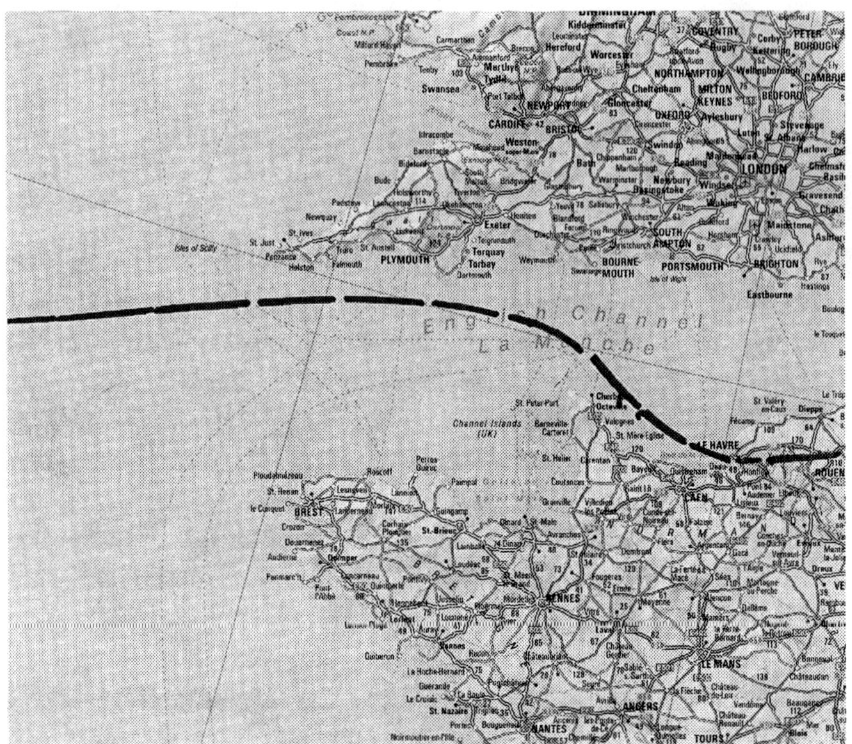

Map of Coast of France

Most of the soldiers decided their destination was England. In the fifth level down Gene did not really care where they were going, just so they reached it safely. One day he heard that they had gone past England and were headed for the coast of France. He knew the invasion had been successful so they would not have to land in a combat zone. Still there was much danger ahead and he could now hear the depth charges exploding around them and the roar of planes overhead. He hoped that these were not German planes as this ship was not outfitted for combat and only had two anti-aircraft guns, one at the stern and one at the bow.

Finally he detected a change in the movement of the ship. The soldiers were told to collect their battle equipment and be ready to leave the ship. The wait seemed interminable. The order came to ascend the ladder. Up five levels and on to the deck. At last, Gene could see the convoy. And the wharf where the ship docked. It was concrete but it was a mess. Big guns of the battleships and the aircraft bombs had made a shambles of the wharf. Most of it could not be used. Luckily, there still remained enough sound concrete to allow a large ship like this to dock.

Convoy ship waiting to unload. Leaving the ship

The next command was to leave the ship. This was not easy since there were no gangplanks. Each soldier with his battle equipment had to climb down a rope ladder swaying on the side of the ship. One misstep and the soldier could easily lose his life hitting the wharf or, worse yet, plunging into the water at least 50 feet deep. Burdened with his heavy clothing and heavy equipment, he had no chance of getting out of the water.

The men were transported through the city of LeHarve to the top of a hill overlooking the city. Here was an abandoned German airstrip and a long line of large tents. It was still winter here and it was very cold. Food was served outside. Also, the open-pit latrines were outside. That night Gene was sick. He visited the latrine so many times that it all began to feel like a dream. In the middle of the night he thought at one time that he was going up to a latrine. Instead, he was scrambling up a large pile of kindling wood. At the top he did what was necessary and then slid down the wood to his cot!

There was no time to recover from sickness. The 1524 ECG was loaded into trucks and hit the road. It was dangerous traveling on roads littered with the wreckage of vehicles and perhaps land mines. But they headed toward Rouen. Some of his companions had the audacity to shout, "Germany, watch out, here we come!"

European Theater - Phase 2

By the time his group reached Rouen, they were sure they were headed for Paris. The Germans had pulled back from the area that included Paris. The 1524 ECG took a circular route around Paris, however, going to Amiens and then to Reims. Here they learned that they would join two armies, the Seventh American Army and the First French Army. The American army was commanded by General Patton and he had the reputation for moving quickly. That meant that the 1524 ECG would move quickly and keep busy. They also learned that they would have five construction battalions (5,000 men) under their supervision. In general, their orders were to follow closely behind the two advancing Allied armies. Their work was to repair bridges, roads, and airfields that the Germans had destroyed as they retreated. In order to do their work as quickly as possible, the 1524 ECG of ninety men was divided as follows: the administration, 5 commissioned officers; the engineers and architects, 25 soldiers; the surveyors, 20 soldiers; the construction men, 15 soldiers; the construction material men, 15 soldiers; the cooks and bakers, 5 soldiers; the support group, 5 soldiers.

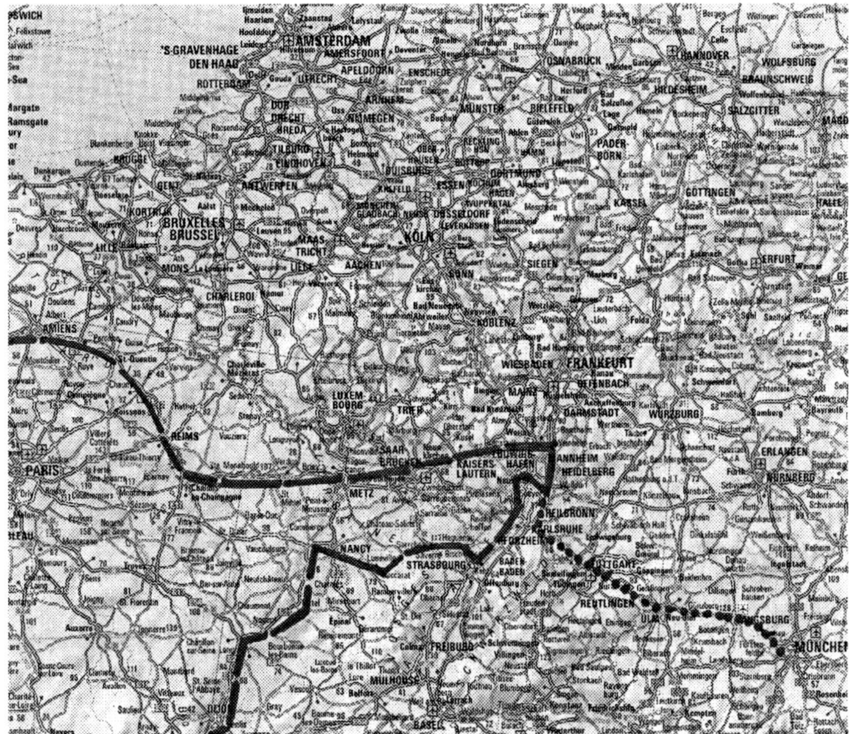

Map of France and Germany

The 1524th ECG would find an abandoned building near the combat zone. They would set up there for the night. Immediately, the surveyors would be assigned areas to inspect. If they found something to repair, they called in the construction men to make a quick analysis of the needed men, equipment, and materials. Meanwhile, the construction material men had been scouring the entire area for material that could be used for construction the next day. The surveyors and construction men would get the necessary measurements and rush back to the architects and engineers. That night all the windows and doors were covered with heavy black cloth so that no light showed the German reconnaissance planes that something important was happening. Then the architects and engineers would make drawings in one night so that plans could be given to the construction battalions in the morning. The reason for needed speed was that General Patton often advanced without his battle tanks and ammunition supplies. The Germans were very thorough about blowing up the bridges behind them as they retreated. In many cases, the needed tanks and supplies would be stalled until the bridge could be made "usable" again. This often required great ingenuity and cooperation by everybody involved. Sometimes it would look like the field men were loafing but the officers knew that after a short rest, these men would plunge into situations where their lives were at stake.

Field men for 1524th ECG having a much needed rest

It often seemed funny to all involved when some of the field men would ride into a town where they had been sent to find it was still occupied by the German soldiers. They would laughingly say, "We never knew who was scared the most, us or the Germans!! All we could think about was how we could get out of there in one piece."

The 1524th ECG moved in a southerly direction for a short distance. At Chalons-en-Champagne they turned abruptly toward the east. It was clear that General Patton was headed direct for Germany. This area was famous for major battles in World War I at Verdun and St. Mihiel near the Meuse River, and Chateau Thierry a little to the east. The 1524th ECG had traveled about 50 miles to Rouen, another 50 miles to Amiens, another 92 miles to Reims, and 24 miles to Chalons-en-Champagne--about 216 miles. It was difficult travel, with the devastation of war on every hand. They were busy repairing bridges and roads. Sometimes stopping for a week or two at one work place and sometimes stopping for just a few days. It was difficult to assess how the combat was progressing. Always there was the rumble of artillery to the east and the sound of bombs dropped by German planes with machine gun fire between Allied and German planes.

But at Chalons-en-Champagne, it seemed that the resistance of the German forces stiffened. Progress was slow and construction work was more difficult and dangerous as the 1524th ECG moved eastward to Metz about 80 miles away. Metz was just to the south of the little country of Luxembourg and about 35 miles east of Saarbrucken in Germany. The danger came not only from the action of the German army but because of the dangerous work in repairing bridges. For example, a concrete bridge of eight arch spans of 150 feet each and 100 feet high had been partially destroyed. Three of the arch spans had been completely removed. It was a crucial link in the advance of the Allied forces. It would have taken one or two years to replace the missing arches with concrete members. The 1524th ECG was allowed one or two weeks to get it in shape for army battle tanks to

Concrete arch bridge to be repaired

use it. It seemed like an impossible task. To the 1524th ECG it was difficult but not impossible. The construction material men found a large number of "meter beams" and heavy wooden timbers. The "meter beams" were structural steel beams one meter (39.34 inches) deep that could span 50 feet. Gene figured that these beams when placed two feet on centers with heavy planks as a deck could take the weight of the tanks and any truck as long as the drivers observed the sign to slow down to 10 miles per hour and to stay 100 feet apart. He then designed the trestle supports to be built of the heavy wooden members at 50 feet on centers. The next day the surveyors provided all the measurements needed and by the end of the day the construction plans were ready. All of the trestle supports were built at the same time with the 20 men of the 1524th ECG construction team supervising about fifteen hundred men of the construction battalions. The trestle supports were built in one week and the cranes lifted the "meter beams" in place above, where five hundred men were ready to place the roadway planks and secure them to the beams. The bridge was ready for traffic in less than ten days. Gene was delighted with the quick result but sad to learn that quite a few soldiers had been killed or badly injured during the construction. The crane operators were amateurs and sometimes misjudged distances, knocking workers off the trestles. Even the construction workers slipped and fell from heights higher than what they were accustomed to. Once an officer sadly remarked, "We lose more men to the construction processes than to German bullets!"

Another example of the type of ingenuity and experience needed occurred when the surveyors asked Gene to come to a bridge that had survived the explosives of a German demotion team. It was a heavy structural steel plate girder bridge with a span of 100 feet over an important railway with four tracks. The officer at the site wanted to remove the bridge and rebuild it. Gene could imagine what the combat officers would say when they heard that all traffic on both the railway tracks and the highway above would be stopped for several weeks. They probably would have him shot by a firing squad the next day.

When he looked at the plate girders, just from experience he judged that the plate girder at the right side was not damaged enough to worry about. The plate girder at the left side had been more severely damaged. It was quite a bit out of line and showed an area where the steel plate web had been bowed out for five or six feet. Tanks were already lining up to cross the bridge. The tank commanders were on the ground shouting curses at Gene and the officer. Gene calmly told them to take a rest for three or four hours while the construction steel workers welded a series of steel angles across the bowed area. Then the first tank would slowly cross the bridge while Gene observed any unusual movement of the plate girder beam. The tank commanders were satisfied. After all, they reasoned, this engineer must know what he was talking about if he would stand next to the repaired plate girder while the tank crossed the bridge. Actually, everything was satisfactory and in only two hours the tanks were rolling across the bridge. Back at his temporary office, Gene often heard German planes bombing in that area. His men would all shout, "There goes the bridge, it just fell down, your repairs weren't enough!" What a poor joke!

After weeks of heavy fighting the 1524th ECG moved ahead to Saarbrucken about 40 miles eastward to a position near the German border. Damage was terrible and the territory was covered with discarded equipment and even crashed airplanes, both Allied and German. But the worst sight was the next city of Kaisers-Lautern about 25 miles farther, just over the German border. The entire city was flattened, not one building was standing when Gene looked in any direction. He asked an M.P. what had happened to cause so much destruction. The M.P. told him briefly this story. The Allied forces knew that the German army would offer very strong resistance to them as they crossed the border. So they subjected the city of Kaisers-Lautern to a combination of heavy artillery fire and aircraft bombing. Then the combat tanks rumbled in, blasting the city with their guns and crushing whatever they could. The Allies surged into the city. The Germans retreated and regrouped. They blasted the city with artillery fire and aircraft bombing. Their tanks rolled into the city, followed by their soldiers. The Allies retreated and regrouped. Again the Allies blasted the city with artillery fire and aircraft bombing. The tanks rolled into the city crushing all resistance. When the Allies reentered the city, the Germans had left for good and the city was crushed. Gene asked the M.P., "Where are the people who lived here?" The M.P. was a battle-hardened soldier and he answered, "The people who could, fled into the countryside, and the remainder are dead under the rubble!"

The 1524th ECG followed the Allied armies to the Rhine River, about 50 miles to the east. It was a tremendous psychological factor in the resistance of the German army. The Allies must not cross the Rhine River! or capture the city of Ludwigs-Hofen on the east bank and the city of Mannheim on the west bank! The Germans could not hold the bridge across the river between the two cities so they destroyed the bridge. The Allies completed the job by sinking the ships in the river.

Destroyed bridge and Ernie Pyle Memorial Bridge

The wooden bridge on the right was the "Ernie Pyle Memorial Bridge." It was a temporary bridge because it could handle only light traffic. It was replaced by the "Gar Davidson Memorial Bridge" which was more substantial. Ernie Pyle was an American writer who was revered by the Americans for his contributions to the army's newspaper. He died during the war.

At Mannheim General Patton received orders from General Eisenhower to turn to the south and go through Karlsruhe, Stuttgart, Ulm, and Augsburg down to Munich (now named Munchan). He was to secure all of southern Germany. He did not see this fulfilled as he died somewhere in this area. The 1524th ECG moved to the south about 25 miles. They went past Heidelberg and crossed the Neckar River to the town of Neckarhausen. On the outskirts of this town they found an abandoned factory in good condition so they established a semi-permanent headquarters there. They expected to move south behind the Allied army so they sent some surveyors toward Munich. Meanwhile they were ordered to rebuild 24 bridges on the Autobahn (the German high-speed automobile turnpike). In the short period of 30 days, they had finished the design of these bridges and the bridges were being renovated by the construction battalions. The 1524th ECG then turned their attention toward Munich and prepared to move to Karlsruhe about 25 miles to the south. But they were ordered to sit tight at Neckarhausen as some big news was about to break. It did. The Germans had capitulated and the European Theater portion of World War II was over.

European Theater - Phase 3

The soldiers were told to keep their helmet and gun with them always. There was to be no fraternization with the Germans. Of course, they disobeyed this order and frequently sought the companionship of the German girls. Gene's friend, Charles Koch, could speak German fluently. The two spent many days together hiking in this area. It was interesting to hear what the German people thought about the war. Every German--man, woman, or child--blamed the war on the Russians! The Russians wanted to conquer the world! The German advice was that the American army should continue eastward and not stop until they had conquered the Russians! If the Americans did not do it now, they would have to do it later! Excuses, excuses.

One day Charlie Koch pointed to the temporary wooden bridge across the Neckar River and asked what had happened to the original bridge. A German was disgusted. He blurted out, "It was the stupid German army! We had a beautiful old historic bridge. The German soldiers were ordered to demolish the bridge and they destroyed the entire bridge!" When the Allied soldiers arrived they were in combat tanks that went right through the water as the Neckar River was only a few feet deep at this place. He added, "It will take years to replace the original bridge!"

Another day Charlie and Gene saw a group of German boys, 10 to 12 years old. Charlie asked them what they were staring at. They replied that they were fascinated by the guns we were carrying. They asked if we ever used our guns. Charlie jokingly said, "Of course." Then to Gene's disgust, with no sign of apprehension on their faces, they asked, "How many soldiers did you kill?" Charlie could hardly believe his ears. He shouted at them, "At least a dozen or two, and if you don't get out of here, you will be next!"

They hiked a few miles back to Heidelberg to visit the famous Heidelberg Castle. It also had a famous brewery that was very popular with the Allied soldiers.

On the way Gene and Charlie took a one-lane dirt road through a small town. Ahead of them were two apartment houses, one on each side of the road. They were close to the road. In each building on the second floor was a German housewife leaning out of the window. As we neared the buildings, the women exchanged some conversation. After Gene and Charlie passed by, Charlie remarked, "I guess that they did not know that I spoke German." The one lady said, "Look at those two sloppy American soldiers, dirty shoes, baggy pants, no hats, what a disgrace." The other one answered, "You are right, they are not like our soldiers. They were always perfectly dressed." Then he laughed and said, "I almost said to them in German, 'That is why your soldiers lost the war!'"

A very enjoyable event occurred about this time. Gene often went for a leisurely walk to the Neckar River after the evening meal. It was about one mile each way and he could find his way easily by walking along the railroad. One day he paused to look more closely at a quaint farmhouse, small but neat, with flowers blooming and cherry trees laden with fruit. Suddenly he saw the face of a little girl at the window. He usually had a snack with him to eat while he sat on the riverbank. In this case, he took out the orange that he was carrying and motioned to the girl to come out to receive her gift. She disappeared but was at the door in a moment. The door was opened and a hand gently urged her out. She quickly walked to Gene, accepted the gift, said thank you in German, and hurried back inside. The next day, Gene walked along the railroad as usual. Sure enough, there was the little girl ready to come out. This time she was accompanied by a German woman. She told Gene that the little girl's name was Brigette and that she was Brigette's aunt. Gene could not speak German and the aunt knew very little English, so Brigette received her gift of a few chocolate bars, then said thank you, and went inside the house. This happened for a few days until one day Brigette's mother came out with the other two. They had a short conversation in a mixture of German and English. Then Gene remembered Charlie Koch and suggested that he come along to speak in German. He agreed and had a nice conversation with the women.

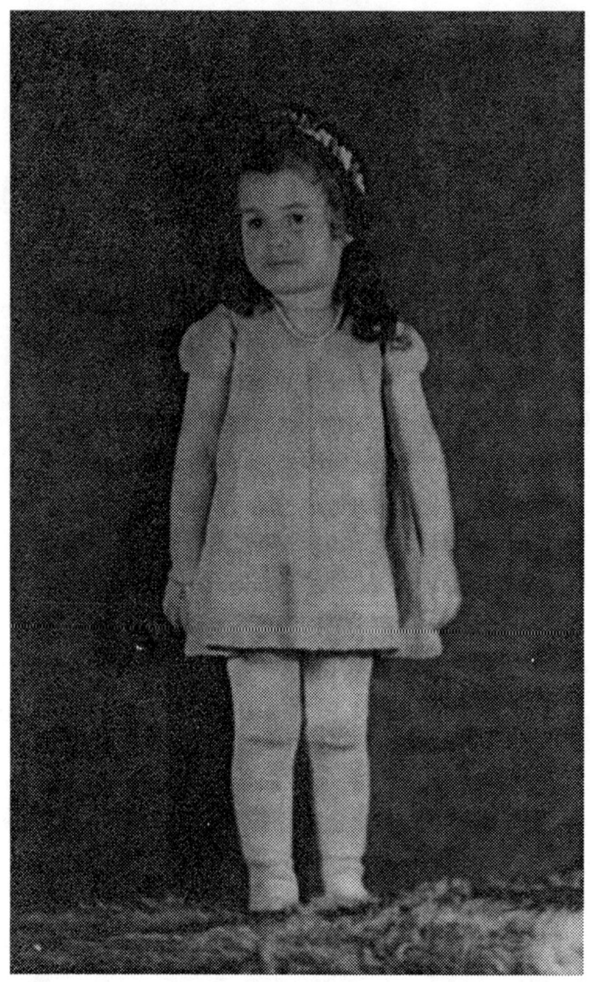

Brigette

A few days later, Gene and Charlie were surprised that no one appeared at the farmhouse as usual. But the next day, all three appeared. Brigette's mother explained to Charlie why they had been missing. The two women took Brigette with them to visit her father in the hospital. He was a lieutenant in the German army and had been shot in the leg during combat. He was happy to see his little daughter and she responded. But she kept looking at the clock. Finally he asked her why. In childlike honesty she told him that "her" American soldier friend came by the house every night at seven o'clock. She "had" to be there to receive the "gift" he always had for her. Gene never met him but he often wondered how Brigette's father felt. Later her father became the mayor of Neckarhausen.

One of the reasons for the "no fraternization" rule was that it was impossible to differentiate between "friend or foe." One day Gene and some of the other engineers were sent to inspect a group of buildings at Freidrichfeld nearby. The buildings were used to house people who had been forced by the German army to leave their home and come to work on the farm.

Allied soldiers now guarded the farm to prevent any workers from leaving the farm until the proper investigation could be made. One of the workers was a young, energetic, buxom girl from Russia. When the Germans invaded Russia they reached Stalingrad where the people put up a ferocious resistance to the Germans. Despite the fact that the Germans surrounded the city and cut off all supplies from entering, they were unable to conquer that city. About 300,000 people in the city lost their lives before the Germans withdrew, taking many persons back to Germany to act as forced labor. One of Gene's young engineers was sexually attracted by the Russian girl. He tried to get her into bed with him. She refused and one of the officers ordered the engineer to leave.

The town of Neckarhausen was a pleasant place to wait. The men of the 1524th ECG exchanged many favors with the German people, always wondering when they would go home. Finally, the word came to pack everything in the trucks. The next day the unit headed back to France. No one knew where they were going but at least, they decided, westward was the right direction.

European Theater - Phase 4

The first stop was in Strasbourg, Germany, about 68 miles to the south. Then Nancy, France, about 88 miles westward. Onward to the south to Dijon, France, about 100 miles farther. The city stood out in Gene's memory because the officers had made no plans to stay here and it was getting dark when they arrived. They noticed a large monastery in the city. Upon inquiry they were told that they could stay there but that it was deserted. They were assigned a small cell each. The bed was made of wooden slats with no mattress. In the morning, the men were glad to leave the cold, musty cell and try to work out the aches and pains.

The city of Lyon was next. It was about 115 miles direct to the south. Another long ride to Avignon, France, about 100 miles away. This 215 miles was beautiful. To the east were the French Alps with snow glistening on the tops of the mountains. Most people consider the Swiss Alps the highest and most spectacular. Then the Germany Alps are rated highly by mountaineers. But Gene thought that the French Alps were the best that he had ever seen. This was truly a highlight of this journey from Germany. From Avignon to Marseilles, France, was about 70 miles but the 1524th ECG turned to the east and climbed to a plain about 10 miles north of Marseilles. The area had been leveled. Unfortunately, the surface was now just a fine sand. Day and night, a strong wind blew up the valley from the Mediterranean Sea. It caused a constant sand storm that got into all of their belongings, even into the food.

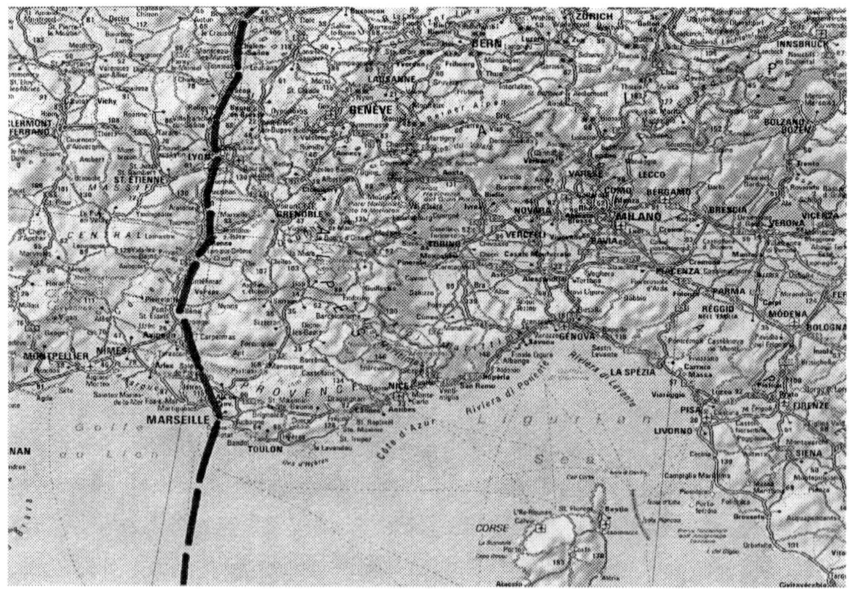

Map of Southern France

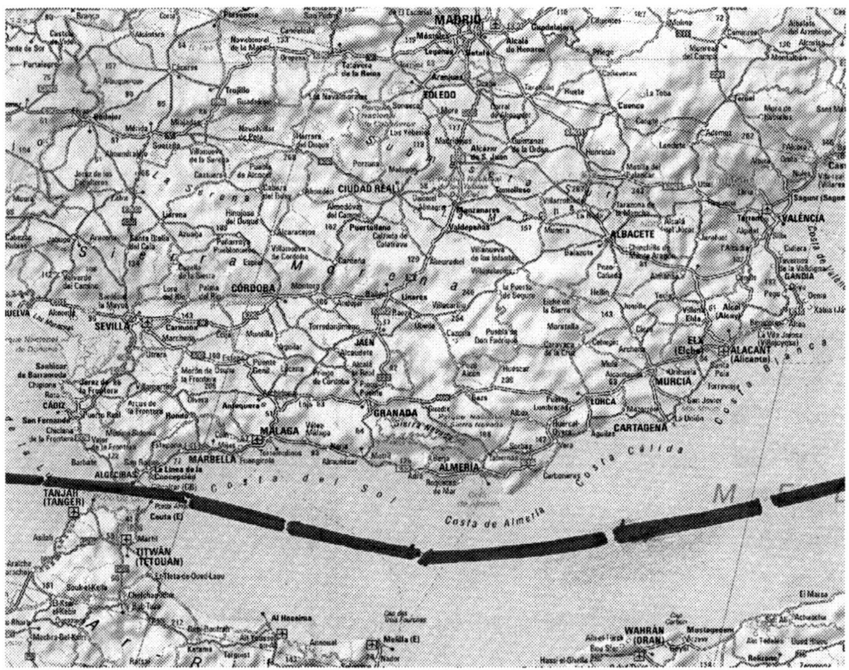

Map--through the Mediterranean

The 1524th ECG had to wait at this site near Marseilles for a week. No doubt for the troopship to get ready for the next voyage. Gene and four of his companions decided to look the area over. One day, immediately after breakfast, they set out hiking toward the east. In the distance (10 miles away) was a hill quite a bit higher than the plain where they were quartered. They went through three valleys and over two hills before starting the climb up the hill that was their destination. It had been difficult walking through farmlands and around farmhouses, through wooded areas, and even across some small streams. But the view was worth the effort. They could look down from the top of the hill to the south and see the city of Marseilles on the shore of the Mediterranean Sea. On the way back they met some French families, all friendly and smiling. Then they reached their quarters and sank exhausted on their cots. Even supper was not attractive. Their legs were as stiff as boards and their feet were blistered.

The word came. Get ready for the final leg of the journey to Marseilles. Into the vehicles and down to the city, 10 miles away. At the wharf was the largest troopship that Gene had ever seen. It could transport 5,000 soldiers. It was armed with two 5-inch guns and six anti-aircraft guns. That night the troopship left Marseilles and headed out into the Mediterranean Sea. First, it went to the south and then very gradually changed its course until it was going directly to the west. The next day Gene had some very unpleasant memories. A friend of his in Pittsburgh had enlisted in the U. S. Navy. He was assigned to duty on a destroyer that was sent to the Mediterranean during the invasion of Italy. The destroyer was hit by a torpedo from a German U-boat and sank immediately. All the sailors were lost.

The troopship reached the Strait of Gibraltar as the sun was going down in the west. The sky was a beautiful mixture of color--purple, orange, red, yellow--and the clear sea water reflected the lights in the sky. Gene was sad when he thought of his friend. But Gene had told him about personal salvation by accepting Jesus Christ as his Saviour. Gene had the deep feeling that his friend had made things right spiritually before his death. He felt better and, also, the realization that they were headed for the U.S.A. buoyed up his depressed inner feelings.

The troopship sailed out into the Atlantic Ocean. The men were sure they would be in the U.S.A. in a week. All the soldiers were jubilant! They had been away from home for two or three years and it would be great to be back. After a few days, a soldier noticed that the ship had altered its course somewhat to the south. He remarked that it was unusual because he figured that they would go somewhat to the north. Then after a few more days, it was certain that they were headed south. Perhaps Florida? But that was wishful thinking. Through the Caribbean they went! Gene could see the frustration on their faces and hear the emotion in their voices. Where were they going? The question was answered in another couple of days when the ship headed into the Panama Canal!

The announcement was made that the ship would stop at the midpoint of the Canal. The men would be divided into groups of 100 and boats would take them ashore where there was a PX (U. S. Army canteen and store). They were ordered to be back at their boats in less than one hour. Anybody who disobeyed would be thrown into the ship's brig (jail) for the rest of the voyage.

That night the ship continued through the Canal. The spirits of the men were uplifted somewhat by the visit to the PX and by the rumor that the ship would go north to San Francisco after leaving the Canal. The next day it seemed that the ship was now going west. It was in the Pacific Ocean but not going to San Francisco!

Pacific Theater - Phase 1

The ship proceeded out into the Pacific Ocean following a zigzag course. Two miles at 30° to the right of the straight course, then 30° to the left of the straight course for two miles, and always eventually on the straight course. The reason for this maneuvering was that the danger of enemy submarines was still a factor. The Germans had surrendered but some of their submarines had not returned to their base. They still lurked in the Pacific Ocean waiting for an unsuspecting victim. And Japan had not surrendered so their submarines were active, especially in the Pacific Ocean. Whatever the real reason, it bothered the soldiers. They wished that the voyage would end, and the constant changing of course aggravated them. They often said, "If it wasn't for this crazy zigzag course, we would have been there." Actually, the soldiers did not know where the ship was going!

Then one day, a shout went up. There on the horizon was land. It looked beautiful with its green forests and picturesque hills. It must be Hawaii was the cry. "We are going to Honolulu," was on every soldier's mind. But the ship kept plowing along until the land was no longer in sight and the ship was again on its zigzag journey.

The officers tried to relieve the monotony by setting aside one hour per week for exercise. This did not last long; everybody had lost any desire for any activity. If the soldier stayed downstairs, he usually just laid on his bed (three-tier bunk bed) and either slept or read a magazine. It was hot and stuffy or maybe it was a case of claustrophobia from being in a closed or narrow space. Usually a person could endure this for

Soldiers relaxing on deck

only a couple of hours, then he would head for the deck. It was always crowded. Soldiers talking to a buddy or staring into space. Some men gambled with cards or "shot crap" (gambled with dice). The officers never interfered; they realized that the men's nerves were on edge. An unwise command could cause a fight to break out--these were battle-hardened soldiers who had seen their fellow soldiers die or had killed the enemy soldiers with little compassion.

Another week and land was sighted. This time the ship headed into the land which turned out to be a series of islands. This was the Philippine Islands! The ship wended its way up through the islands until it reached Manila Bay. Then it was docked at a concrete wharf where all the men disembarked. This journey from Marseilles, France, had taken 36 days!

The men from the 1524th ECG stood on the wharf while the rest of the 5,000 soldiers left for their assignment areas. Later the 1524th ECG joined with them again. Now Gene stood on the wharf and looked at the city of Manila. A good portion of it had been destroyed shortly before when the Americans had invaded it and defeated the Japanese there. One thing especially caught his attention. Around the semicircle of Manila Bay at the water's edge had been a row of majestic government buildings constructed of massive stone and concrete. The Japanese had used them as their headquarters and had fortified them carefully to repulse any attempt by the Americans to recapture them. When the Americans arrived, the battleships remained out of the range of the Japanese guns and subjected these buildings to a terrific bombardment with their 18-inch guns. The result was the complete destruction of these buildings as well as the adjacent portion of the city. All that remained was a tremendous pile of stone and concrete rubble.

Just then a small dilapidated Filipino coastal steamer tied up at the end of the wharf. The men of the 1524th ECG boarded this vessel (with some misgivings since it looked as if it was ready to sink). The rest of the day was spent chugging up the coast for 150 miles to Batangas. Here they left the vessel and hiked up to a large level area where they were to stay.

Pacific Theater - Phase 2

The officer in charge ordered dinner. It was now late in the afternoon. The dinner was frozen C-rations and coffee. The 1524th ECG was told to lay prefabricated wood wall sections on the ground as a floor for each tent. The ground was partially covered with grass so Gene felt that this would be an easy task. To his surprise, the ground surface was 8 inches of sticky brown mud (it rained often at this season of the year). The men did their best but the wood floor was soon covered with mud from their shoes. Luckily, they had laced-up-over-the-ankle shoes. If they had not, the sticky mud would have pulled the shoes off their feet! It was now dark but they

1524th ECG Quarters

could not stop. The tents had to be erected and the two-tier bunk beds brought in. Each man received a smelly, moldy, straw mattress which he threw on his bunk, covered it with his blanket, fashioned a pillow using his jacket, took off his muddy shoes, lay down on his bunk, and immediately fell sound asleep.

The next day the site was trimmed up a bit. Some paths of crushed stone were laid out. Then the men were told about their assignment. It came as a complete surprise. The 1524th ECG was to assist in the design and construction of a complete camp for 250,000 soldiers. That meant living quarters, training areas, supply buildings, hospital facilities, etc., and everything from scratch. Unfortunately, the commissioned officers showed their inexperience with this type of assignment. During the European Theater, the assignments were usually the repair and construction of bridges and aircraft landing strips. Here, this was different and the commissioned officers were at a loss to even get started. Fortunately, Gene had a group of noncommissioned officers who were architects and engineers with experience with this work before the war.

An example of this ineptitude showed up when the 1524th ECG had to provide an adequate water supply. The second lieutenant and Gene climbed a hill near the camp and found a nice stream flowing down the hill. At a convenient place they decided to build a reservoir to store a week's supply of water for the entire camp. The second lieutenant did not know what to do, so he told Gene to get busy and design the reservoir. The second lieutenant was Nathan Levinson and his superior was Major Graves. The next day Lt. Levinson kept asking Gene if he had the drawing finished. Near the end of the day Major Graves asked Lt. Levinson if the design and drawing were finished. Lt. Levinson grabbed the drawing from Gene's desk and rushed up to Major Graves. Now Major Graves was a construction man but he knew nothing about reservoirs so he asked Lt. Levinson to explain what was on the drawing. Lt. Levinson told him how he had designed the reservoir and how he had made the drawing. After a few minutes of explanation from Lt. Levinson, the major stood up and shouted, "Levie, you don't know what you are talking about! You did not design this reservoir. Go back to Gene Dotter and find out how he did it, then come back to me!"

Work proceeded for the next few months. The camp grew in size quickly. Men flooded in every day. Some of these men were part of the 5,000 who had come from France with Gene. They had had a few months of special training and were waiting here for assignment. The men of the 1524th ECG now were told why the camp was established. Ten camps of 250,000 men each were being made ready for an invasion of Japan. They were arranged in a circle around Japan. Also, a number of airfields had been established with many bombers and fighter planes. Scattered in the circle around Japan were ports filled with battleships and other types of combat vessels. At a certain time the invasion would start. It would be the largest invasion in history. The vessels would descend on Japan from different directions and open up a barrage of large cannon that would shake Japan from one end to the other. At the same time thousands of aircraft would drop their heavy bombs, followed by hordes of small aircraft like dive-bombers, etc. Vessels would now bring in the 2,500,000 invasion soldiers and multitudes of combat tanks and artillery units. Japanese blood would flow in the streets like water. The Americans knew that the Japanese would not give up without a desperate fight so they were reconciled to having heavy losses on their side. They realized, however, that this tremendous invasion would probably end the war.

Suddenly an event took place that changed the lives of many people around the world. After years of experimenting with nuclear fission, the U.S.A. perfected an atom bomb. After much debate, the president, Harry Truman, agreed that this was an excellent time to test the bomb by dropping it on a city in Japan; in fact, two bombs were dropped, one on Hiroshima and one on Nagasaki. The devastation was unbelievable. It struck terror in the hearts of the Japanese people. They realized that every city in Japan was a potential target. They immediately sought terms of surrender.

Many people in the U.S.A. felt that using the atom bomb was inhumane; but the men in uniform did not think that way. They considered the terrible loss of life on both sides if the invasion had been carried out. Also, only two cities were affected by the atom bomb. The invasion would have affected many more cities.

Now the war was over; it was time to go home.

New men stopped arriving. The expansion of the camp came to a halt. The soldiers had plenty of leisure time. The officers organized trips to Manila and to other places of interest. Sports flourished; basketball and volleyball were the most popular. Usually at night, under the lights, when it had cooled down after the heat of the day. But the biggest item of interest was the time when a soldier was informed of the day when he was going home. The army had a system for determining when a soldier left the camp. It was called the "Point System." As the name implied, each man accumulated points that were determined by the number of months in the Armed Forces, the theaters, the major battles, decorations, etc. Then, of course, the number of ships available made a huge difference. Usually the men went across the Pacific Ocean in a Liberty ship. It was small, probably could take only 1,000 men each trip; and it was slow, its speed only 15 to 20 miles per hour. That meant at least two to three weeks per trip. And there were about 250,000 men at Batangas.

Gene liked to keep busy so he did many odd jobs around the camp. He even sold candy at the PX. It was several months before he had enough points to qualify for the next trip to the U.S.A. When he got the word, he packed up his duffel bag and was ready the next day to leave. No good-byes or words of thanks from the officers, just climb into the truck and go to the wharf where the Liberty ship was the only vessel. One officer with a megaphone stood at the gangplank shouting out one name at a time. The jubilant soldier picked up his duffel bag and struggled up the gangplank. This took quite some time as the officer had to check the soldier's army serial number on his "dog tag." Finally, as the sun was disappearing, all the men had boarded the vessel except Gene. He stood all alone on the wharf. The officer said, "I will have to get a vehicle to take you back to your outfit. You are not on the list and there are no bunks left!" Suddenly there was a loud roar. The 1,000 men on the ship shouted, "Let him on, let him on, let him on...," over and over. The officer didn't know what to do. He was a very considerate man so he turned to Gene and said, "If you are willing to sleep on the deck, you can get aboard." Gene replied, "Yes sir, yes sir!" And hurried up the gangplank to the cheers of the men.

Eighteen days later the ship docked at San Francisco. It had been a tough journey sleeping on the steel deck with no place to wash or even to eat. Gene was glad to be back in the U.S.A. but he thought that the questioning period was kind of stupid. "Where do you want to be discharged? Would you like to remain in the army? Would you accept a promotion if you elected to stay?" All Gene could think of was to get back to Guttenberg, New Jersey. So two days later he boarded an army bomber that had been stripped clean; in fact, there were no seats, just two long benches, one on each side of the interior. They took off at 5 A.M. and took the southern route, Los Angeles, Dallas, Atlanta, and finally Camp Dix at Trenton, New Jersey. At the top speed of 150 miles per hour, the plane took a day and a half to reach Camp Dix. Just in time for another questioning period, a physical examination, dinner, and a good night's sleep. In the morning, Gene was given his final pay, a train ticket to New York City, and his honorable discharge.

Pacific Theater - Phase 3

Although Gene had received an honorable discharge at Camp Dix, he considered himself as part of the U. S. Army. The Armed Forces had notified all men being discharged that they were eligible to receive a sum of money to be used to finance education. This was known as the G.I. Bill and Gene was determined to use it to pay for all the expenses at the Massachusetts Institute of Technology while he studied there for a Master of Science degree in the field of structural engineering.

The head of the Civil Engineering Department at M.I.T. was Dr. John Wilbur who had a love for bridge design. When he interviewed Gene he was entranced by the tales of how the 1524th ECG had repaired so many German bridges, particularly those of the German Autobahn. The class of 1947 at M.I.T. consisted 100 percent of men who had graduated with honors when receiving their Bachelor of Science degree. This provided stiff competition for Gene and would have prevented him from entering M.I.T. except that he had graduated from Newark College of Engineering with honors and Dr. Wilbur appreciated immensely his service in the European Theater, especially while replacing all those bridges.

Gene graduated from M.I.T. in the summer of 1947. He immediately left the Boston area for New York City. A friend of his was driving to his home in New Jersey and he offered Gene a free ride. They had often discussed their religious beliefs and his friend probably desired this last extended opportunity for another exchange of views. The friend was a member of the Christian Scientist Church. The denomination, founded in 1866 by Mary Baker Eddy, was known for its position of healing based on the teaching that cause and effect are mental and that sin, sickness, and death will be destroyed by a full understanding of the divine principle of Jesus's teaching and healing. Their discussions often began with both men being in accord that Jesus was the Son of God. But they soon moved along separate paths. Gene felt that a person away from God must repent of his sin and accept Jesus by faith that He was his personal Saviour. Then as a Christian, he must follow God's will in his life for whatever is before him. His friend felt that there was no sin, sickness, and death because it was a figment of their minds. But his friend was troubled because sin, sickness, and death were tangible factors in his life; in fact, his wife had divorced him just a short time before. The foundations of his faith were crumbling and he was at a loss to ascertain where to go. Gene advised him to go to Jesus, the solid rock, and put these problems in His hands.

* * *

The question of "What is Truth?" had now become a more penetrating factor in Gene's life. As a soldier, he had been faced with the situations where subterfuge and conniving were an essential part of obedience and discipline toward a superior officer. Also, many of the "Great Disappointments" in Gene's career in the army could have been eliminated if some officer had examined the situation truthfully. So he came to the question of what truth is, as defined in the dictionary:

1. a. Fidelity, constancy.

   b. Sincerity in action, character, and utterance.

2. a. (1) the state of being the case--fact.

   (2) the body of real things, events, and facts--actuality.

(3) a transcendent (lying beyond the limits of ordinary experience) fundamental or spiritual reality

b. a judgment, proposition, or idea that is true or accepted as truth.

c. the body of true statements and propositions.

3. a. the property (as of a statement) of being in accord with fact or reality.

b. true.

c. fidelity to an original or to a standard.

4. a. the quality or property of keeping close to fact and avoiding distortion or misrepresentation.

b. veracity, verity.

A mark of a truthful person is sincerity in what is said or what is done. A person who is free from adulteration and hypocrisy and of an honest mind. The officer in training caused them to support the Armed Forces standards whether right or wrong. Most enlisted men were not above reproach because they had a constant problem with falsehood, deceit, and deception.

Gene arrived at this conclusion, based on his war experiences: the truth must be regarded as precious. As the Old Testament of the Holy Bible says:

> The law of thy mouth is better unto me than thousands of gold and silver. (Psalm 119:72)

> Buy the truth and sell it not; also wisdom, and instruction, and understanding. (Proverbs 23:23)

He was also impressed by the need for constant observance of truthfulness:

> The lip of truth shall be established for ever: but a lying tongue is but for a moment. (Proverbs 12:19)

> Stand therefore, having your loins girt about with truth, and having on the breastplate of righteousness. (Ephesians 6:14)

III. PART THREE

Early Professional Life

1. MY SON--THE CONSTRUCTION ENGINEER

World War II had ended and Gene was free to resume his engineering career. He had returned to New York City where one of the executives of a large engineering company offered him a place to start. Gene gave it much thought and decided that he needed more construction experience. After all, the ammunition plant in Terra Haute, Indiana, for E. I DuPont deNemours had lasted only two months before the U. S. Government terminated the project. So Gene formulated a plan to follow up on his professional career. It was as follows:

a. Construction of industrial buildings.
b. Construction of steel mill buildings.
c. Construction of steel supply warehouses.
d. Construction of monumental buildings.

Gene afforded himself the luxury of a few days of vacation at the New Jersey shore, but he was anxious to begin work as soon as possible. He had not had a civilian job for five years so he hurried back to New York City. In a few days, he was hired by a construction company.

Kidde and Company, New York City, New York

From New York City to Philadelphia by way of Trenton, New Jersey, was an exceedingly busy set of railroad tracks. The train traffic flowed copiously in both directions. Gene was sent to Trenton to act as a surveyor-engineer for this company. The chief surveyor had been a fine employee but now was an alcoholic. When hired he did not have even one clean shirt or pair of pants. Part of his first week's pay was spent on decent clothing. The rest probably went for alcohol.

One day the crew of four surveyors was laying out a new building. The chief surveyor called out the angles and distances while the other three placed stakes at the corners. In keeping with Gene's desire to learn as much as possible, he had carefully examined the construction drawings before the other men had started to work. It dawned on him that the figures that the chief surveyor was providing were not the ones that he had seen on the drawings. He quietly gathered the men around the drawings and told the chief surveyor that something was wrong. The chief surveyor vehemently objected but Gene quietly persevered. It was apparent that the chief surveyor had had, as they say, "a liquid breakfast." He was reading the construction drawings upside down! A few days after that he thought he had screwed a transit to its tripod; but when he picked up the surveying instrument, the transit fell off the tripod and landed on the ground. He carefully looked around to see if anybody was observing his actions, then he quickly fastened the transit to the tripod and walked away as if nothing had happened. The superintendent would have excused him for dropping the transit but he could not overlook a surveyor dropping a sensitive instrument and not having it checked by an experienced transit repair mechanic. Gene never saw him again. Gene was sad because this man was actually very pleasant, often smiling, and often quoting classical literature and poetry. But alcohol and drugs can reduce the best person to a poor shadow of his original self.

This project did not last long but it taught Gene some practical lessons. One of the surveyors came happily trotting along a path. He was to pass five very large roof trusses that were stacked flat on the ground. One projected about one foot or so into the path. The surveyor walked into the projected end without a pause. He fell flat on his back, out cold. Ten minutes later when he came to, all he could say was that he was thankful that he had not knocked out an eye. Gene agreed. He then put this event into spiritual terms by saying that God wants us to be aware of any secret sins in our life and do something about them before it is too late.

The assistant construction superintendent had some laborers remove some old, soft fill where the floor of the warehouse was to be situated. It was getting late so he had already ordered the concrete to finish the floor. To his surprise, the trench became a small, underground stream of water. The assistant superintendent did not have the time to investigate the problem. He shouted to the laborers to place the concrete. Quietly he whispered to Gene that he thought the concrete would prevent the water from rising. Gene thought that someday the water would appear; in fact, the floor slab would settle and crack. He observed, "Be sure your sins will find you out" (Bible quote).

The construction superintendent was Edward Pavlo. He had been a star football player in college. Upon graduation, he married a beautiful classmate who came from the quiet life of socialite. Ed was signed by the NFL New York Giants to play as a defensive lineman. He was really not big enough so he was soon released. In the next ten years he had played for five or six teams. Then he realized that his success was very limited and he took a construction job with the firm of Kidde and Company. It suited him as he was a rugged, quiet person--actually quite gentle. His wife was not able to withstand the rigors of a football player's life. And now, being the wife of a construction superintendent did not appeal to her. She began to have mental problems.

The company held a Christmas party at their headquarters in New York City. Mr. and Mrs. Pavlo attended. Some of the people from the Trenton project were there. Gene was not there. The next day he heard that an employee had consumed too much alcohol and had attempted to attack Mrs. Pavlo but had been restrained, had apologized, and had been forgiven by Mr. and Mrs. Pavlo. Somehow this incident triggered a thought in Gene's mind. Five years before he had met a young lady in Pittsburgh. He decided to move to Pittsburgh to work and find out if Elizabeth Wood still thought highly of him.

Pittsburgh Industrial Engineering Company (PIE)

This was a small engineering and construction company that specialized in handling small projects for the larger steel companies that did not want to be bothered with them. The work was usually done in the steel mills near or over steel rolling lines. The men who worked in the mills had to rest quite often because the steel billets that came sliding down the lines were red hot. The heat exhausted these men so they were often resting when Gene's crew came in. Soon Gene and his crew were exhausted also and they would sit around covered with perspiration.

Sometimes the work entailed climbing high above the steel rolling lines. This was very dangerous as there were no catwalks. Gene had to inch his way carefully out onto a roof truss about 200 feet long and at least 50 feet above the floor. The bottom angles that he walked on were usually two angles, back to back, with six-inch steel horizontal legs to step on. And the angles were covered with a thick black slippery sediment deposited by years and years of rolling steel down below. The idea was to keep from slipping and falling while working with measuring tapes to obtain the necessary dimensions. Gene always breathed a huge sigh of relief when work was complete and nobody had fallen.

Gene with transit

It was not long before Gene decided to leave this company. Not because of the danger but for another reason. Gene had often noticed that the boss of the field crew would leave without explanation and be absent for a few hours. The other men did not seem to mind; in fact, if they finished their task and he was not present, they would find a comfortable place and sleep for a few hours. When Gene asked where the boss was one day, he was told that the boss had started his own surveying company and would take care of his own personal work whenever he felt that it was necessary. PIE would pay for this as the men all worked on a weekly wage basis, not an hourly basis. Gene thought that this dishonest procedure should be stopped. So he had a talk with one of the partners of the company. To his amazement, he was told that the company policy was to allow this behavior. Mr. Parker said, "If a worker is wise enough to handle two jobs, we approve of his conduct. Why don't you try to arrange something for your advantage?"

Gene did not need any further "advice." He quickly decided that this was not honest, and he found that this would not fit into his plans to become a consulting engineer.

Wheeling Corrugating Company, Wheeling, West Virginia

This company was a division of Wheeling Steel Company. The parent company had decided to expand their outlet system. The first building was to be in Richmond, Virginia. It was really a warehouse for Wheeling Steel products but it had a large office area at the front. Gene was hired as an architectural engineer to supervise the general construction for the owner. He was to be in residence. This position was usually called "the clerk of the works." It appealed to Gene for it afforded him an opportunity to learn about architecture as well as structural engineering. He carefully studied the construction drawings and the specifications. These were known as the Construction Documents. He was prepared to answer any questions. Unfortunately, some answers came only from experience, not the documents or a textbook.

The construction was being carried out by the Hudson Construction Company with headquarters in Hudson, Virginia, about 200 miles to the west of Richmond. The construction superintendent was from Hudson. He was an excellent administrator with a great deal of construction experience. Unfortunately, he was in charge of four projects, each about 50 miles apart. It meant that he visited each job only two or three times each week and only for a few hours during each visit. For most of the week the chief carpenter was in charge. He was an experienced construction man with a nice personality. The problem arose again, which seemed to be always present in the construction field: he was an alcoholic. Most days he was sober. Around Wednesday he couldn't hold out and he got drunk that night. Thursday and Friday he was sober again, ready to leave Richmond for Hudson as soon as the work on Friday was over. That suited Gene for he was eager to return to Pittsburgh for Saturday and Sunday.

One day Gene was invited to ride to Hudson with the chief carpenter. He quickly accepted the invitation for it was a good opportunity to see what that area of Virginia was like. He went to the local hotel while his friend went to stay at the home of his fiancee. Gene regretted this move for he found the bed full of bedbugs. When he moved to the sofa to get away from the bedbugs, he found that it also was "occupied." The next day he moved to a cleaner place but he was awfully tired after being up all night. He was glad when Sunday morning arrived. After breakfast, they joined the carpenter's fiancee at church, had a nice dinner, and headed back to Richmond. This couple was in their forties but unmarried. They had been engaged for over 15 years. Gene surmised that the question of alcohol and its hold on the carpenter was too much of an obstacle for marriage. Another alcohol-blighted life.

The entire construction time was eight months. The Hudson Construction Company was careful to complete this project in a very workmanlike manner. Their personnel were always courteous and anxious to satisfy the owner. If there was a problem, it was not Hudson. To Gene's surprise, the suppliers from the Richmond area had a problem dealing with a northern owner. It seems that many people in Richmond (the South) were still living in Civil War days! An unusual weather system was noticed by Gene one day which could have reflected the personality of the people. Early in the morning the weather forecast was for cold weather. Most construction workers would have a jacket on when they started work. By noon these men would have shed the jacket and would be working in shirt sleeves. On this particular day, there was a very noticeable line of demarcation that divided the city into two parts. The northern half was covered with heavy dark clouds and was covered with several inches of snow. The southern half had a ordinary blue sky with bright, warm sunshine. This kind of reflected the attitude of the North and the South.

Gene was satisfied with his work experiences on this project, but he did not wish to continue working for Wheeling Corrugating Company. It was time to return to Pittsburgh.

Mellon-Stuart Company, Pittsburgh, Pennsylvania

In the year of 1949 this construction company had achieved an enviable reputation as a major builder. They had completed the Gulf Building which was 40 stories in height and were finishing a permanent U. S. Army camp in Pennsylvania and a major library building for Ohio State University. Their latest project was a Veterans Administration Hospital in Altoona, Pennsylvania, about 100 miles east of Pittsburgh, Pennsylvania. The first phase had not proceeded well and the Federal Government was complaining about the progress. One of the actions by Mellon-Stuart was to hire Gene as a construction engineer with the hope that he could expedite construction progress. Also, they requested Ned Mellon, a member of the famous Andrew Mellon family, to establish an office at the construction site as a public relations move.

It was not long after Gene arrived that he realized that the estimators had made a grievous mistake. There were three major buildings with deep basement areas. Somehow the estimators had gained the erroneous opinion that all the basement excavations were in soft, clean dirt that could be removed by bulldozers and by hand. Instead, the material was solid rock that could not be ripped out by a big, powerful backhoe. It was slow, costly work, often requiring explosives to loosen the rock. One of Gene's first tasks was to convince the V.A. that Mellon-Stuart should receive an extra $200,000 to cover the added cost of excavating.

The buildings were on a beautiful ridge overlooking a wooded area with several smaller ridges in the distance. During the day Gene could pause for a moment and look into the distance and see wild deer on the hillside. That excited Gene to see the wild deer, but he was also excited about this project. The main hospital building was five stories high and the framing was largely steel but with poured concrete floors. The construction superintendent was T. Piper who had many years of experience. He taught Gene often new things about construction. Usually with a caustic tone to his voice and a fat stub of a cigar in his mouth.

Gene boarded in a local home during the week, then went to Pittsburgh on Friday afternoon. He returned to work early Monday morning. Mellon-Stuart had a van that the men going to Pittsburgh could use. Most of the time the chief accountant, Bill McKinney, drove. He decided to drive southward until he reached the Pennsylvania Turnpike and then westward to Pittsburgh. Once it was a warm summer day about five o'clock in the afternoon. The man seated next to the driver had fallen asleep. Gene, seated behind the driver, suddenly noticed that the van had slowly drifted from the slow lane into the fast lane. He became concerned when the van moved farther to the left onto the concrete berm. He shouted to McKinney, "Mac, Mac. You are asleep." McKinney awoke with a start, jerked the steering wheel to the left and sent the car careening across the grassy median strip. Still hurtling along at sixty miles per hour, the car raced along the fast lane going in the wrong direction. It was miracle to see car after car zoom past the van with horns blowing (and drivers swearing). Finally McKinney collected his wits enough to turn to the right across the median strip and headed back in the right direction--still moving at sixty miles per hour.

Another day as they were driving along the Pennsylvania Turnpike, McKinney told the man next to him to stop smoking. A few minutes later he repeated the request. The man told him that he was not smoking. Then McKinney said that he thought the smell of burning was coming from the back where Gene was sitting. Gene said that it couldn't be him. Then he noticed that his suitcase, made of a heavy type of cardboard, was sitting on the van floor next to him. He idly turned it over. To his astonishment a large circular hole had been burned in the bottom and the clothes inside were smoldering and smoking. The springs of the van had relaxed and allowed the wooden body of the van to settle down onto the drive shaft where the friction had burned through the floor and through the bottom of Gene's suitcase without anyone knowing what was happening.

Mellon-Stuart headquarters requested Gene to pack up his belongings and come to Pittsburgh to help the estimating department. He worked at this new job for two months, then he was told that large losses in the last four projects had taken the available capital of the company and it was about to go bankrupt. One course to follow was to have Edward Mellon, the president, to request a large loan from the Mellon Bank. To Gene's surprise, the president of Mellon Bank, a member of the Mellon family, refused to approve the loan. The reason, that was known only to insiders, was that Ned Mellon was no longer considered as a member in good standing with the Mellon family. During World War II, he had divorced his wife of many years (who was considered as a member in good standing with the Mellon family) and married a nurse that he had recently met.

The company managed to survive, however. Ned Mellon, the president, was given a minor position and another man, Donald Peters, assumed the presidency. Mellon Bank probably then gave the loan although there was reliable information that a large mechanical engineering and construction company had bought controlling interest in Mellon-Stuart. Gene did not care for these manipulations so he requested a change. He was well liked by Don Peters, Ned Mellon, T. Piper, and others. He was offered the position of assistant construction superintendent of a large hospital project, Butler County Memorial Hospital. He accepted readily for this was a tangible promotion. The negative factor was that

George Porter, the construction superintendent, was very difficult to work with. After a few months though, it was apparent that Porter was very sick and probably could not live more than a year. Gene never really knew what happened to him because Don Peters promoted Gene to construction superintendent on another project.

The new project was a moderate-sized Catholic school building in Perrysville, Pennsylvania, near Pittsburgh. The Catholic church was on Perrysville Avenue and the school was to be behind it. It was a poor site because the ground sloped at a steep grade and there was no entrance to the bottom of the valley where the school was to be built. First, a winding one-lane dirt road was cut into the side of the hill. Then the hole for the school basement was excavated. Trees, bushes, dirt had to be removed. It was now late Fall and it rained frequently. The excavating contractor often had to winch his bulldozer out of the mud. Finally thc hole was completed and a level road was cut along the top of the hole. The footings for the columns and the walls were dug and prepared for the concrete. A ready-mix truck slowly made its way down the steep, winding dirt lane and stopped at the level lane along the one side of the hole which was about twelve feet deep. Gene went to the edge of the hole between the side of the truck and the hole which was about fifteen inches wide. He rested his hand on the side of the truck and peered into the hole. To his horror, he felt his hand move as the truck began to slide into the hole. He had about five seconds to decide what to do. If he jumped down the twelve feet into the hole, he knew that he would not avoid the truck falling on top of him. He could not run out of the way of the truck so he breathed a short prayer for divine intervention and turned to jump. Then God answered with a miracle. The truck moved about six inches toward the hole and stopped with just enough room for Gene to remain standing and then inch his way out of danger. The truck driver jumped out of the truck, as white as a ghost, and said, “I sure thought that the truck was going over.” Gene answered, “Thank the Lord for His mercy toward us!”

It soon began to snow and further construction work here was impossible. Gene came faithfully every day to look over the situation. Then he went up to the basement of the church where the church janitor had provided a chair and a light. He spent most of the day talking to the janitor or reading a book. After a month of inactivity, he called Don Peters, Mellon-Stuart president, and told Don that he was quitting. When Don asked him why he was leaving, Gene said that he was wasting his life here in this basement. Don wanted him to take another position during the winter but Gene refused. He had the definite feeling that God wanted him to leave the construction business. He had two degrees in structural engineering and it was time to start using his education in his primary professional area of work.

2. MY SON - THE STRUCTURAL ENGINEER

Before World War II, Gene had worked in Pittsburgh, Pennsylvania, for the Bethlehem Steel Company. He had attended the Union Gospel Church in Wilkinsburg, Pennsylvania. Here he met a young lady, Elizabeth Wood, whom he found very attractive. She was still attending high school and Gene had just graduated from college. It seemed wise for him to wait until she had graduated from high school before he got too serious. Then he traveled away from Pittsburgh and eventually volunteered for the U. S. Army. After four years in the army, he attended the Massachusetts Institute of Technology. When he graduated in June, 1947, that same day Elizabeth graduated from the University of Pittsburgh with the highest honors. She was asked by the Dean of Women if she would consider a position in her office. Elizabeth accepted gladly and worked there for two years.

Meanwhile Gene worked in Trenton, New Jersey, but returned to Pittsburgh in 1948. Gene and Elizabeth (Betty) found that they had much in common; in fact, they were convinced that God had brought them together for the purpose of marriage. So in 1949, while Gene was working in Altoona for Mellon-Stuart, they were united in marriage. They established a home in Penn Hills, near Pittsburgh. Betty went back to work at the University of Pittsburgh for the Foreign Student Exchange office. Gene continued his work for Mellon-Stuart until he left them in 1953. He wanted to work in the field of structural engineering. Also, he felt that construction work was a divisive force in their marriage and in their religious service for the Lord. So Gene's professional career now began in earnest.

Leland W. Cook, Pittsburgh, Pennsylvania

Gene was immediately hired by this consulting engineer. Leland W. Cook had often joined with Robert Zern to offer consulting structural engineering services to architects. Now they had been hired by the architectural firm of Kaclik and Graves to work on a very large project for Allegheny County, a new county hospital. Zern had one assistant,

James Younkins, a graduate of Penn State, so Cook hired Gene as his assistant. Gene was a good draftsman. He took Lee Cook's calculations and his notes and produced a set of structural drawings that all the architects thought were excellent; in fact, some architects returned with more work because they thought that the drawings were so good. It was difficult work. The office was not air-conditioned. In the summer, the windows were opened for needed ventilation and that resulted in the drawings being constantly covered with dust. Or the warm temperature meant perspiration on hands and arms which stained the drawings.

There was little time for rest. Payment from the architect was based on the percentage of the construction cost. Other factors made an impact on whether the project ended in the black or the red. Some architects did not produce decent reference drawings. Many errors were present on what they gave to the engineers. Often they were late in sending the reference drawings and they insisted on the engineering drawings being submitted on the scheduled date. Some architects telephoned constantly with the question, "Are you done yet?" In order to finish on time, it meant some night work. Gene often had a quick evening meal and hurried back to work until 9 P.M. And Gene always tried to get to the office by 7 A.M. This allowed him one hour for Bible study before starting work at 8 A.M.

The pay was poor. Gene had earned more with Mellon-Stuart. Lee Cook was rather tight with his money. He paid at the beginning of each month. Often he would forget to pay Gene. After a week had gone by, Gene would quietly enter Lee Cook's office. After a few minutes, Lee would ask him what he wanted. When Gene reminded him that he had not given him his monthly check, he would reply, "Do you have your hand in my pocket again?"

Despite the negative aspects of the work, Gene loved the job. The variety of the projects was amazing. After completing the hospital for Allegheny County, Lee and Gene worked on an addition to the Pittsburgh International Airport, a bridge for a new airplane runway, a new classroom building at the University of Pittsburgh, a new hospital for McKeesport, Pennsylvania, a parking garage for Wierton, West Virginia; a new high school for Butler, Pennsylvania, and numerous buildings in the Western Pennsylvania area. All this time, Gene attended all the technical structural engineering seminars that he heard about. He was especially careful to continue his connection with the local A.S.C.E. (American Society of Civil Engineers) and to glean whatever he could from the national technical meetings. He had observed that only a few practicing structural engineers were interested in the A.S.C.E. meetings. They had been taken over by the academic population. Usually the program consisted of the latest research project of the structural engineering professor at the local college. This was very dull listening for the average structural engineer; but Gene decided that even if he found only one new idea in a whole day of seminars, it was well worth the effort.

After three years of association with Lee, Gene asked for a raise in pay. Lee obliged with a 10 percent raise. After another three years had gone by Betty reminded Gene that it was time to talk with Lee again. One day he quietly brought up the subject which Lee calmly ignored. Gene had no intention of begging. He had heard that Alcoa (Aluminum Company of America) was looking for structural engineers. They were offering a pay scale substantially higher than that offered by Lee Cook. Gene applied at Alcoa and was accepted. He hurried back to Lee and explained his need for a higher salary. He told Lee that Alcoa had offered what seemed fair to him. To Gene's surprise, there was absolutely no discussion. Lee just leaned back in his chair, smiled, and said, "I guess a little engineer like me can't compete with the big boys."

This incident brought back to Gene's memory something that Lee had said to him. Lee had read a letter from the church where he was a member. The pastor had asked if Lee would serve as an elder in the church for another term. Also, the pastor had included a request from the treasurer of the church for Lee's annual contribution toward the expenses of the church. Lee then laughingly had said to Gene, "I'll send a check and also indicate that I will serve as elder, even though I will not attend any meetings." He then added his favorite scripture (?), "After this life, then the fireworks."

Gene wondered what kind of church that could be. A member who sent an offering once per year. An elder who never attended any church meetings. A person who couldn't quote scripture correctly.

Alcoa (Aluminum Company of America), New Kensington, Penn.

The Board of Directors were looking for new uses of aluminum. In New Kensington, about twenty miles north of Pittsburgh, a new division consisting of about twenty recent college graduates was organized. The purpose of this division was to be available to any company that had formulated some desire to use aluminum. One of these men suggested that Alcoa look into structural shapes made of aluminum rather than steel. They figured that aluminum could be a better metal in some cases because it would not corrode and rust like steel. Also, it was much lighter than steel. The negative side to aluminum was that it had a much lower modulus of elasticity, it was difficult to weld, and it was more expensive to produce.

A new division of eight men was organized: a division leader, his assistant, and six structural engineers. Only one person had any practical experience with structural engineering design. That one person was Gene. The other persons were recent college graduates who had been hired because of their outstanding academic records in college. The wisdom of that was open to debate.

The first project was to design electric transmission towers with aluminum members (angles) rather than steel. The initial cost of a tower was higher. The bid tendered by Alcoa always was rejected because steel was cheaper; however, when Alcoa produced information showing that aluminum towers did not have to be repainted like steel, they were much more attractive. The towers also did not have to be taken out of service in order to allow painters to have access to the high members carrying the long spans of electric cable.

"Inside politics" took over in electric transmission companies--and in Alcoa. The result was that another avenue for using aluminum was tried. The second project was to design an aluminum structural framing system for a building where chemical corrosion would attack a steel framing system quickly. Even though the division leader and his assistant had no experience with the design and construction of buildings, they insisted on having absolute supervision of the project. The assistant division leader was especially difficult to work with. Gene soon lost his patience with his tedious ignorance. He knew that Alcoa had an Engineering Design and Construction Division that handled all of the company's internal building design and construction. He met with the division leader and asked if he could transfer into this division. He felt well qualified to be there and he knew that he would like the work much better. The division leader said he would consider the request. Instead, he immediately contacted Gene's superior and told him that Gene was trying to transfer without official permission. That amounted to a grievous "sin" in a large corporation like Alcoa. From then on Gene was a "persona non grata." Gene didn't really care, for he had decided that he no longer wished to work for Alcoa. He was convinced that he would rather be a "large frog in a small frying pan than a small frog in a large frying pan."

As far as his five fellow structural engineers were concerned, they could care less. They had no intention of staying in this division. It amused Gene to see how they wasted hour after hour discussing how they could rapidly get into the upper echelon of administration; in fact, they even spent much time figuring out how much their pension would be at retirement (in about forty years).

The project was not a success. The division leader and his assistant were transferred to minor positions. Shortly after, three of the structural engineers left Alcoa. Two remained for a few years but then disappeared. A few weeks after his transfer request was refused, Gene heard from Jim Younkins, the former assistant of Robert Zern, the consulting engineer. Jim had left Bob Zern to become chief structural engineer for a large architectural firm in Pittsburgh, Deeter and Ritchey. He needed help so he invited Gene to join him.

Deeter and Ritchey, Architects, Pittsburgh, Pennsylvania

Downtown Pittsburgh is situated on what is called "The Golden Triangle." The triangle is formed by the Allegheny River meeting the Monogahela River and forming a point in the land between the rivers. The rivers then become the Ohio River. This flows southward and westward to meet the Mississippi River eventually. Before the 1950s, the triangular piece of land was a mess. Small industrial shops, saloons, houses of prostitution, and flophouses for transients flourished on every hand. Then in the 1950s the "Renaissance" began. A committee of outstanding citizens began a vigorous effort to clear this eyesore and replace it with some high-rise office buildings and top-rate hotels. One of the strong supporters was Alcoa. Because of their heavy investment, they had much to say about the architecture of the new buildings.

Russell Deeter was an architect employed by Alcoa. He realized that this project would provide years of lucrative work so he resigned from Alcoa and formed his own firm. Dahl Ritchey was an acquaintance who showed much skill in the field of architecture. It was natural for the two to pool their resources and become the leading architectural firm in Pittsburgh.

Ordinarily they would have contracted with consulting engineering firms in the fields of structural, mechanical, electrical, etc., design. Instead they decided to form their own groups of engineers. Jim Younkins was hired to lead the Structural Engineering Division. He had some drawbacks. He had graduated from Penn State with a degree in Architectural Engineering. As of this time, he had not really made up his mind whether he would be an architect or an engineer. Gene had tried to convince him to concentrate on one field and to continue some advanced study in that field. He would not do this, but he appreciated that Gene had done this so he invited Gene to leave Alcoa and work for him. So in 1962 Gene joined the firm of Deeter and Ritchey.

Gene worked nicely with Jim but he noticed that he was doing quite a bit of his own work in the evenings. Actually, he was working as an architect with a friend in West Virginia. One day Jim told Gene that he wanted a raise in pay (Jim had five children) so he was going to approach Dahl Ritchey about this. He was going to put a little pressure on Dahl by intimating that he could get a higher salary somewhere else. That afternoon Jim said to Gene that he was on his way to Dahl's office. He returned in about ten minutes and sat at his desk without saying a word. Finally Gene went over and said, "How did it go?" Jim looked at him with a sort of dazed expression on his face. He said, "I think that I just got fired!" Later he said that he had mentioned that he had an offer of a higher salary. Dahl had jumped out of his chair with a pleased look on his face and had said, "That is great, take the offer, take the offer right away!" and shook his hand vigorously. So Jim cleared out his desk and left the next day.

Fortunately, Gene was familiar with all the structural projects in the office. There was one project just starting for which Jim had done the preliminary work alone. It was an exhibition building for the National Cash Register Company to be erected at the 1964 New York City World's Fair in Flushing Meadows, New York. Jim had told Gene that he would take the information home and do the design calculations at home. Several weeks later Russell Deeter asked Gene for a progress report on the NCR building. When Gene told him that Jim was working on this project, he was very unhappy. He told Gene to call Jim and tell him that the office needed the finished design in one week; NCR was being pressured by New York City.

Jim worked every evening at home on this design. At the end of the week he slipped into the office very early in the morning and left his design results on Gene's desk. When Gene came to work, he took only one look at Jim's work and knew that it was entirely incorrect. Gene rushed into Russ Deeter's office to tell him the bad news. Russ was furious. He had been given one more week by NCR to produce a preliminary structural drawing that could be submitted to New York City. Russ had to meet Robert Moses, an outstanding administrator for

New York City, who was now in charge of the World's Fair buildings. And who had chosen ten buildings to be in a select area. One of these was to be the NCR building.

Russ was at a complete loss about how to proceed. He looked at Gene and asked him what he thought. Gene told him that the NCR building was very complicated and had to be solved on a computer. Unfortunately at that time (1963) there was no computer around Pittsburgh that could handle this problem. Russ then admitted that it seemed to be impossible but could Gene try in a week to get something ready for New York City. Gene agreed and explained the procedure that he would use. He knew of a firm in Boston, Massachusetts, Jackson and Moreland, who could set up the 1,000 simultaneous equations in two days. They would go to M.I.T. where there was a computer that could solve the equations in two more days. Then Jackson and Moreland could work with Gene for two days to apply the results to the framing plans. That left one day for Gene to make some preliminary structural framing plans. Gene then said to Russ, "If you trust me to produce, then we must get up to Boston immediately." Russ merely said, "Let's go."

The schedule laid out by Gene was followed exactly. The preliminary plans were approved by NCR and by Robert Moses for the City of New York. The final construction documents were accepted with one important change. One end of the building had a cantilever of 42 feet. The calculations indicated that the deflection would be excessive when loaded with spectators. Jackson and Moreland did not know what to do. Gene told them to put some steel columns in the window mullions and rerun the new computer input. It solved the problem. The final drawings were sent to a plans reviewer in New York City. When he saw the structural drawings, he turned to Gene and said, "I hope that you know what you are doing, I don't! I'll approve the plans because you are certain that the design is adequate."

The construction moved along smoothly. Deeter and Ritchey were pleased because NCR was pleased. Also, they were impressed with the fact that a number of adjacent buildings had been designed by the

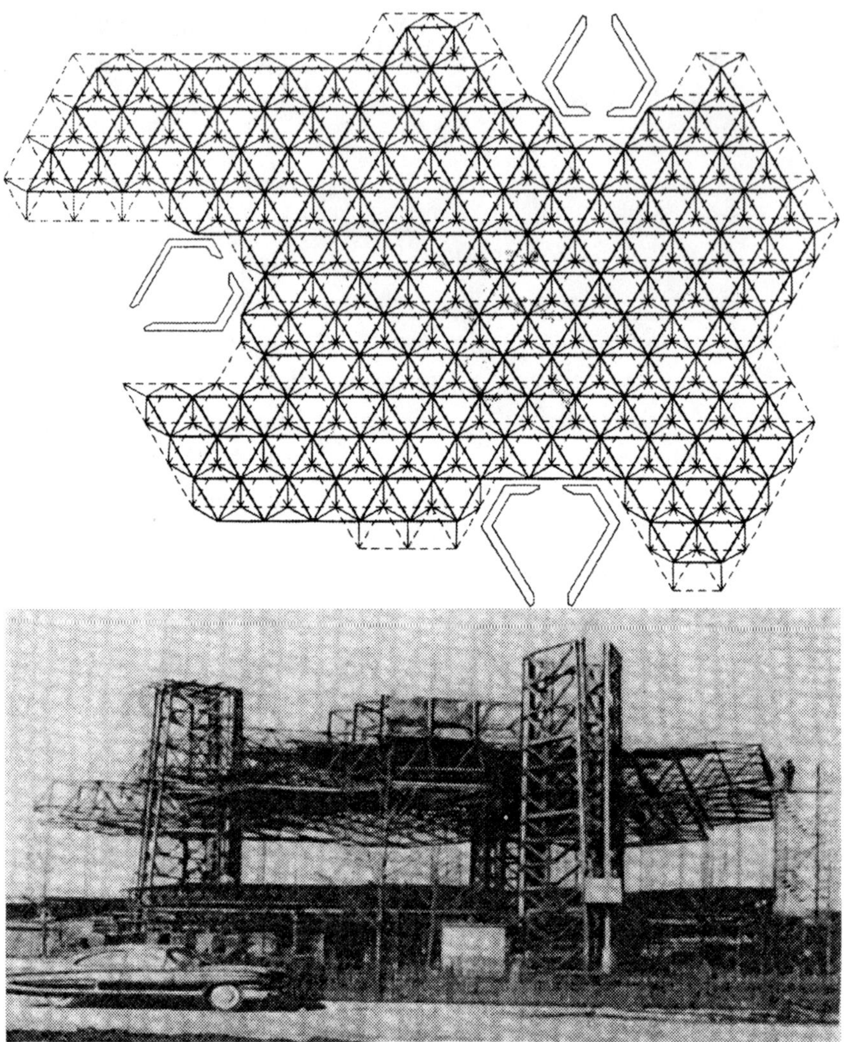

NCR Building floor framing

foremost architects and engineers in the country. The day before the opening of the World's Fair arrived. Russ Deeter was escorting a group of NCR executives around when one of them noticed what appeared to be a weakness in the floor framing over a set of windows. The steel framing there appeared to be about 12 inches lower then the remainder of the floor framing. All the executives were alarmed. Perhaps the framing was inadequate there and would fail when the people arrived the next day. A quick telephone call was made to Gene. He was told to rush out to the airport and take the next plane to New York City. He arrived that evening at the NCR building. He suggested that a surveyor come very early the next morning. The surveyor checked the elevations and told Gene that the floor framing was level (therefor strong enough to support the people) but that the window trim had been installed incorrectly. The installer had left it that way as he did not have any replacement and the World's Fair would open the next day. Gene told Russ Deeter to open the doors at the scheduled hour of 8 A.M. Then Gene spent the whole day visiting as many exhibits as possible before heading back to Pittsburgh.

The World's Fair was extended for one year (1964-1965). In 1966 Russia hosted a special conference on the structural design of unusual buildings. Gene was invited and accepted the invitation. Upon his arrival in Moscow, he was immediately taken by private limousine to his room at the hotel. Everything was first class as the host considered him to be a prestigious guest. The only thing that they couldn't produce was a glass of milk with his evening meal. Everyone drank vodka. In the street many drunks lay on the sidewalks until a policeman came and tossed them into the sidecar of his motorcycle.

The next day Gene was taken by plane to Leningrad where he joined a group of forty Americans participating in the conference. The next day was free so the group was taken to visit the Hermitage, a famous museum. There were a number of beautiful Bible paintings on the walls. One of the paintings showed King David speaking to his friend, Uriah. David had committed adultery with Uriah's wife, Bathsheba; and David had just ordered Uriah to the front of the next battle in hopes he would be killed. The Russian woman explaining the paintings got David and Uriah reversed. She was insulted when Gene told her that she was wrong. Gene was surprised when his companions told him to be quiet.

On Sunday Gene asked at the hotel registration desk how he could get to church. He was told that there were no churches. Gene was certain that there was at least one Protestant church. It was known as the Baptiste Church. He was determined to find it, so he asked at least six or seven taxi drivers to take him there. All declined. Finally one driver said that he would do it. They drove for almost an hour. Gene got the impression that the taxi driver wasn't sure where the church was. Suddenly he stopped and motioned to Gene to get out and go down a long street of tenement apartment houses. It was 9 A.M. but there was not a single person in sight. With some misgivings, Gene walked down the street. He came to a large, plain, brick building with the windows completely closed with steel plates. At the front of the building near the sidewalk was a pair of large steel doors. Nothing daunted, he quietly slipped up to the doors and tried to open them. To his delight, a door opened easily. To his surprise, inside was a large church. Every square foot--seats, aisles, vestibules, balconies, etc.--was filled with people either seated or standing. A man (usher?) took him to the pastor in the basement offices. The pastor could speak some English. He greeted Gene and introduced him to a young lady who spoke English and sat in the balcony with him translating quietly the entire service which lasted about four hours. When the service ended around noon, the people cried and prayed with arms upraised, showing a real desire to remain in this hallowed place.

The professional conference was a success. All of the talks were translated into English. The Russian talks were helpful. The thing that Gene appreciated most was the cordial manner of the Russians. Some of them would have liked to correspond with him concerning some other phases of structural engineering, but he never heard from them again. He surmised that they were discouraged by the authorities.

The group returned to Moscow. Gene had a few days before he was to speak in England. He hiked around Moscow. The Russians had closed all churches and used the buildings as schools, museums, and libraries. Communism used Lenin's saying, "Religion is the opiate of the people." One thing that Gene wanted to see was Red Square. When he arrived there, he was surprised to see a double line of people stretching at least one mile long. The people were patiently waiting to view Lenin's open casket in Lenin's Tomb. Gene did not want to waste a day waiting in line so he walked near to the entrance and was about to turn away when a Russian army soldier at the door asked if he was an American. Gene said yes, so the soldier stopped the line of people while Gene entered. Behind the tomb in front of the Kremlin wall was a row of graves. One of them contained the body of an American scientist who had helped the Russian people for many years.

Gene did not think that he could enter the Kremlin but he went to the main entrance gate anyway. To his pleasant surprise, he was ushered in without any delay. He found that the interior area consisted mainly of buildings that had no political significance. One place that he visited was St. Catherine's Church. Another was a museum where the crowns and miscellaneous jewels of the former czars were on display. The buildings used for political purposes were not open but Gene had no time left anyway.

Before going to the next conference, Gene flew to East Germany. Then he went through "Checkpoint Charlie" to West Germany and into West Berlin. It was interesting to see the Brandenberg Gate which was then closed because of the Berlin Wall. Just one day of sightseeing and he flew to Hamburg in northern Germany. He was anxious to find some trace of where his grandparents, the Wiereshausens, had lived. It was a beautiful city. It was situated on the Elbe River which was navigable by ocean-going ships. From the hill on which the city of Hamburg stood, Gene could see a long line of thirty tugboats carefully cleaned and painted. Farther away from the river was a lake that was provided a nicely landscaped area for family picnics. Gene was once asked if he could choose the nicest looking city in all of his travels. Without any hesitation, he chose Hamburg.

On Sunday morning, Gene attended the service of what appeared to be an evangelical church. He did not understand much German so it was difficult to follow what was said. After the service, he spoke to some people who understood English. They told him that there would be no evening service at that church; however, a small group of people from the church conducted an evangelistic service at a nearby village of

Hungarian vagabonds. He was welcome to ride along with them. He agreed to go; in fact, he was asked to say a few words about his trip to Russia and why he happened to be in Hamburg. He also managed to get in a few words about his relationship to Jesus Christ. All of this was translated from English to German by a member of the church group.

The people from the church offered Gene a warm welcome but they could not help him concerning the original location of a Wiereshausen family. So Gene bid them farewell and flew to London, England, the next morning. And then on to Surrey College about twenty miles south of London, where the technical engineering conference was to be held. Gene had one free day so the next day he spent the whole day in London visiting places that he had heard about. He had admired David Livingston for his missionary exploits in Africa, so he visited the grave of Livingston at Westminster Abbey first. Nearby was Parliament, St. Paul's Cathedral, the Tower of London, and the London Bridge over the Thames River. Fortunately, he heard that he could see the changing of the guard at the residence of the Queen of England. The pomp and pageantry of the ceremony was well worth the effort of getting through the crowd to find a good spot to watch the marching military men and the bands. He visited a number of other places before he staggered exhausted back to the college.

Gene spoke at the conference. He was well received. Now he could take a few days to visit some famous places in England. Just then, he received a telephone call from his office at Deeter and Ritchey. Come back to Pittsburgh as soon as possible. The firm was having some trouble with the initial phase of the construction of a new Engineering Hall at the University of Pittsburgh. Gene had designed the foundations for this fifteen-story building and he needed to be back to supervise their installation.

When Gene arrived at the Pittsburgh airport, he was met by Betty, his wife. They went to the University of Pittsburgh to check the foundation construction. It was late in the afternoon and it was raining hard. All the workmen had gone home. Gene was on his own. He plunged out into the rain and stomped around in the mud. It occurred to him that the man excavating for the basement did not understand the procedure that had to be followed. The excavation would go down over forty feet and the face of the excavation would have to be supported as it was dug or else it would topple into the hole. The man doing the excavation was digging the hole without any concern about the stability of the face of the excavation. At a depth of about 12 feet, he noticed that the face was beginning to topple in on him and he became alarmed and called for help. The next day Gene told him that he could not dig straight down but cut at a 45-degree line. When he reached the basement floor, he would stop until a footing was placed and a steel beam bracing would be inserted. Then the argument started. The excavator thought that he should have been made aware of the bracing so he could have added the cost to his bid. Gene told him that excavators knew what to do without being told by the structural engineer.

After this argument was settled, the company placing the footings announced that the steel piles to be driven were not strong enough. The piles were provided by U. S. Steel Company and their estimator had been warned by Gene that about 25 feet below the proposed basement floor was a strata called indurated clay which was harder than rock. He had disregarded the advice and now U. S. Steel would have to substitute a stronger pile for the same price. The estimator told his boss that his doctor had advised him to leave work for six months because of a mental breakdown. U. S. Steel allowed him to take a six-month leave of absence and requested Gene to substitute an entirely different type of footing. When Gene agreed, he examined the soil mechanics investigations very carefully. Also in a used bookstore he found a small technical pamphlet that was out-of-date. It explained why the ground at this new Engineering Hall was so unusual. The writer had made a study of the ground from the Monongahela River at Braddock through Wilkinsburg, past East Liberty, to Oakland where the University of Pittsburgh was, and then back to the Monongahela River. He then concluded that 10,000 years before, during the Ice Age, a valley had been cut along this path into the hard rock and now was filled with soft soil, almost like mud. Gene had never heard this before but he quickly observed that it answered questions in his mind about the excavation at the site of the new Engineering Building.

This project was a headache for Gene. The general contractor made some serious mistakes, then blamed them on Gene. They accused him of being incompetent. A neutral engineer was hired as an arbiter and absolved Gene of any errors.

Gene worked with Deeter and Ritchey for six years. He enjoyed every aspect of his work although he rarely received much credit for his efforts. One day Russ Deeter was conducting an "open house" for a large hospital building addition to Childrens Hospital in Pittsburgh. He was explaining to Gene's wife, Betty, some of the architectural features. Suddenly he stopped and said, "I can show you the architecture that we are proud of producing but I cannot show you another feature of the building that we are proud of: Gene's outstanding structural solution to the framing of this building. That is hidden behind these walls. But make no mistake, it is there." Russ Deeter often introduced people to a new building by saying, "This building is the result of the work of Deeter and Dotter."

Dr. Bowman, the Chancellor of the University of Pittsburgh, had resigned. As his replacement, the Board of Trustees had hired Dr. Edward Litchfield. He was told to upgrade all of the individual schools at Pitt. Money was no problem. He hired vice chancellors for six of these schools at Pitt and offered copious advice to them on the program for the future. One thing he initiated was a School of Oceanography. The school was to be at Virgin Gorda, an island of the British Virgin Islands. It was leased for 99 years and Deeter and Ritchey was picked by Pitt to be the architects and engineers. Gene went with the architect and they were amazed at the beauty of the surroundings. The school buildings were placed on a bluff about 100 feet above the clear surface of the Caribbean Sea. Often sailing ships came in with all sails blowing gently in the warm breeze. They brought only vacationers who loved to help the sailors. There were no developments on the island which was 30 miles out from Charlotte Amalie, the capital city of the U. S. Virgin Islands.

The foundations and ground floors had been placed for several of the buildings when the Board of Trustees suddenly terminated Dr. Litchfield's contract; however, he had signed his name to the lease of the island so Pitt had to withdraw. Dr. Litchfield was the head of the Board of Directors at four large U.S. industrial companies. He decided to finish the proposed buildings as a "trysting place" for the Board of Directors' meetings. He worked out agreements with the four companies. Construction continued and he was pleased with the progress.

Dr. Litchfield had recently married again. His first wife had died from cancer. He had three children from the first marriage. He had his own plane and a permanent pilot. In the late Fall, he took his mother-in-law, his wife, and his new son, about two years old, to Chicago. As they approached the airport on the shore of Lake Michigan, it began to snow heavily. The pilot became confused and landed in the water about one mile out from the shore. The plane dove to the lake bottom and was never recovered. All aboard were drowned. The only body recovered was Dr. Litchfield's several months later. Work on the "trysting place" was halted until the lease options could be investigated. The construction on the project was never resumed.

The association of Gene with the firm of Deeter and Ritchey ended in an unusual way. The chief mechanical engineer was eating lunch at a restaurant in Pittsburgh when he had a heart attack and died. Shortly after, the chief estimator left the firm. Then the chief electrical engineer started his own business. The firm decided to terminate the engineering division as, already, the chief structural engineer (Gene) was considering a move.

Alfred C. Achenheil, Mount Lebanon, Pennsylvania

One of the outstanding Christian professional men in Pittsburgh at this time in the 1960's was Dr. Alfred C. Achenheil. He was a professor in the Civil Engineering Department at the University of Pittsburgh. He was active in the fields of Geology and Soils Mechanics. Also, he had founded a consulting engineering firm in Soil Mechanics and it had developed into a very successful endeavor. Dr. Achenheil's firm had done some consulting work for Deeter and Ritchey. He met Gene and invited him for lunch a few times. They became friendly, especially when they realized that they were both Christians. One day Gene had a hole in the sole of his shoe. The upper portion of the shoe was still usable so he bought a pair of rubber soles and fastened them to the soles of his shoes. Later, he went for lunch with Dr. Achenheil at a prestigious men's club in downtown Pittsburgh. Dr. Achenheil asked Gene about his early life. In the course of their conversation, it came out that Gene had fixed the hole in his shoe by adding rubber soles with glue. Then right in the midst of the millionaires eating lunch at this dignified dining room, Dr. Achenheil lifted his foot in the air and showed Gene that he also had affixed rubber attachments to the soles of his shoes. He told Gene that he never wasted the Lord's money. He then suggested that someday he and Gene ought to be in business together.

That time came more quickly than they expected. The engineering division at Deeter and Ritchey was terminated and Gene went to work at Dr. Achenheil's office. The arrangement was that Dr. Achenheil remained as the president and there would be a vice president of Soil Mechanics and a vice president of Structural Engineering (to be Gene).

The main project at Dr. Achenheil's office was a development undertaken by a Pittsburgh investment company at North Hills, Pennsylvania. The architectural work was being done by John Schurko and his assistant, Ana, from Argentina. Both of these architects were very capable. It consisted of a number of stores and a large mall with a central office tower forty floors high. At the top of the office tower was a rotating restaurant which had a nice view of Pittsburgh about fifteen miles away.

The investment company had collected about ten million dollars. The investors were anxious for quick returns so they hired a construction company to begin excavation immediately. This was a bad move as most of the excavation was in rock. If they had waited for test holes, they could have moved the buildings to take advantage of easier excavation. Soon most of the ten million dollars was gone with very little to show for it. Also, Gene had left the Achenheil office. He did not want to leave but he had two reasons for doing so. The first was that Gene was 48 years old and he felt that, if he ever was to be a consulting engineer in his own office, he would have to start without any delay. The second was that he had never in all his career worked with women. It was not good for Gene to associate with so many women.

3. MY SON - THE HUSBAND

Betty was an excellent wife. She was very intelligent and a good public speaker. She had been a devoted Christian almost all her life. Her father had a beautiful Scottish tenor voice and Betty was a gifted pianist so they always cooperated well with the church music program. She was the only child of two very loving parents. Gene, on the other hand, had had a different childhood. He had trouble fitting into the close family that Betty loved so much. The result was that Betty's mother soon grew distant in her relationship with Gene. And Gene never learned to break down the barriers between Betty's parents and himself.

Betty loved Gene with no emotional reservations. Gene was different. He appreciated her outstanding Christian character and her exceptional ability. She once said to Gene in a moment of absolute candor, "I don't think that you really love me, you place my ability before everything else." Not quite right, but close.

Actually they spent all of their time in the Lord's work. They had an inexpensive small home. They led a sacrificial life with their income designated as the Lord's money with every possible dollar given for church expenses or missionary endeavors.

As a young child, Betty always desired to be a teacher. At the University of Pittsburgh she graduated from the School of Education at the top of her class. Gene recognized her ability and decided that they should wait a few years before marriage so that she could have some experience in her professional field. In addition to working at the University, she taught in Sunday school classes as well as women's classes at the church.

It was Gene's feeling that she really excelled in the organization of Christian material and people. In 1967 Gene joined the Gideons, and shortly afterwards Betty joined the Gideon Auxiliary. The tightly structured organization of the Gideons and the Auxiliary suited Betty perfectly. Officers served three years at a position before moving upward. Betty served two or three years in each local position--secretary, treasurer, and president. Then two or three years in each state position--secretary, treasurer, and president. Her ability was recognized at the national level, so again, two or three years as secretary, treasurer, and president.

As president of the Gideon Auxiliary numbering over sixty thousand women, Betty had many responsibilities. She often traveled to the Gideon headquarters in Nashville, Tennessee, for Gideon or Gideon Auxiliary planning meetings. At one time, she and her cabinet rewrote the auxiliary guidebook. The Executive Director of the Gideons, M. A. Henderson, after reviewing the revamped guidebook, was led to say, "In my thirty years of service, I have never seen a better auxiliary president than Betty Dotter."

During her term of three years as President of the Auxiliary Betty visited every state in the U.S.A. at least once or twice. She would speak several times at each state convention. Gene rarely went with her as each trip lasted Friday, Saturday, and Sunday. When he did attend a convention, much to his amusement he was always introduced as "Mrs. Dotter's husband."

On the other hand, Betty never went with Gene on his business trips. Also, she went only once on a missionary trip. He had been invited to speak at a combined convention of the Mexican and American Societies of Civil Engineering in Mexico City. When Gene explained that two of their close missionary friends in Mexico, Jane and Neil Nellis, Wycliffe Bible Translators with the Zapotec Indians, would be in Mexico City, she decided to go. Imagine her great delight when she stepped off the plane and found Jane with a huge bouquet of beautiful flowers for her. Then Jane and Neil took Betty and Gene to the hotel where Jane loudly exclaimed in Spanish at the registration desk, "Take good care of these two people, they are my special friends."

Later the Nellises took Betty and Gene to visit the Wycliffe Bible Translators Center at Ishmaquilpan about 100 miles north of Mexico

City. On the way back to Mexico City they visited the ruins of the Aztec Indian pyramids. Then they stopped at the town nearby. They were told of a miracle that had happened at a Protestant church about one half mile from the town. It seemed that the town was the center of Catholic fanaticism. One day when tempers were out of control, a group of twenty Mexican men decided to burn down the Protestant church and kill any worshippers who were in the church. Armed with guns and other weapons they climbed the hill to the church, shouting and cursing at the Protestant believers. When they reached the church they were amazed to see the church entirely surrounded by Mexican soldiers with rifles pointed at them. The men threw down their weapons and ran pell-mell down the hill, frantically shouting for mercy. The mayor of the town was angry so he went to the Mexican Army barracks in an adjacent but larger town. He demanded to know why the commander of this army unit had sent such a large detachment of soldiers to protect a Protestant church. The captain looked at the mayor in disgust and said, "You must be drunk. I have never sent any soldiers to your town or to any church." The mayor was convinced that he personally had seen the soldiers. He left mumbling that it must have been a miracle!

Betty immediately knew that it was a miracle. She remembered the account in the Old Testament of the Holy Bible where Elisha opened the eyes of his servant to see how God was protecting them with horses and chariots of fire around about them.

Betty was absolutely honest in everything that she said and did.

* * *

Gene considered Betty as the most truthful person that he ever met. From a previous definition, that would mean that Betty expressed always sincerity in action, character, and utterance. And Gene had observed her fidelity to an original or a standard through the many years of their life together. Gene could say that Betty was trustworthy or worthy of confidence because she was dependable.

Gene, however, would still need to determine the truth or falsity of the proposition or statement that Betty had accepted. He would have to arrive at the "truth-value" of her beliefs. In some professions such as computer logic or judicial examinations, there is a combination of facts known as a "truth table" which shows the truth-value of a compound statement for every truth-value of its component statements.

p	q	p	p*q	pvq	p+q	p q	p+q
T	T	F	T	T	F	T	T
T	F		F	T	T	F	F
F	T	T	F	T	T	T	F
F	F		F	F	F	T	T

Truth Table

truth-value	= the truth or falsity of a proposition or statement
T	= truth
F	= false
denial	= negation in logic

negation = a negative doctrine or statement

conjunction = a complex sentence in logic true if and only if each of its components is true

inclusive = broad in orientation or scope

inclusive disjunction = a statement of a logical proposition expressing alternatives that usually takes the form p v q, meaning p or q or both

exclusive = whole, undivided

exclusive disjunction = statement of a logical proposition expressing alternatives that usually take the form p+q, meaning p or q but not both.

conditional = true only for certain values of the variables or symbols

biconditional = a two-way implication

For a truth table, Gene used the two propositions or statements:

p = Christ the truth q = God of truth

The choice came from a study of the Holy Bible as follows:

A. Christ the truth

(1) John 1:14: And the Word was made flesh, and dwelt among us, and we beheld his glory, the glory as of the only begotten of the Father, full of grace and truth.

(2) John 14:6: Jesus saith unto him, I am the way, the truth, and the life: no man cometh unto the Father, but by me.

B. God of truth

(1) Deuteronomy 32:4: He is the Rock, his work is perfect; for all his ways are judgment: a God of truth and without iniquity, just and right is he.

(2) II Samuel 7:28: And now, O Lord God, thou art that God, and thy words be true, and thou hast promised this goodness unto thy servant.

IV. PART FOUR

The Consultant

1. MY SON--THE ACHIEVER

Gene's definition of the word "achieve" was as follows:

> to carry out successfully, to accomplish,
>
> to get the result of exertion, to win,
>
> to attain a desired end or aim.

An architect was once asked how he would describe briefly the meaning of success in his life. His answer was one word, "accomplishment." Gene thought about this and he added to this by stressing that the result should be brought about by resolve, persistence, or endeavor. He would have added the word "perform" because he would have defined this as follows:

> to adhere to the terms of,
>
> to carry out,
>
> to do in a formal manner or according to prescribed ritual,
>
> to follow an action or pattern of behavior.

A person cannot shape his entire life according to secular definitions only. Gene was careful to include his religious thoughts and beliefs with his secular desires. To be a success as a consulting structural engineer was always in his mind, but it was always tempered with the religious.

Education

During his first job, while in Pittsburgh, Gene realized that he had a wonderful opportunity to delve further into the field of engineering by attending the evening classes offered at Pitt. He believed that a consultant should have more knowledge of the electrical, mechanical, and chemical fields so he took a basic course in electrical engineering design. He completed the course but left Pittsburgh before he could go any further; in fact, it was about a year later when he volunteered for service in the U. S. Army that another opportunity came his way. He began a 17-week basic training period at Fort Belvoir, Virginia, and he felt that his evenings would be comparatively free. He took a correspondence course offered by the University of Wisconsin. It was largely a review of a course in structural steel design that he had taken at the Newark College of Engineering. To him, it was worth taking, even if it was just to see another professor's method of teaching. Unfortunately, combat experience in the U. S. Army Corps of Engineers did not allow time for taking correspondence courses.

When he was discharged from the army, Gene was accepted at the Massachusetts Institute of Technology. He finished three trimesters and received the degree of Master of Science in Civil Engineering. This university was recognized as the best engineering institute in the United States. It was difficult to keep up with the professors. A student left his class in the late afternoon, went across the street to the Graduate House where he had a room. He studied for an hour and went to the dining room for the evening meal. After an hour's rest, it was back to the books until midnight. Some of the students enjoyed skiing in the New England hills. Only a few dared to go, however. A broken leg or arm could wipe out an entire year of study.

Gene went to Trenton, New Jersey, to work. He took two courses (one year) in the evening school at Columbia University. Trenton was 55 miles from New York City. Gene's schedule for three evenings each week was very tight. He had to board a train in Trenton at 4:30 P.M. which took him to downtown New York City at 5:30 P.M. He then ran through a tunnel and boarded a subway at 5:40 P.M. which got him uptown at 134th Street about 15 miles away at 6:10 P.M. Then a 10-minute run to the class which started at 6:30 P.M. and lasted for three hours. At 9:30 P.M. he was on his way back to Trenton.

In the early part of 1948, Gene went back to Pittsburgh. There he studied architecture by correspondence with I.C.S. (International Correspondence School) for two years. He dropped his studies at I.C.S. because he wanted to concentrate on studying for the degree of Doctor of Philosophy (Ph.D.) His teacher urged him to continue as he seemed to have special talent for architecture. But Gene enrolled instead at the Columbia Pacific University in California to study via correspondence courses for the Ph.D. He spent three years and completed the necessary course work. When he submitted his doctoral dissertation, it was refused because his professor thought that it was not academic enough. Gene thought that it was very practical, especially for a field like structural engineering.

Dr. Tung Au had been elevated to the position of Head of the Civil Engineering Department at the Carnegie Institute of Technology. Gene had met him a number of times at American Society of Civil Engineering (ASCE) meetings and other technical seminars. Dr. Au readily accepted Gene as a graduate student and Gene finished eight courses (two per year) in four years of evening school. At that time Gene requested Dr. Au to have him upgraded to the classification of graduate student preparing for matriculation for the Ph.D. Dr. Au looked at him in surprise and said, "Why do you want to do that? You must be almost 40 years old! You are well known now as a structural engineer. You do not need a Ph.D., it would be wasted time and money for you and for us!" Gene tried to reason with him but to no avail. So he did what many other students did, he went over to Pitt and started over again.

Pitt had also recently appointed a new Head of the Civil Engineering Department. This man, Dr. Joel Abrams, was an outstanding teacher, probably the best teacher that Gene had ever had--even at M.I.T. He enjoyed explaining the details of his lectures and he always made certain that his students understood what he said. If he had a problem, it appears that he was not a good administrator. When Gene went into Dr. Abrams' office, he could not find a place to sit down. The chairs, desks, huge conference table, and even much of the floor was covered with piles of books five to ten high and technical papers that seemed to have no order at all. A few years after Gene finished the program that was laid out for him to complete his course work for a Ph.D., Dr. Abrams left Pitt and never was heard from again. He told the department that he felt that he was not intended to be an administrator. He would find a teaching position that he would enjoy and feel that he could excel there.

When Gene had finished three courses each year for ten years, he met with Dr. Abrams to discuss his future at Pitt. He showed Dr. Abrams a list of the subjects that he had completed:

1. Scientific German
2. Basic Calculus
3. Advanced Calculus
4. Advanced Modern Mathematics
5. Probabilities, Combinations, and Permutations
6. Foundation Design
7. Basic Soil Mechanics
8. Advanced Soil Mechanics
9. Dam Design
10. Physical Geology
11. Advanced Geology
12. Earthquake Resistance Methods

13. Thin Shell Structures

14. Advanced Dam Design

15. Free Form Concrete Structures

16. Advanced Structural Analysis

17. Dynamics of Structures

18. Advanced Solid Mechanics

19. Finite Element Applications

20. Structural Concepts

21. Advanced Finite Element Topics

22. Behavior and Design of Steel Members

23. Behavior and Design of Steel Structures

24. Behavior and Design of Reinforced Concrete Members

25. Behavior and Design of Reinforced Concrete Structures.

26. Bridge Design

27. Advanced Problems in Reinforced Concrete

28. Tall Building Design

29. Advanced Topics in Structural Engineering

30. Dissertation Preliminary Investigation

Gene was convinced that this was sufficient and that it was time to appoint his doctoral guide from the structural engineering professors. Dr. Abrams agreed to do this but he required Gene to first accept a teaching assistant position for one or two years at a salary of $3,000 per year. Gene refused. He mentioned that he had earned a B.S. and an M.S., spent four years in the U. S. Army Corps of Engineers, and had twenty years of experience working as a structural engineer. Dr. Abrams replied that Pitt did not confer a Ph.D. on any student who did not serve as a teaching assistant and who did not agree to commit himself to a permanent teaching position. After some discussion, Dr. Abrams offered his final suggestion: find a smaller college that will accept the credits at Pitt and will not require you to assume a teaching position; in fact, there are some good colleges who will consider the years of your engineering experience as equivalent to some courses and even equivalent to a doctoral dissertation.

Later Gene completed several on-line courses (computer arrangement). Then in the year 2002 he reviewed his status in his field of engineering. Briefly it could be summed up:

1. B.S. in Civil Engineering

2. M.S. in Civil Engineering (structures)

3. Litt.D. (Honorary Doctorate of Letters)

4. Correspondence Schools - 7 years, 14 courses

5. Evening Schools - 16 years, 41 courses

In 2004, Gene learned of Suffield University in Idaho. This university is recognized as a premier nontraditional learning institution. It is considered nontraditional because its state of the art on-line programs enable their students to earn a degree with no classes to attend and no required courses that do not relate to the on-line degrees being sought. They offer one-on-one faculty mentoring and consulting. Suffield University faculty examined the graduate credits that Gene had accumulated and approved those relating to a doctoral program.

At Suffield University they realize that some of the most effective learning does not come from a textbook, but from actual experience and hands-on learning. This includes knowledge obtained from previous occupational training, military service, and work experiences. The National Distance Learning Accreditation Council (N.D.L.A.C.) and the Professional Board of Education (P.B.O.E.) accredit the degree programs of Suffield University.

In addition to his two professional degrees, B.S. in C.E. and M.S. in C.E., and the many university credits in Gene's professional field, he could present his four years of experience in the U.S. Army Corps of Engineers and forty-six years as a registered structural engineer in ten states of the United States. Gene had successfully completed all requirements of the Suffield University Board of Examiners. On the basis of his academic experience, methodical working, and educational ability, the degree, rank, and academic status of Doctor of Philosophy with distinction in Structural Engineering was conferred on Gene in May of 2005.

Employees

A number of outstanding titans of industry and religion have written books about people who have been fired from a job and have not allowed this setback to permanently negate their future. They have gone on to achieve success in their field or even in an entirely new field of endeavor. Gene agreed with this premise but he subscribed to something further. He was certain that a person would not get fired if he put all of his energy and skill into his work and became recognized for his ability and his standing in his field. Of course, Gene agreed that it may be God's will in a person's life that will change his life completely. Gene knew that he had to be in the position spiritually where he could ascertain the will of God through the help of the Holy Spirit.

It was now time to begin a new phase of professional life. Gene had labored diligently for 25 years as a structural engineer for other individuals and organizations. Now he was sure that he should establish his own office as a consulting engineer. He felt that it was the leading of the Lord in his life. He would have to discuss this with his wife, Betty. She was a real Christian but she was often reluctant to make a change in their work habits; nevertheless, he wanted her to understand what he had in mind. One evening they spent several hours reviewing the pros and cons of this move. Then they had a season of prayer. Finally, both agreed to make the change.

Shortly afterwards, Gene resigned from his position of Vice President of Structural Engineering at the office of Dr. Alfred C. Achenheil. He rented one small office in a building where the architect, John Schurko, had his office. Schurko talked it over with Dr. Achenheil who graciously agreed to allow Gene to complete the project in North Hills with Schurko, as the consulting structural engineer. Unfortunately, a series of bad decisions in management by the investment company brought about an abrupt halt to the project. Meanwhile, a student at Pitt completed his study for the Master of Science degree in Structural Engineering and asked Gene for a job. He was informed that Gene had not received any payments yet on the North Hills project. He replied that he would work for nothing until Gene had received some money as payment for their work. So Charles Fedon was hired as the first employee in the office of Eugene V. Dotter, Consulting Structural Engineer.

When the project in North Hills was halted, the two engineers sat quietly reading textbooks, etc., for the next two weeks. Then Gene offered a short, inaudible prayer to God: "God, I am sure that you directed my path to this place. Now I do not understand why I sit here with nothing to do. Please send some work to me soon or else I will feel that I made a mistake and I will make a change." In a few minutes, the telephone rang. It was a man in Charleston, West Virginia, who was a friend of Dr. Achenheil. He told Gene that he had heard from Dr. Achenheil that Gene now had his own office. If Gene was not too busy, he, Robert

Ainsley, would arrange for a meeting soon, where Gene would start a project on a new building for the West Virginia State Board of Colleges. Gene thanked him and agreed to come when called.

Gene put the telephone down and prayed, "Heavenly Father, I thank you for providing these projects for the future. But at the present I have no work and no income." In a few minutes the telephone rang. It was a man that Gene had known at Alcoa. He had been a member of the new division called Product Development that was trying to interest companies to use more aluminum. After Gene had left Alcoa, this man had stayed for several years. Then he came to the conclusion that there was no future for him at Alcoa so he quit and got a job at U S. Steel Company. He had somewhat the same responsibilities but had a permanent office in Pittsburgh. U.S. Steel had divided the country into twelve areas where their representatives each had an office at a central city. The representative would visit the architects in their area and offer to make a preliminary study of the structural framing of a new building, free of charge. The architect frequently agreed because there were no obligations, just a sort of friendly exchange of ideas. The representative would obtain the building information and send it to the home office in Pittsburgh. But Ronald Fluger, Gene's friend at Alcoa, had only one employee working for him. This employee was an engineering graduate but had his twenty years of experience in sales positions. Ron Fluger was at a loss to decide how he could prepare a preliminary study of building framing from twelve representatives. Suddenly he was inspired from above to call Gene Dotter. He learned from a mutual acquaintance what the telephone number was and felt compelled to call Gene at that specific moment.

After a few minutes of friendly conversation, he explained his predicament and asked if Gene would help him. Ron would receive the information; his one employee, Henry Flieshman, would come to Gene's office with the information including some of Ron's suggestions; Gene or Charles Fedon would make up the preliminary study; then Henry would come over (only three blocks away) to talk about the study and take it back to Ron. It would go to the representative without any names, just as a study from U. S. Steel Company. Gene would receive a check from Ron Fluger immediately! And Ron was ready at this minute to send Henry with the first preliminary study request! Gene thanked his Heavenly Father for such a quick solution to his dilemma.

Now that they were really working on several projects, the one office was too small. Gene was about to expand his office space when he received a telephone call from his former employer, Leland W. Cook. Lee was working at an office building nearby. To Gene's surprise, Lee asked if he would locate in an office suite next to him. Lee was 75 years old and he figured that he needed someone to help with his engineering work and he did not want to hire another full-time engineer. Currently, he had a full-time draftsman. So if Gene would rent an office near him, he would give Gene any work that he could not handle himself. Gene did not want to do this but he decided to help Lee and show him a good Christian testimony. On Monday of the next week, Gene and Charlie packed up their remaining equipment and went to the Investment Building only a few blocks away. They arranged their new office space, then Gene went across the hall to see Lee Cook. To his surprise, Lee was not in his office. He asked the draftsman, Bill Mayer, about Lee. Bill told him that on Friday Lee had a very serious stroke at the office and it was doubtful that he would survive. Gene rushed over to the hospital but was not able to see Lee as he was in intensive care. Gene went back to Lee's office and worked with Bill for several hours to get Lee's projects in order. Then he settled down with Charlie to consider how they would keep both offices functioning.

Lee Cook continued to improve until after several weeks at the hospital he was allowed to go home. His doctor told him to rest for a month, then he would decide if Lee could go to the office. At the end of the month, Lee was weak but very anxious to get to the office. His wife brought him in at about 9 A.M. and he talked with Gene and Bill for an hour or so, then looked over the projects that were being worked on. He felt tired and his wife suggested that she take him home for lunch. He assured Gene and Bill that he would be back in the afternoon or the next morning. He sat back in his reclining desk chair for a few minutes, smiling and pleased to be there. Then he went home and never returned. Gene was told that Lee had cancer and he was terminal. A few days later, he telephoned and asked Gene to visit him at his home. Gene was surprised at his weak condition. Lee probably realized that he would never be back at the office. He had two requests: (1) offer Bill Mayer a permanent job as draftsman and (2) give Mrs. Cook a portion of any fee derived from Lee's connection with architects or other engineering associations. He related some of the pleasant things that he had experienced during his professional career. Then he said that he was tired and wanted to rest. His wife quickly helped him to his bed. Gene wanted to speak to him about his relationship to Christ but there was no opportunity. He never saw Lee again.

The next day Gene offered Bill a permanent job as draftsman in his office. At first he refused, saying that he could continue working as he was. He said that he had a close relationship with all of Lee's architectural connections. He would do the drafting and he would hire engineers to do the calculations. Gene carefully explained to him that the State of Pennsylvania required a permanent registered engineer in all offices listed as performing structural engineering work. Gene added that Bill was a very intelligent draftsman with a good grasp of engineering procedures. All he needed to do was to take a course or two at Pitt in structural engineering design and pass the examination. Gene promised him that Bill had his approval and Gene would help him at his studies and at the registration examination. For some reason, Bill considered himself unable to complete the requirements successfully. He refused and accepted Gene's offer of employment.

Bill was a terrific draftsman. He never loafed and he always wanted to be busy; in fact, after eight hours at the office, he would take his drawings home. After the family dinner, he would send his two children into other rooms to do their school homework, etc., and he would settle down at his drafting board for at least three hours of work. The next morning he would be ready and anxious to start again at 8 A.M. He often came into the office to work on Saturdays. Perhaps the fact that he was paid by the hour with time and a half for all hours over 40 per week gave him an incentive to work so much. He always made a beautiful drawing and was also a very careful, thorough checker. He had 21 years of experience with Lee Cook when he accepted the invitation to work with Gene.

The firm of Eugene V. Dotter had a strong desire to furnish top quality structural engineering services to all clients whether large or small or even if they could or could not pay for the services. Gene, the president and owner, had a close bond to each employee. He considered it to be his Christian duty to treat every employee fairly and to help each person to become a better person in his secular profession as well as his spiritual, religious attitude with God and brother employees. In 1985 the firm of Eugene V. Dotter, Consulting Engineers, was incorporated in the Commonwealth of Pennsylvania. During the fifteen years since its founding, the firm had experienced consistent growth. Each new employee had a unique experience and Gene tried to offer personal help to all who entered, whether they remained as permanent employees or left because of various reasons. Briefly, they are (in Gene's personal opinion only):

Charles Fedon, Chief Structural Engineer

Previously employed by Koppers Company, Pittsburgh; Mackin Engineering Company, Pittsburgh; and Alfred C. Achenheil and Associates, Mount Lebanon. Upon graduation from the University of Pittsburgh with the degrees of B.S. and M.S. in Civil Engineering, Charles worked briefly with the three companies listed here but then desired to work only with Gene. His father was a tile contractor. Charles was an only child. His mother was the domineering force in the family. Charles always seemed to resent her and it had much to do in molding his life.

Charles M. Boyle, Senior Structural Engineer

Previously employed by the Pennsylvania Department of Transportation, Pittsburgh; Chatham Engineering Corporation, Pittsburgh; Younkins

Engineering Services, Pittsburgh; and Peter F. Loftus Corporation, Pittsburgh. After graduation from the University of Pittsburgh with the degree of B.S. in Civil Engineering, Charles worked for sixteen years with the companies listed above. He was a very capable engineer but did not seem to have much ambition to advance in his profession. Perhaps his marriage was instrumental for he was blessed with a talented wife, lovely children, and helpful parents. He was out of work and satisfied with unemployment compensation when Gene insisted that he get back into his profession and come to work with Gene. He considered the request carefully and finally accepted.

Iskender Mericli, Structural Engineer

Graduated from Robert College, Istanbul, Turkey, with a B.S. in Civil Engineering and from the University of Michigan with an M.S. in Civil Engineering. Previously worked for 37 years with the Bureau of Airport Construction, Ankara, Turkey; Green Engineering Company, Sewickly, Pennsylvania; Pittsburgh-Des Moines Steel Company, Pittsburgh; Kopper Company, Inc., Pittsburgh; and Comstock Engineering, Inc., Pittsburgh. He had been laid off from Comstock when he approached Gene about work. He did not fit into Gene's type of engineering. Iskender was much more experienced with industrial projects rather than the monumental buildings of schools, hospital, etc. He was a very likable fellow, however, and he was sending his son through a Catholic Theological Seminary. So Gene agreed to hire him for a few years. Then Comstock Engineering asked him to return. He accepted happily--with Gene's approval.

Chandrakant A. Shah, Structural Engineer

Graduated from the College of Ahmedabad India, with a B.S. and an L.D. in Civil Engineering and from the University of Wisconsin with an M.S. in C.E. Previously worked for 26 years with Dr. R. N. Vakil, Consulting Engineer, Ahmedabad, India; Design Circle, Gandhinagar, India; Central Designs Organization, Gandhinagar, India; Dennis Roth, Structural Engineer, and R.A. Zern, Consulting Engineering,

Pittsburgh. Bob Zern retired after his wife passed away and left his office and books to Chand Shah. His office was in the same building with Gene so after a few weeks Gene paid him a visit. An architectural firm wanted to have Gene provide structural engineering services for a large addition to Mellon Institute in Pittsburgh; however, the architects were told by the U. S. Government that they had to have a "minority" firm do the work. They asked Gene if he knew a firm that fitted this request. He thought of Shah. He asked if he wanted to take on this lucrative project. Shah refused, saying that he had no one to do the drafting. Gene assured him that he had several draftsmen who would work for Shah. Shah again refused, saying that he might not be able to do the work economically and be forced into bankruptcy. Gene again assured him that there was no danger of this happening. Then Shah said that he needed time to think this over. Gene agreed and suggested one week. Shah still couldn't make up his mind. The architect gave Shah another week. Then he was exasperated and told Gene that he didn't care what the U.S. Government said, Gene would get the contract!

Shah remained at his office for one month. He could not continue for some unknown reason so he closed the office and went to work for Dennis Roth, but Roth drank alcohol in the office which displeased Shah. And Roth insulted Shah by demeaning his religion. So Shah left the Roth office and asked Gene for a job. Gene did not have a need for him but he hired Shah for anticipated growth. His analysis concerning Shah was that Shah was a good engineer but was too methodical and slow. When Gene retired, he did not ask Shah to be one of the new officers of the firm. Shah knew that he had no future with the new administration so he resigned. Actually, it was a smart move for him.

Robert J. Conway, Structural Engineer

Previously employed by Babcock Contractors, Pittsburgh; Dravo Corporation, Pittsburgh; Pullman Swindell, Pittsburgh; Galletta Engineering, Pittsburgh; Jacob Engineering, Pittsburgh; and Rust International, Pittsburgh. He graduated from Cornell University with the degree of B.S. in Civil Engineering. He was a Christian, a member of a Christian and Missionary Alliance Church in Pittsburgh. One day he saw Gene at the church and asked him if he could do some "moonlighting" work (after regular hours) for Gene. He explained that he and his wife had one child, a retarded boy. They thought that their son needed another boy in the family. They did not anticipate the birth of another boy so they wanted to adopt a boy from Korea. They needed $1,000 soon. Gene said that it would be excellent if Conway would help him with the design of the addition to the Mellon Institute. The Conways appreciated Gene's offer. Then one day Rust International announced that the corporation was moving south to Alabama. Any employee could come south and resume his position with the company. Bob Conway did not want to move so he was fired. He applied to Gene's office and was accepted. His experience was mainly along industrial plant design but Gene knew that he could include him in the office. Later, Bob was one of the three employees in charge of the office after Gene retired.

Wayne Airgood, Structural Engineer

Mrs. Airgood had a son, Wayne, that she wished to learn to play the piano. She thought of her good friend, Betty Dotter, who was an excellent pianist and who would teach children for only one dollar per lesson (actually to pay for the music books). The trouble was that Wayne did not want to learn to play the piano. So Mrs. Airgood told him to wait in the car while she took the lesson. He did not care for that arrangement so he came into the house, took a lesson, and decided that it was not so bad after all. About a year later, his father suddenly had a heart attack and died. Wayne's whole world fell apart. He was a sophomore in high school but he had absolutely no interest in school.

He barely made it through the year. He paid no attention to his mother and began to get into trouble on the streets. As he entered his junior year in high school, he told his mother that he was through with her, music, school, everything!

When Betty told her husband, Gene, about Mrs. Airgood's sad problem, he told her that he had the solution. Mrs. Airgood should get permission from the school to have Wayne's study periods combined into two or three times per week at the end of the days. Then she was to take Wayne to Gene's office and leave. She could come back about 5:30 P.M. to take Wayne home. Gene figured that Wayne needed some men to associate with on a man-to-man basis.

And if he liked the work, perhaps he would consider this as his profession for later life. The plan suited Wayne and he enthusiastically showed his mother and his teachers at high school the drawings that he had made. Throughout his junior and senior years at high school, his attitude improved at school and at home.

When Wayne graduated from high school, his mother spoke to him about attending college. At first he did not want to go; but when she explained how it was necessary if he wanted to be a structural engineer, he chose Geneva College, a Reformed Presbyterian school with a good Civil Engineering Department. Each summer he came back to the office to work for two months. Finally, he graduated from college. As soon as possible, he appeared at Gene's office to ask for a permanent position. To his surprise, Gene said, "No!" Then Gene explained that Wayne had never worked in any other engineering office and he should work somewhere else before choosing the place he liked best. Gene gave him a list of structural engineering offices and told him that he could return in two or three weeks if he needed any advice. Instead, he came back in two days. He said that he did not want to go to any other office. He was hired and went to work immediately.

Wayne was fortunate. He made the calculations for several small projects. Then he was an essential part of the team working on a tremendous addition to the Medical Department at the University of Pittsburgh. Gene retired in a few years. His last advice to Wayne was that he should join a larger firm where he could mature further as a structural engineer. Wayne took that advice and is now a valued employee of a consulting engineering firm with headquarters in Cleveland, Ohio, and a branch office in Pittsburgh, Pennsylvania.

Daniel P. Sweeney, Structural Designer and Draftsman

A lady from the church where Gene had attended called him to ask if he would give a young man a job. He was about to be married to a fine Christian young lady. He had worked as a draftsman with the Allegheny County Engineering Department. Because of politics, he was laid off. Dan had completed three years in Civil Engineering at Carnegie-Mellon University so Gene was curious why he had not completed the four years. Dan told him that his father had left and Dan needed money. Gene hired him as a draftsman but recommended that he finish his education before it was too late. Dan had a problem concentrating on his work but it was eliminated by changing his location in the room and asking Bill Mayer to supervise him more closely.

Dan did not finish at Carnegie-Mellon University but he did take some courses at Pitt and at the local community college. Bill Mayer helped him tremendously. His drafting had the look of a professional. Bob Conway took some time to help him with his work in structural design.

Dale Seng, Junior Structural Draftsman

Near Pittsburgh there was a Christian organization that offered personal advice to members of broken families or to troubled individuals. Gene was familiar with the people who were in charge. One day he received a call from the director who asked him if he could hire a young man (28 years old) and train him to be a draftsman. This young man, Dale Seng, had never had a job in his life. His mother was employed in a menial position in a county hospital. His brother was unusual and later was placed permanently in an insane asylum. When Dale was ten years old he found his father hanging from a rafter. He had committed suicide. This may have caused a mental breakdown, but his problems may have come from his family background. Gene felt sorry for Dale and, as a good Christian, was willing to try to help Dale.

Dale had made a profession of faith in Jesus Christ as his Saviour. He attended church regularly. He moved out of his mother's apartment and found his own place to live. He did not handle his finances very well. One item that he always carefully observed was to buy a theological commentary when needed. His problem was that he could read a book carefully and retain absolutely nothing. It seemed that he had no power of deduction so one simple task at a time was all that he could handle. An example of his thinking occurred when the first satellite landed in California after circling the earth, etc. Dale was out of the office on an errand. When he returned, he asked Betty where all the other employees were. She told him that they were at the restaurant on the third floor watching the satellite land in California. He paused to think that over. Then he made this remark to her: "I did not know that you could see a plane landing in California from the third floor of our building (in Pittsburgh, Pennsylvania)."

All the people in the office knew his problem. They kept him busy doing the odd jobs like wrapping packages, going to the stores, etc. Betty sometimes became very exasperated when, for instance, she sent him to buy some drafting paper and he returned with a dozen boxes of rubber bands. He would smile and say to her, "They were on sale." She would smile at him and say to him, "This office here needs to be cleaned. Please sweep the floor and wash the walls."

The employees of Dotter Engineering Company were proud of the fact that nobody was ever discharged or ever quit his job. Several persons did leave but because of special personal reasons:

1. Robert Roth, Senior Structural Draftsman. Bob worked with ten different companies and had 32 years of experience. Actually,

however, he was a mechanical engineering draftsman doing that type of work like piping, heating, and air-conditioning. He was temporarily out of work and Gene converted him to a structural engineering draftsman. When he was offered a job in mechanical engineering drafting, he discussed it with Gene and he was told that he would do better if he left.

2. Anthony Moscollic, Structural Engineer. When Tony graduated from Pennsylvania State University, Gene noted that he had received a degree in Architectural Engineering. He advised Tony to choose Structural Engineering or Architectural Engineering and pursue that one field instead of both. Tony went to work for Gene. In one year, he decided that he really liked architecture better and left to follow that line of work.

3. Eric Schmitt, Junior Structural Draftsman. Frederick Schmitt was an architect who was a friend of Gene. His son, Eric, graduated from high school and refused to go to college. Fred asked Gene if he would try to make a structural draftsman out of him. After a month or so, Gene was told by other draftsmen that Eric had the ability but that he either was absent from work or he fell asleep at his desk. In spite of many warnings from Gene, Eric continued his wayward behavior. So he was dismissed with the invitation that he could return when he thought that he would improve. Actually, he was helping a friend fix cars until midnight or later. Gene suggested that he find work with some type of machinery. Eric went to computer school and began repairing computers. He had a special affinity for all kinds of computer activity. Soon he was promoted to a much better job.

4. David Farbishel, Structural Engineer. The firm of Alpha Engineering Company specialized in surveying and water supply designs. Dave graduated from Penn State with a B.S. in Civil Engineering. His first job was as a surveyor with Alpha. Gene was acquainted with Alpha and one day he was asked if he could give David an engineering position.

David went to work for Gene and proved to be an excellent structural engineer. He was engaged to marry a Chinese girl that he had known from the Presbyterian Church which they attended. She graduated from nursing school. Shortly after, they were married. She was hired as an anesthesiologist at a large hospital nearby. Everything looked fine as they bought a house and began a happy married life. Both were Christians with a good testimony. Something happened to her that was a surprise. She wished to be accepted by her fellow nurses, so she often had lunch with them. They always had an alcoholic drink and they urged her to drink with them. At first she refused but then took one drink. It was soon evident that she had no resistance to alcohol. She needed more and more. She expected David to join her in the evenings. He refused to take a drink and she became furious. One evening she attempted to stab him with a carving knife. The police were called. They took her to jail and he was advised to leave home. As a result, he left his job and went to Canada.

When he returned a year later, he felt led to go to the theological seminary and enter the ministry. He divorced his wife. He served for ten years as the pastor of a church in Texas. The church organized a work trip to Russia. While there he met a young lady who went with the group back to Texas. Soon afterwards, they were married.

Work Experience

In addition to serving as a structural consultant for architects, Gene also served industrial firms and government agencies. He was a special consultant for the American Institute for Steel Construction (AISC). He was registered with Technical Advisory Service for Attorneys as an expert in structural engineering and construction. He was a life member of the American Society of Civil Engineers and served on the Committee for Determination of Allowable Stresses in Steel and in Concrete. He was a member of the American Concrete Institute (ACI), American Welding Institute (AWI), and the American Consulting

Engineers Council. Gene also was appointed as a member of the Bureau of Standards and Appeals, City of Pittsburgh.

The first year that Gene began his career as a consulting engineer, he had one hundred projects. After twenty years, he had three hundred projects in the twentieth year. In other words, he had an average of 200 projects per year or a total of 4,000 projects. Some were small, just an hour or two. But some were large, lasting months. It would be impossible to describe every project or to show a picture of what it looked like, so he has included just a comparative few.

Gene was valued as a friend and consultant at a number of religious denominational headquarters. They included the Catholic, Greek Orthodox, United Methodist, Primitive Methodist, Lutheran, and Church of Jesus Christ of the Latter Day Saints. He also helped some architect friends who worked on buildings for Muslims, Buddhist, and Hindus.

It was exciting to "trouble shoot." Frequently Gene was asked to look at a building, decide what was causing a problem, and provide a solution. Gene was once requested by the Geneva College to teach a course in structural engineering. The head of the Civil Engineering department asked him to look at the "Old Main," the central auditorium and office building, that was leaning and caused much alarm at the school; in fact, the President of Geneva College had hired a structural engineering firm from Philadelphia to provide the solution. This firm decided that the roof and attic over the auditorium should have more supports. They suggested adding columns through the auditorium and the stage of the auditorium. New foundations would have to be constructed, the offices below the auditorium rearranged, new framing systems designed at each floor level, and the auditorium seating severely curtailed. The cost of construction would have been about $350,000 and the disruption to the school program would have been extensive.

After a few hours of inspection of the roof framing system, Gene decided that the wood was getting old and losing its strength. As it lost its strength, it moved in its weakest direction. This was toward the front of the building where the leaning was noticeable. He decided that it could not be restored to its original position without replacing the entire attic and roof. It would make more sense to leave it as it was and strengthen the roof framing so that it would not continue to move. This could be done by adding some trusses to those already in place, then bracing all of the trusses together, old and new, to form a solid roof mass. Gene knew a specialty carpentry company who could do this work in the attic without disturbing the floors below. The estimated construction cost would be about $35,000 (only one-tenth of the cost estimated by the Philadelphia firm), and with no disruption to the school program. The construction work was started immediately. Twenty-five years later, there had been no movement since the work was completed. A successful ending.

A deterioration of wood with its loss of strength and consequent movement was a problem often faced on old buildings. This occurred in old churches, especially Catholic churches that usually had very high ceilings and architectural features like domes and arches in the ceiling. Gene was once called to a Catholic church where the priest had noticed in the ceiling a pattern of cracks that was constantly growing. Gene looked up at the ceiling at least forty feet above and told the Father that he would come back in a few days later with an architect. At the appointed time Gene arrived on time but the architect was late; however, the Father had arranged for a mechanical engineer to come to check on the piping. Two mechanical engineers were there, so Gene decided to go with the other two up above the ceiling. In order to get close to the truss where the cracks were appearing, they had to climb over a dome in the ceiling. Gene warned the two men to step very carefully on the wood ribs. They assured him that they were fully acquainted with the dome layout. The three looked closely at the truss and Gene could see that the truss needed some repair work. On the way back, on the way down from the top of the dome (about ten feet down), one of the men grew careless and tried to run down the ribs. He slipped and fell through the ceiling which now was about 45 feet above the seats down below. Fortunately, his two legs went through the ceiling to his hips but he was left with his crotch straddling a rib which for some reason did not break. Gene and the other engineer very carefully pulled the fallen engineer out of the broken ceiling. He was shaking from the experience. He realized that he had been very close to death or a serious injury. They took him over to the parsonage and sat talking to the priest about the need to repair the truss and especially the hole in the ceiling. The priest assured them that an artist in Pittsburgh would patch the ceiling and paint any missing figures on the ceiling like angels or apostles, or Bible scenes, etc.

Meanwhile the architect arrived and got quite a shock. He went into the church calling Gene's name. All was silent as he moved through the seats. Then he reached the place where the broken plaster and broken lath lay on the floor. He looked up at the ceiling and saw the hole. He was panic stricken and ran to the parsonage. He rushed into the parlor and shouted, "Gene fell through the ceiling, he must be dead! Where is he? Where is he?" Then he saw them all seated together, talking calmly. He gulped a few times, and slumped weakly into a chair.

Concrete also behaves like wood in that it has a plastic deflection. This means that it will deflect in proportion to the load applied, but as time goes by, the molecules of the material will rearrange themselves and allow a secondary deflection which becomes a permanent set and can be as much or even more than the primary deflection. A good example was the School of Engineering at the University of Pittsburgh. The first floor was almost all devoted to a library. In order to have more natural lighting, the entire front of the building was a window wall similar to a store front. It was divided into fifteen-foot lengths by vertical mullions formed by steel posts. The posts were connected to the floor and to the concrete floor above. The building was in use for only the short time of six months when it was noticed that the posts were bowed and in another month the glass windows popped out and fell on the ground. Gene examined the situation and reported that the top of the mullion posts had been connected solidly to the concrete above. They should have been connected with bolts in slotted vertical holes so that they could move downward as the secondary deflection took place. All the connections had to be rebuilt. No further problems.

A man bought a section of land in an area of Pittsburgh where many rich families lived. They had monumental brick-and-stone homes but he decided to build a home of glass and sheet steel panels between large window sections. It was a nice home with a price of $750,000. It incurred the wrath of the residents with homes costing in the multiple million dollar range. He hired an architectural firm in New York City and the house was designed and constructed. Soon afterward, he hired Gene to determine why the glass was breaking and the floors and walls were cracking. Gene reported that the building had no lateral stability. When the wind blew, the building leaned or twisted excessively. The architect refused to accept responsibility for the problems. So the owner filed a complaint with the American Arbitration Board. Gene was an expert witness for the owner. He told the judge and the panel of technical persons that the architect had not hired a structural engineer even though it was readily apparent that this unusual building needed special lateral bracing. After a few days of discussion, the decision was made in favor of Gene and the owner. The owner was awarded $5,000 to be paid by the architect. Gene was angry. He told the owner that the architect should have been required to pay for all revisions or additions to bring the building up to normal requirements. He also asked the judge why the award was so small. The judge just laughed and refused to answer, although he was a friend (perhaps?).

Church Buildings

Church of Jesus Christ of Latter Day Saints, Freeport, Pa.

The denominational headquarters had carefully compiled standard design drawings and specifications for any church complex to be built in any area of the U.S.A. They then hired the architect, structural engineer (Gene), mechanical engineer, electrical engineer, and the landscape architect to prepare working drawings for the church but following the standards that they had prepared. Their work was meticulously supervised by a member of CJCLDS who had much experience with building churches of their denomination. The denomination's area leader gave the members of the new church several opportunities for input but only within the standard boundaries set by the denomination. The architect and the local engineers also had an opportunity to suggest changes, but again only within the established standards. The members of the church were always satisfied with the appearance of the church and especially with the construction costs which were kept very low by the standardization of concepts, materials, and methods.

One unusual characteristic of this building was that all of the framing was wood. The walls were wood studs with brick veneer. The roof framing was a combination of wood purlins and wood trusses. All of this was carefully laid out on the standard drawings. Gene had to check the sizes and location of the structural members to insure that they were adequate for this project.

Another commendable feature was the location of the gymnasium (basketball court). It was about the same size as the nave and had the same wall and floor features. It was placed directly behind the nave and separated by a moveable partition. The nave could seat three hundred persons. The gymnasium could seat another three hundred persons by merely opening the door and using three hundred folding chairs.

A few years before, Gene had done the structural engineering for an addition to a church of another denomination. The project of several million dollars cost was placed in the hands of the "Building Committee" composed of eight church members and the pastor. After many disorganized meetings, it was decided to get an architect. Nobody knew how to proceed. And nobody would have had any idea if the architect was capable or not. Fortunately, a church member with some experience with construction knew an architect that he felt was competent. So he began a more systematic procedure. And Gene was his choice as consulting structural engineer.

Gene tried to explain a logical approach to future construction of church buildings to several denominational headquarters. But to no avail. The leaders were not interested in the engineering approach. As one perceptive president of a denomination said, "Gene, you must realize that all of these men are ministers, well versed in religious matters but not in secular projects."

United Methodist Church, Scottdale, Pa.

A beautiful stone church building went up in flames and burned completely down to the basement except for some exterior walls. The members of the church insisted that the new church incorporate all of the remaining walls into the new building. This added somewhat to the complexity of the architect's task and, to some extent, the structural engineer's task. Also, the cost of new construction had to be close to the settlement allowed by the insurance company. A number of the former architectural features like the expensive stained-glass windows and the cut stone walls had to be eliminated. Fortunately, the soil bearing values were high and excavation was a minor problem. The architect substituted a pleasing brick pattern for the exterior walls.

This suburban Methodist church was a carefully detailed and well-executed example of an approach to design which was on the generally conservative side of current efforts. It was very similar to St. Andrew's Church, Park Ridge, Illinois, which is shown on page 175 and 189. Serving a middle-sized congregation, the combined seating totals 590 using both the meeting area at the rear of the nave and the church parlor as overflow areas. The site is a level lot, pleasantly shaded by maturing trees and generally free of difficult design determinants except

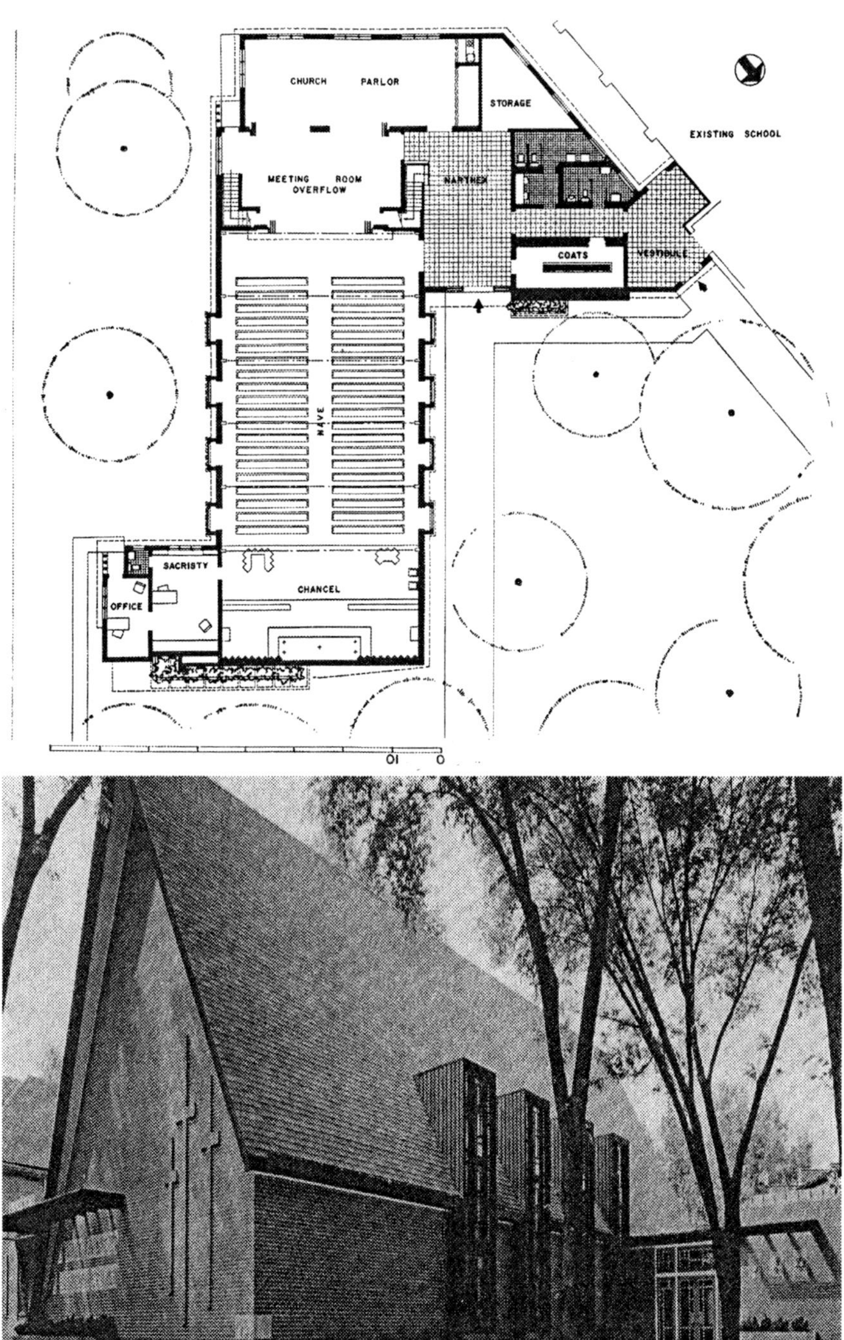

United Methodist Church

for the rather busy road that influenced the retired position of the main entrance.

The roof structure was of exposed laminated wood rigid frames, purlins, and beams carrying 2" x 6" T and G "V" joint planking. Roof surface was asbestos shingles. The laminated structural framing members are technically known as three-hinged arches and are of three principal types: Tudor (used in this church), Gothic, and Continuous. Spans usually range between 30 and 100 feet, although much wider spans are possible. In providing permanent structural framing for both roof and sidewalls, these arches add greatly to the beauty of the interior.

Commercial Buildings

J. C. Penney Department Store, Columbus, Ohio.

A shopping center is a carefully integrated area of merchandising facilities. The types of merchandise to be offered must be ascertained before any other planning starts. Today's shopper tends to purchase needed items from stores in close proximity to one another. No longer are they content to drive from store to store to make purchases. A popular plan to meet these demands is the grouping of a variety of stores, so the customer can easily walk from one to another. The selection of the site is a very important preliminary planning factor. A careful study must be made of such features as the shape of the plot, orientation, access roads, availability of utilities (sewers, water, gas, electricity), slope of the land and drainage possibilities, and soil conditions influencing construction costs.

The center should be built around one or two large stores such as department stores. The addition of small shops adds to the completeness of the center and gives it a balance of services. This frequently includes restaurants and banks. Large stores attract great numbers of customers.

For this reason, they should be situated so that customers, to reach them, must pass the many small shops in the shopping center. In this shopping center, there were two large stores, the J. C. Penney Department store and a Sears Roebucks store, each positioned at opposite ends of the shopping center. Fine for J. C. Penney but poor for the small shops.

The planning for the J. C. Penney Department store surprised Gene right from the start. The J. C. Penney headquarters was in New York City, the architect's office was in Pittsburgh, and the new department store was in Columbus, Ohio. A few weeks after the architect had been chosen, he was requested to come to New York City with his structural engineer. When they arrived at the conference room, the architect was asked to produce the preliminary drawings. He replied that he had not been instructed to bring, or even to prepare, these drawings. The angry retort was, "In that case, get out of here and come back when you are prepared!"

The architect and Gene hurried out and took a taxicab to JFK airport. On the way it started to snow. By the time they arrived, it was snowing harder; in fact, all planes to Pittsburgh had been canceled. They were told to try Newark airport so they boarded a bus and managed to get there in about three hours. By that time, all planes to Pittsburgh had been canceled. Their choice now was to use a train overnight and arrive the next day. It looked as if the snow would stop falling soon so they elected just to sit and wait.

While working on the preliminary design, Gene noticed that the shopping center construction was almost finished. All of the new construction of the J. C. Penney Department store--foundations and steel roof framing--would have to be given special attention to avoid existing construction. A study of subsurface soil conditions is always necessary but this had not been done because the area taken by the J.C. Penny Department store had not been chosen yet. When the test holes were drilled, the soil samples showed that a strata with 5,000 PSF bearing capacity could be used economically; however, it varied in elevations so the footings had to be placed at different elevations.

The J. C. Penney Department store headquarters gave the architect typical layout drawings for the first and second floors. The columns were spaced at 50-feet centers in both directions. There was a basement so the framing for the first and second floors was about the same with the Live Load equal to 100 PSF. The roof was similar but the Live Load was only 50 PSF. The floor girders were prefabricated structural steel trusses with floor beams at 5-feet spacing, spanning from truss to truss. The structural steel for the roof was similar to the floor but the structural members were lighter in weight. In general the framing was on a systematic grid except for the framing for the escalators, elevators, and exterior special framing such as entrance canopies and exterior spandrel walls. The floor system used load-bearing cellular-steel units for electrical distribution and heat and cooling distribution. The cellular-steel decking was placed upon the structural members of the building. On top of this, placed at right angles, was a crossover header. This carried wiring across the decking and permitted it to extend into the cellular units, thus allowing electrical outlets and telephones to be placed wherever needed. These outlets could be easily moved at any time.

CBMC (Christian Business Men's Committee) of Pittsburgh invited Mr. J. C. Penney to speak at an annual dinner meeting. Gene was asked to meet him at the airport and to take him to one of the better hotels in Pittsburgh. Mr. Penney was a small trim man ninety years of age, with beautiful white hair. He spoke freely to Gene about a number of miscellaneous items. In a friendly manner, Gene asked him a question: "Mr. Penney, I often buy clothing at the J. C. Penney store in Pittsburgh. Do you use clothing from the Penney store in New York City?" Mr. Penney smiled and then turned over his hat which had a hatband with the Penney marking. He then opened his coat to show the Penney signature. Then his suit coat was opened to proudly show another Penney marking. Without a pause, he said, "If I could, I would show my shirt, socks, underwear, shoes, and tie--all bought from the local J. C. Penney store." He was a Christian man with a sincere testimony for Christ. He also was a proud man with a straightforward testimony for the J. C. Penney Department stores and their merchandise.

Medical Facilities

Canonsburg General Hospital, Canonsburg, Pa.

About 25 miles south of Pittsburgh was a city called Little Washington. It was growing rapidly and the residents felt that the necessary public facilities like the hospital were outdated and too small. So the city, county, and state joined together to plan for a new hospital in Little Washington. They hired an architectural firm in Pittsburgh which began preparations for preliminary drawings and reports. One report went to the city, county, and state group and another report was sent to the Federal Hospital Investigation Board. The local group accepted their report whole-heartedly. After several months the Federal Board refused to accept their report on the grounds that the existing hospital was adequate for the needs of Little Washington; however, they suggested that the future hospital would be acceptable if the site was moved about 20 miles to the east along a busy highway. The local group needed the Federal financial aid badly and they knew that actually the two hospitals would be easily accessible to Little Washington. They readily accepted the suggestion and changed the name to Canonsburg General Hospital.

Because of the hilly terrain, the new hospital included both one-story and two-story areas. The allowable soil-bearing pressure was easily adequate for inexpensive reinforced concrete spread footing for the columns. The most economical spacing of 25 feet between columns was used. The framing was of light structural steel beams for the second floors and roof. The first floor needed no framing as the concrete floor slab was placed on the ground. Most of the bedrooms were placed on the second floor and the work areas with heavier specialty equipment were on the ground floor (first floor). A general idea of the needed floor areas on the ground floor was as follows (square feet):

X-ray room - medical	300
Dark room - medical	100

X-ray storage	150
Minor surgery room	200
Operating room	400
Supply room	150
Employee lounge	250
Laboratory room	300
Nurses' station	200
Waiting room	400
Examining room	150
Consultation	200
Toilets	300
Kitchen	2,000
Dining room	2,000
Library	400
Janitor	200
Emergency room	2,000

After the hospital had been in service for one year, the architect and the structural engineer were asked to review some unusual occurrences. Many pipes had broken, electricity had failed, X-ray machines had shifted, operating room equipment tilted, and partitions and floors were cracked and sloped. Gene was told that the top surface of the column base plates in many areas, which had been at the same elevation as the top of the floor surface, were now two or three inches below. The feeling of the hospital administration was that the whole hospital had settled the two or three inches and almost nothing was working properly. It appeared that Gene was about to confront some angry administrators and a serious law suit.

The architect spent an hour reviewing the damage while Gene walked through the second floor and then examined the column base plates. When the architect returned, he told Gene that he had not come to any conclusions about what had happened. Gene surprised him by stating that he was quite sure that he knew what had happened and it would probably get worse unless the proper steps were taken. Then he explained his conclusions. The second floor and roof had not moved. The column footings had been placed on a shale which had excellent bearing capability. It was very unlikely that the framing beams and columns had settled at all. But he could remember that the site was quite hilly and often the valleys had to be filled with soil material brought from long distances. Gene had worked on several projects where the soil material was expansive. He suggested to the architect that the fill material that had been placed under many areas of the ground floor slab was expansive and had raised the floor slabs the two to three inches and would do more damage unless it was removed. He told the architect to bring to the building the soil consultant that had worked on the hospital project.

Later the soil consultant confirmed Gene's suspicions. He had taken a sample of the soil under the floor and it was expansive. The sale receipts pointed to the firm where the fill had been obtained. When the soil consultant investigated the firm, he was informed that several other projects had experienced the expansion of the fill on their buildings so they had sued in court and obtained large amounts of money from the firm to pay for the damages. The firm had then declared bankruptcy.

The soil consultant who had approved placing the bad fill and the building contractor who had hired his firm were now responsible to make all necessary repairs. They arrived at some wild ideas like tunneling under the floors without disturbing anything above. When requested for his solution, Gene answered without hesitation:

1. Choose a convenient area.

2. Remove all equipment, etc., on the floor and place in an adjacent area.

3. Excavate floor slab and expansive soil.

4. Replace soil, slab, and equipment.

5. Repeat at another area until every area that had been damaged was replaced.

Office Buildings

Comstock Center, Pittsburgh, Pa.

The front of this building was about 300 feet from the east shore of the Allegheny River. The south side of the building was about one-half mile from the junction of the Allegheny River and the Monongehela River. At this point the Allegheny River was about one-quarter of a mile wide. Geologists have said that during the Ice Age, the glacier scoured out a valley about one mile wide. Later mud and small aggregate filled in the valley and then the river made a channel for itself. This resulted in a quarter-mile of soft material on each side of the river. The building was in this soft material and required the use of steel H piles to support the building.

The building was very unusual as it was ten floors in height and most of the floors stepped back from the floor above. It was only about 70 feet wide because of existing buildings on each side. Parking was at a premium so it was decided to use a basement for parking. To excavate the soft earth, it was necessary to use sheet piling as the exterior of the basement walls. Cars entered the basement from the rear; in fact, to provide an entrance, a piece of land 70 feet wide was purchased from the rear of the building to the adjacent street. And a portion of it was sloped in order to allow vehicles to descend to the basement level.

There were no interior columns, just the two rows of exterior columns at the sides of the building. This was true for the ten floors above grade as well as the basement. In order to achieve the necessary lateral stability, the 70-foot floor beams had to be designed with moment connections at the columns. Of course, it was necessary to have two sets of stairs and two elevators. This complicated the parking in the basement and it caused a bad error to occur on one of the floors.

Gene was called to the side after the concrete had been placed on the fifth floor. The construction superintendent noticed that the floor at one of the elevators had an unusual slope. He checked with a transit and found that the floor at that point was eight inches higher than it was supposed to be. The connection of the floor beam to the column had been installed upside down which raised the form deck eight inches and therefor the floor slab was eight inches too high. It could not remain that way so the superintendent asked Gene to explain how it could be fixed. Gene suggested in simple terms the following procedure:

1. Place heavy wood plank on the fourth floor slab.

2. Position several adjustable steel scaffolds under the fifth floor slab around the connection that was wrong.

3. Raise the scaffolds slowly until they were carrying the slab.

4. Remove the faulty connection, reverse and install correctly.

5. Slowly lower the slab down until it was resting on the properly installed connection.

This was done and it worked perfectly.

Gene later said that on a square foot floor area basis, this building was the most expensive that he ever worked on.

Two Chatham Center, Pittsburgh, Pa.

On the west side of Wood Street, near where it entered the downtown business district of Pittsburgh, was an office building named One Chatham Center. Adjacent to it was a large concrete parking garage three stories high. Several times Gene was called upon to inspect the garage and to recommend repairs to the floors, beams, and columns. Pittsburgh experiences many days in winter when it is snowing or the temperature drops below freezing. This bad weather caused the concrete to deteriorate especially due to the road salt brought in on the car tires.

The owners of Chatham Center decided to construct another office building to be sixteen floors in height, 200 feet long, and 100 feet wide. The architect pointed out that the site did not have enough room to accommodate a building of that size. The architect suggested placing the building on the parking garage. Gene was hired to give an opinion on the feasibility of this idea. In a short time he told the owners that the parking garage was not strong enough to support any building whatsoever; however, by coordinating the location of the columns of the new building with the structure of the garage, the columns could pass through the floors of the garage without weakening the floors or even interfering with the traffic movement or parking of the cars. The biggest problem would be to provide new column footings but this could be solved with some extra expense. The owners agreed with the approach and the architect began the design process.

The new building was architecturally simple, no extra extensions, just a plain rectangle with a metal and glass facade. The spacing of the columns in the parking garage was thirty feet in each direction, so the spacing of the columns in the new office building was made thirty feet in each direction. Hence the size of the building was somewhat larger than anticipated. It was 210 feet long and 120 feet wide which was agreeable to the owners. The structural design was also simple. Pittsburgh is in Seismic Zone 1 and does not require earthquake design. Also, it is not subject to hurricanes so the wind design is nominal, 25 pounds per square foot. Office Live Load surprisingly is rather small, only 50 pounds per square foot. Office walls were plaster with steel studs which is only about 15 pounds per square foot.

In the parking garage it was necessary to check the structural strength of the floor at every place where the columns forming the new office building passed through. Later, during construction, after the new columns had been placed, the floor openings were repaired and the existing floor was used to provide lateral support for the columns. Most of the new columns came through where it was relatively easy to cut the hole in the floor and then repair the concrete.

The difficult problem was to decide how to choose the type of footing for the columns of the new office building. The soil was a mixture of small and medium-size rock aggregate with allowable bearing value of 5,000 pounds per square foot. For the parking garage, the column footings were about 8 feet by 8 feet. On this basis, the column footings would have to be 20 feet by 20 feet for the office building. This was not economical although it was possible to get the footings between the existing footings. Something else had to be introduced into the thinking. Gene remembered reading about using a grout forced into the soil between the aggregate to increase the allowable soil bearing capacity. A concrete grout would increase the value from 5,000 to 10,000 pounds per square foot and the column footing would then be 15 feet by 15 feet. This still seemed to be rather large so Gene investigated using a chemical epoxy. This would have increased the soil bearing capacity to 15,000 pounds per square foot and the column footings would then be 12 feet by 12 feet. This method was adopted and the project proceeded with little interruption.

Parking Garages

Bayfront Parking Garage, Erie, Pa.

Two major objectives in designing a parking facility are efficient use of space and rapid handling of incoming and outgoing automobiles. This parking garage was in Erie on the shore of Lake Erie where there was a large amount of snow and ice during the winter. So a third major objective is to provide a floor slab that is relatively impervious to water and salt brought in on the tires of the vehicles. Even though many parking garages have a separate circular ramp for moving the vehicles from floor to floor, Gene decided to use two side areas that are sloped gently about nine feet in 130 feet with parking for automobiles on each side of an aisle for both up and down traffic. The two ends of the garage were level but with the same width as the sloping sides. The width of each ramp was about 62 feet which consisted of the parking stalls of 9 feet by 21 feet on each side plus an aisle for two-way traffic (up and down) of 20 feet. A 60-degree angle of the parking stall was used. One elevator and two stairways were provided. The spacing of the columns was 18 feet and they were placed in three rows, a row on each side of the garage and a row down the middle. The garage was five stories in height with a floor-to-floor height of 9 feet. This height was determined by the depth of two feet for the concrete beams spanning across the 62 feet from column to column, and the floor to the soffit of the beam giving a clear height of 7 feet for automobiles. The concrete floor slab spanning between the beams was 8 inches thick with the top of the slab at the elevation of the top of the beams. The description of the garage here, shows that the first two major objectives have been satisfied. The solution to the third major objective of proving a floor slab that was relatively impervious to the entrance of road salt and water from rain or melting snow was then considered.

All concrete cracks to some extent. Most cracks are too small to be seen with the naked eye. Cracks may be due to shrinkage of the concrete beam or slab when it is drying after it has been placed. The usual way to eliminate this tendency is to use adequate curing methods or the concrete beams or slabs may exhibit a pattern or cracks due to temperature changes such as warm, sunny days and cold, freezing nights. In any event, Gene decided to use a new concept for reinforced concrete.

Prestressed Concrete

Through the use of high strength materials and improved methods of design, there is a reduction of cross-sectional dimensions and consequent weight savings. There are limitations to this development, due primarily to the presence of tension cracks which occur under service load conditions. The undesirable characteristics of ordinary reinforced concrete have been largely overcome by the development of prestressed concrete. As explained by Winter, Urquhart, O'Rourke, and Nilson in their textbook, Design of Concrete Structures, a prestressed concrete member has been defined as one in which there have been introduced internal stresses of such magnitude and distribution that the stresses resulting from the given external loading are counteracted to a desired degree. Concrete is basically a compressive material, with its strength in tension a low and unreliable value. Prestressing applies a precompression to the member which reduces or eliminates undesirable tensile stresses that would otherwise be present. The entire cross section can be used to resist bending, and cracking under service load conditions can be minimized or even avoided entirely.

Prestress force was applied to the concrete beams and slabs by tying together with wires or cables the jack bases at the ends of the concrete members. These ties of high strength steel were passed through a hollow conduit embedded in the concrete. The conduit was then filled with a noncorrosive grease that allowed the movement of the ties. One end of the prestressing tendon was anchored, and all of the force was applied by a jack at the other end. After attainment of the desired amount of prestress force, the wires were wedged against the concrete, and the jacking equipment was removed for reuse. The magnitude of prestress force in concrete members was not constant but diminished with time at a gradually decreasing rate. The reduction of the initial prestress force to the final effective value was due to a number of causes. The most significant were elastic shortening of the concrete, concrete creep under sustained load, concrete shrinkage, relaxation of the stresses in the steel, frictional loss between the tendons and the stressing operation, and loss due to the slip of the steel strands as stress was transferred from the jacks to the anchorages at the end of the beams.

Prestressing was accomplished using high-tensile wire with an ultimate strength of 250,000 psi at a working stress of 150,000 psi. Concrete of substantially higher compressive strength was used, 5,000 psi, instead of ordinary reinforced concrete compressive strength of 3,000 psi. Gene was very much satisfied with the use of prestressed concrete.

Recreational Facilities

Falling Water Reception Center, Ohiopyle, Pa.

Frank Lloyd Wright was the greatest architect of the 20th Century, though some thought he was the greatest of the 19th Century, while he himself asked, "What about the 21st?" Wright was born in a close-knit Welsh clan in the Wisconsin town of Richland Center in 1867. He lived almost 92 years, designed over a thousand buildings, and saw six hundred of them to completion during his 72 years at the drafting board. In 1936 Wright designed his best-known building, Fallingwater, a country retreat for Edgar J. Kaufmann, Sr., at Bear Run, Pennsylvania. Hovering above a waterfall in a lovely ravine, its dynamic demeanor held in check, anchored into the ancient rock ledges by tall piers of native stone. Ledgelike floors and terraces of concrete are cantilevered out over the waterfall, overlapping one another. The largest of these cantilevers carries a lair-like living room where a big boulder emerges out of the flagstone floor beside the fireplace. And through a glass-encased "hatch," a hanging staircase flutters down to the stream.

In 1976 Gene was asked by the office of Edgar J. Kaufmann, Jr., to inspect Fallingwater and recommend necessary repairs. Most of the concrete was exposed to the snow and rain and the freezing temperatures of the severe winters. For these areas Gene recommended that all deteriorated concrete be removed down to the solid concrete and any rusted reinforcing rods be replaced. In some places prestressed concrete could be used and this would eliminate cracking and spalling of the concrete. Where this could not be done, the replacement should be an epoxy which resisted the severe weathering effects, especially the constant humidity of the waterfall under the cantilevered concrete. He also recommended that a specialist concrete repair company be hired to place scaffold under all exposed concrete and the concrete be checked by hammer impact. Then it would be repaired with epoxy, and be coated with an epoxy solution over all the concrete area.

Edgar J. Kaufmann, Jr., did not use Fallingwater as a residence any longer. He donated it to the state and it was used as a memorial to Frank Lloyd Wright, the architect. Many interested families visited the site. So the state decided to build some recreational facilities where the visitors could get food, examine photographs of Wright and his

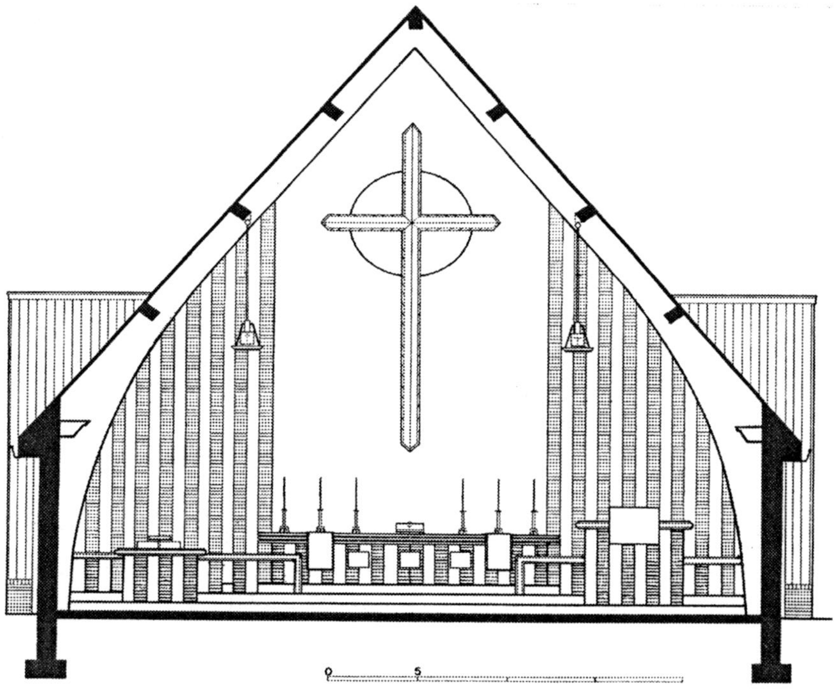

United Methodist Church

many projects as well as construction photos of Fallingwater, etc. The architect was hired and he chose Gene to be the structural consultant. He decided to use five one-story buildings about 50 feet by 50 feet in area. They were constructed entirely of wood except for exposed concrete columns. They were arranged in a semicircle and connected by suspended wooden walkways. When finished it was very attractive and blended into the landscape very nicely.

The architect made one grievous error. He had adequate toilet facilities, but for some unknown reason he decided not to use water to flush the toilets. Instead he used a new concept where the toilet was packed at the bottom with straw which soon decomposed and slid away carrying the waste material (during the night). Signs were conspicuously erected warning smokers not to throw lighted cigarettes into the toilets. One week after the buildings were open to the public, a visitor thought that the cigarette that was thrown into the toilet was extinguished. It smoldered for a few hours, then during the night it and the straw burst into flame. The watchman had gone home after closing the facility at 10 P.M. So one by one each building and the walkway went up in smoke. When the watchman came in the morning all that remained was a field of charred concrete columns.

The facility had to be rebuilt exactly as before--except for the toilets! Gene checked the concrete columns and found that they could be reused so it was not a total loss.

Educational Facilities

Reizenstein Middle School, Pittsburgh, Pennsylvania

The mayor of the city of Pittsburgh strenuously opposed the choice of the architect by the Board of Education. The mayor had examined his credentials and judged him to be lacking in architectural experience. Also, his business ability was poor--his office workers often had not received their monthly pay. Several times the mayor had cautioned the Board but they did not listen.

When the architect received the contract for the school project, he offered the structural engineering contract to a friend of Gene's, James Younkins. Jim refused to take the job and suggested that the architect speak to Gene. The reason why Jim did this was because the architect owed him his fee from another project; in fact, Jim heard that the architect owed every consultant some money. Some people even said that the architect owed everybody in Pittsburgh some money! But Gene felt sorry for him and told him that he would work with him on this project. The mayor was furious when he learned that this architect was actually starting this major school project.

The architect hired another architect to be his assistant. The two decided on a new concept for the building design. All interior spaces were to be open. The school principal would place movable partitions where desired. Gene was told to place steel columns at 100 feet spacing in each direction. The building was only one story in height except for certain designated areas. The roof framing was steel trusses spanning from column to column and with subsidiary trusses at 5 feet spacing. Gene worked for two months without preliminary architectural drawings. Then he was told to submit his final drawings in two weeks. His structural drawings were the only drawings submitted on the designated day. The mechanical consultant and the electrical consultant refused to submit their drawings until they had received 75 percent of their fee. The Board of Education allowed the architect one additional week. Then they paid him 75 percent of his fee so that he could give his consultants 75 percent of their fee. He gave Gene only 35 percent of his fee.

The project was advertised for bidding with the estimated price of $10 million and an allowable overrun of 5 percent. The Director of Construction for the Board of Education was happy when the low bid was about the estimated price. But he could not understand why Gene told him that because of the inadequate drawings, the final cost would exceed his expectation. The extras received from the building contractor would be enormous.

The construction was started but the architect had disappeared. The Director of Construction promised that the consultants would receive their final 25 percent if they would help during the construction phase. He then hired another architect to replace the original architect. The second architect was dishonest. He waited until the construction had proceeded far enough that he did not need the structural consultant. He told the director that Gene had not performed according to the construction documents and should not receive the rest of his fee. The director accepted this false story and not only refused to pay Gene but accused him of being dishonest. Actually, the director gave Gene the impression that he and the architect were covering up the truth. As Pilate said, "What is truth?"

The project was finally completed. A year later the original architect appeared in Pittsburgh with the tale that he had been seriously ill. He was sued by the Board of Education for the extras incurred on this project, not $500,000 but $2,500,000. And a few days after he appeared, Gene called him about the portion of the engineering fee that was unpaid. He assured Gene that his son would be at Gene's office in 30 minutes with the check. Gene waited for several hours but the son never appeared. Again he called the architect and was told that the son had started to walk the three blocks to Gene's office when he put the check on the fender of a parked car and bent over to tie his shoelaces. Before he could straighten up and retrieve the check, the car had disappeared with the check. He sent another check to Gene the next day. The bank refused to honor it and marked it NSF. The architect was sued and the court's decision was that he was a free man as long as he continued to pay his debts. He made one payment then stopped. Gene's lawyer checked with the district attorney and found that some unknown person had removed all judicial papers from the architect's file! As Pilate said, "What is truth?"

Hotels

Sheraton Motor Hotel, Marshall Twp, Pennylvania

This motel was built in an excellent location. It was between a major highway from Pittsburgh to Erie and a major business area with only one-quarter of a mile separating them. It was not different from the majority of motels because its layout was similar. The sleeping rooms portion of the building was five stories high and the adjacent area containing a large banquet hall and some small dining rooms and conference rooms was one story high.

The framing of the sleeping rooms area was unusual. The walls of the rooms were spaced about 25 feet apart. They were made of high-strength concrete block with no grout or vertical rods and 8 inches in width. When a building was above five stories (to six or seven) the cells were filled with grout and when a building was above seven (to eight or nine) the cells were filled with grout and contained one vertical reinforcing rod in each cell. The blocks for one story were laid, then a floor of cellular concrete deck was placed, spanning from wall to wall. The space between the ends of the two rooms of deck was filled with grout which was allowed to penetrate into the open cells of the deck and formed a solid support for the next story of block. Vertical and horizontal rods were added in order to ensure lateral stability. The top surface of the deck was covered with 2 inches of grout to form a smooth floor surface.

The type of foundation depended on the allowable soil bearing pressure. The soil pressure here was low so Gene decided to make the wall footings 8 inches deep and continuous from one end of the building to the other. The allowable soil bearing pressure was only 2,500 PSF but using the method that Gene suggested, the soil bearing pressure was only 1,000 PSF.

The roof framing at the banquet hall was primarily laminated wood. Most of it was exposed and gave a pleasing look to the ceiling. One day Gene was asked to look at one of the laminated beams which appeared to have deflected more than usual. Fortunately, it was one of the small beams over a supply room. It had a large deflection. The beam was near a steam pipe which had a small leak. For several years the end of the beam was subjected to a constant cloud of moist steam. Finally, the beam fibers were weakened and the beam began to deflect.

It was noticed by an employee and Gene was called. He supervised the installation of a new beam.

Research Facilities

Medical Research Facility, Pittsburgh, Pennsylvania

This building was an addition to a Medical Research Facility at the University of Pittsburgh. It was on the side of a hill, across the street from the University Medical School. The new addition was similar to the existing building. The height was three floors and the room layout matched that of the existing building. The framing was a standard structural steel arrangement of beams and columns, with the column spacing of 25 feet which was a very economical spacing. The Dental School was also near this new building. The new addition had two serious problems.

Much of the University of Pittsburgh was situated over coal mines. The mines had been abandoned as the usable coal had been removed. The problem was to ensure that the roof of the mine was supported adequately. The first step was to examine the mine drawings at the Bureau of Mines. This not only gave the exact location of all mines in this area but also the elevation of the mine floor. If the distance from the ground surface down to the mine roof was less than 200 feet, Gene would use some method of bridging across the mine or shoring up the mine roof by filling the mine with concrete. If the distance was over 200 feet, Gene would have some test borings made and use the appropriate type of footings. In this case, the distance was about 700 feet and the material over the mine was a shale that afforded a natural bridge across the mined area. Gene used ordinary reinforced concrete footings for the walls and columns.

The other problem was actually outside the building. People exited from the building to the sidewalk of a side road that had a very steep grade down to the busy road between the building and the medical school. It was always difficult to cross this road, and in the winter it was especially difficult to go down the sidewalk of the side road with all the ice and snow. The Medical Research Facility was a very important building. It was the building where Jonas Salk was working on a cure for Polio. It had to be easily accessible at all times. So it was decided to use a covered walkway from the Medical Research Facility down the hill to the busy road where a covered bridge crossed the road. Medical personnel left the research facility on a covered walkway that remained at that elevation even though the side road sloped rapidly downward. By the time the covered walkway reached the busy road, it was high enough to use the floor of the covered bridge at the elevation of 18 feet which was the accepted regulation for truck height. Many students coming down the side road from classes in another building used the bridge and many students coming from the medical school for a laboratory class at the research facility were thankful for the bridge.

Jonas Salk continued his research work until he was successful in finding a cure for Polio. He was credited with saving thousands of lives, especially of children.

Residential Housing

Morse School Housing, Pittsburgh, Pennsylvania

This building was an addition to the Morse School which was no longer used as a school. It was similar to the sleeping rooms portion of the Sheraton Motor Hotel. It was used to provide small apartments for the elderly. The building was five stories in height. Prefabricated concrete cellular deck was used for the structural floor. The deck was supported by 8-inch concrete block walls at 25 feet apart. It did not use the usual 2-inch concrete topping but only a thin application of grout to fill any joints and level up the floor for the carpet.

The soil was a compacted mixture of small and large aggregates with an allowable soil bearing pressure of 5,000 PSF. This was adequate to make the use of standard spread footings economical. They were 5 feet wide and 14 inches thick and were reinforced in both directions.

This type of building construction was simple and inexpensive. The architectural fee received from the Federal Government Agency was very low also. Instead of the usual 7 percent of the construction cost, it was only 3.5 percent. Accordingly, the structural consultant received only 0.35 percent instead of 0.70 percent.

Retrofit Projects

Station Square, Freight Shops, Pittsburgh, Pennsylvania

This building was one of four existing buildings abandoned when the B and O Railroad decided to close their terminal on the east bank of the Monongehela River. It was originally used for freight storage so it had one set of tracks down the center of the building. Five freight cars were left in the building and used as shops for the public. The remainder of the pit for the track was filled in with earth and covered with a concrete floor slab. The building was 100 feet wide and 800 feet long. On one side of the freight car shops was the main central aisle 15 feet wide. To obtain more shopping space, framing for a second floor was erected of structural steel and the steel floor deck was placed with 2.5 inches of concrete. The other side of the freight car shops had an aisle 10 feet wide and shops but without the new second floor.

The existing roof framing system was inspected for rusted steel members that were replaced if necessary. The footings for the new columns of the second floor had to be carefully designed. The soil was practically mud with an allowable soil bearing capacity of only 1,000 PSF. The footings were 10 by 10 feet square and 2 feet thick. Probably some settlement has occurred.

2. MY SON--THE MISSIONARY

Home Missions

On October 15, 1949, Betty Wood and Gene Dotter were married in the Union Gospel Church of Wilkinsburg, Pennsylvania. They were convinced that God had brought them together and they were determined to serve God financially, physically, and spiritually. As one mission group had put it:

I will give whatever God asks me to give;

I will go wherever God asks me to go;

I will do whatever God asks me to do.

They continued to be very active in the church: Sunday School teachers and superintendents, youth work, officers of the church, Bible study leaders, Bible expositor speakers, and even janitorial work when necessary. Gene was sure that God would use them in any place if they were willing. An illustration showing God's hand in their menial work happened one wintry evening.

It was Saturday and it had been snowing. After the evening meal, Gene gathered some tools and paint and went down to the church. He knew that he would probably have to scrape some loose paint off a wall and make some repairs. Also, it was a section of Pittsburgh where there were broken homes, single parents, and gangs of bad kids on the streets. Sure enough, he found some places on the walls to repair. While working in the quiet solitude, he heard the sound of a snowball hitting one of the stained-glass windows. He was quite upset as this happened often and sometimes meant a broken window. To repair a stained-glass window was expensive!

So Gene jumped off the ladder and ran to the main door. He flung the door open and saw three boys across the street looking at the place where the snowballs had hit. They probably thought that he would shout at them and go back into the church. Instead he ran across the street, grabbed two boys and sternly said, "Who threw a snowball?" They were shocked. They managed to answer, "We didn't do it!" Gene thought that he should teach them a lesson. He inquired, "What are your names? Where do you live? You are going to pay for the broken windows!" He released the two boys in order to get a pad and pencil from his pocket. As quick as a wink, the three darted off in different directions. One boy jumped over a fence and ran down behind a street of two-story homes. Gene went into the church to finish repairing the wall.

During the next week Gene was led to make some effort to find the three boys to give them a lecture about their mischief. He started with the boy who had jumped over the fence. That kid was ten to twelve years old with a rather handsome face. No doubt he lived in one of these houses on this street. When he reached the fourth house, he was startled to see a police car in front of the house. Two policemen were coming down the stairs from the second floor. Gene explained that he was from the church. They brushed him aside and told him that they had been called to stop a fight between a man and his wife. Then they added that the man worked as an erector of billboard signs during the week but spent the weekend roaming the streets in a drunken stupor. The wife was known as the town prostitute. As they talked, the woman came down the stairs with her suitcase. She was going away with another man. She had told her husband that she would never be back to see him or their four sons.

Gene was hesitant about bothering the man and his sons. Then he realized that God had sent him there so he went upstairs. The door was opened by the boy that he was seeking. He did not want to let Gene in but Gene assured him that he would not bother his father about the snowball incident. Gene found the father resting on his bed. He had cancer and was dying. He was open to the gospel so they had a nice talk about salvation through the blood of Jesus Christ. Gene visited the family every few days until the father died in about a month. The town took charge of all the arrangements for the funeral and for the sons.

Betty and Gene were certain that they should be busy for the Lord outside the church as well as in the church. Whenever the opportunity came, they did not hesitate to pray about it and then go to work.

Christian Businessmen's Committee (CBMC)

The CBMC is a nationwide organization of men. Once every month the local group met at a hotel for dinner at a private dining room. The speaker was an outstanding businessman, such as J. C. Penney and R. J. LeTourneau, with a sincere Christian testimony. Each member was requested to invite a friend or business associate. The speaker spent most of his time telling about his professional life, then gave a short but clear salvation testimony. After the meeting, the guests had ample time to discuss with the speaker or with the person who had invited them to the dinner, the talk that they had just heard. A friend of Gene had asked him to invite his brother-in-law (an architect client) to a CBMC dinner. The architect was an atheist who constantly spoke in sarcastic terms about church or any Christian discussion. He did go with Gene but left the meeting very quickly. Several weeks later the architect talked to Gene about attending another dinner meeting. Gene asked if he enjoyed the last meeting. The architect responded, "It was great. After the dinner meeting I visited my brother-in-law. Praise the Lord, I accepted Jesus Christ as my Saviour." That architect has been an outspoken Christian for the last forty years.

Women's Christian Fellowship (WCF)

One evening a group of women met with Betty in the YWCA at Wilkinsburg, Pennsylvania. They enjoyed the Bible study so much that they decided to meet with her every month. The YWCA is no longer there but the meetings are still held every month. They were moved to Penn Hills and then to Turtle Creek.

The women enjoyed the Christian fellowship and the depth of Bible teaching.

The Gideons International

Two traveling salesmen met at a hotel. There was only one room available so they agreed to share the room. Before retiring for the night they read the Bible and prayed. Then in the morning they both expressed the desire to meet again; in fact, they had an idea that it would be helpful if there was an organization of traveling salesmen that would encourage Christian fellowship. A short time later the organization was started. At first it was just for fellowship but then it was decided that the primary purpose of the Gideons was to distribute the Bible. It was logical to stress the placement of Bibles in hotels and motels. This was expanded later to hospitals and doctors' offices. Soon the membership grew tremendously when the regulations were changed to include not only salesmen but any person (not a minister) who supervised at least two subordinates in his secular work and was a member in good standing of a church.

The Gideon organization is over one hundred years old. About 50 years ago it started a new ministry of distribution of copies of the New Testaments in schools, prisons, colleges, the armed forces, and in personal ministry. Gene and Betty have been active members for forty years. During that time Gene has spoken about the Gideon work in three hundred churches and has spread the gospel of Jesus Christ with at least 50,000 Bibles and 100,000 New Testaments. Betty helped the Auxiliary's work with the distribution of Bibles in doctors' offices and New Testaments to nurses and hospital personnel. Her greatest work was her presidency of the Gideons Auxiliary International.

Wycliffe Bible Translators

A young man went to Guatemala as a missionary. He spent a major portion of his time with a tribe of native Indians. One thing became clear to him: these people found it very difficult to understand the message that he brought because it was in Spanish while they knew only their tribal dialect. He found that the local people only spoke their language, as it was not written. He began to investigate how he could produce the Bible in the language of the people. He found it to be a task far too large for only one person. So he recruited people to go to groups of people around the world who had no written language. They had to live with the tribes, often in jungles or seemingly inaccessible places. One missionary told how she arrived at the last civilized town, was transported up a small river by canoe for seven days, hiked through a forest for ten days, and then climbed over mountains for another ten days before reaching a lost civilization of thousands of Indians. She spent ten years listening carefully to the people speak. Then it took another ten years to construct a written language from the sounds she heard spoken. Finally, after another five years, she was able to give portions of the Bible to these people in their own tongue.

This work necessitated the efforts of many people in the U.S.A. or Canada to provide support for the Wycliffe translators. Betty and Gene volunteered to be the Wycliffe representatives in Western Pennsylvania. Their task was to provide lodging for the translators passing through their area, arrange for services at churches for the translators, and to organize at least one banquet every year, open to the public. One outstanding banquet speaker was Dr. Oswald J. Smith, pastor of the Peoples Church in Toronto, Canada, a man with a real missionary heart who came to Pittsburgh to speak.

The first Wycliffe missionary to visit Betty and Gene was Neil Nellis about 50 years ago. He and his wife, Jane, were laboring in southern Mexico among the Zapotec Indians. He came from hot, humid Mexico to a wintry afternoon in Pittsburgh wearing only a summer suit. The first task was to provide a warm overcoat. Then a hot dinner and a restful bed. He stayed with Gene and Betty for one month, making some good contacts as he spoke in various churches. The Nellises were asked to retire at age 65 but stayed for five more years. It was now mandatory to retire so they promptly joined the Indian Mission and remained with the Zapotec Indians, translating more of the Bible along with songs, poems, and study books for fifteen years. Jane Nellis had both legs amputated but remained in Oaxaco City for three more years when she died at the age of 88. Neil is still living in Oaxaco City with his married daughter who is serving with Wycliffe.

Ron Gluck had served in the Army Air Force as a fighter pilot. After three years he left the Air Force and married Ruth who lived near Pittsburgh. They joined Wycliffe Bible Translators in the Jungle Aviation and Radio division (JAARS) where he served as a pilot transporting Wycliffe personnel and materials in New Guinea. Ron and Ruth were transferred to a new base for Wycliffe in Nigeria, Africa. He needed a single-engine light airplane for this work. Gene and Betty organized a committee of ten local persons with the intention of raising the money to buy an airplane. The committee heard of a dentist in Pittsburgh who wished to sell his airplane that met all the requirements. They raised $40,000 and bought the plane. After a few changes, it was loaded with fuel and a Christian pilot employed by United Air Lines took a vacation and flew the plane nonstop to Nigeria. It was named "Friendship for Nigeria."

Meanwhile Gene went to Nigeria to supervise the construction of a hangar for Wycliffe. Unfortunately, the Nigerian government issued a proclamation that only Nigerian pilots could fly a plane in Nigeria. Obviously this was against Wycliffe policy. All strategic materials like airplanes had to be under the control of Christian personnel of Wycliffe. This issue was quickly settled when the neighboring country of Cameroun announced that Wycliffe could bring their plane to Cameroun where this country would also supply a new hangar and had no restriction on the pilot's nationality. The plane was flown to Cameroun and renamed "Friendship for Cameroun."

Ron and Ruth served in Cameroun for eleven years, then were transferred to Washington, D.C. They are serving as liaison persons between Wycliffe people in the U.S.A and the countries of Africa.

Prison Fellowship

This organization was founded by Charles Colson after he was released from prison. He had been an accomplice of President Nixon in the Watergate scandal and had served a number of years of a ten-year sentence. The ministry of this organization is:

> "To exhort, assist, and equip the Church in its ministry to prisoners, ex-prisoners, victims, and their families, and in its advancement of biblical standards of justice."

For many years Gene had the privilege of speaking to the inmates at the Pittsburgh City Jail. This was at some of the Sunday morning church services which were attended by two hundred to three hundred men. On some Sunday afternoons, Gene spoke at the Allegheny County Work House to a smaller group of one hundred to a hundred fifty inmates. Then on some Sunday mornings Gene spoke at the Pennsylvania State Correctional Institution which houses the more hardened criminals. During this time, Gene attended two training sessions where he became qualified as a volunteer for Prison Fellowship. Before serving regularly, Gene retired from his profession as consulting structural engineer. He and Betty went to Florida to live in Fort Myers.

Prison Fellowship Serving Florida suggested that Gene help the volunteers at the Southwest Florida Juvenile Detention Center. The residents at the institution were between eight and eighteen years of age. They usually numbered from fifty to one hundred boys and fifteen to twenty girls. Gene's task was to conduct the Sunday morning church service and to present a Bible study. One other volunteer presented a musical program and another volunteer gave a salvation testimony. In the fourteen years that Gene took part in this service, he distributed about 12,000 New Testaments, 2,000 Bibles, and 25,000 pieces of gospel literature.

Because of his faithfulness with his efforts at the detention center, Gene was invited to be the volunteer chaplain at the Lee County Boot Camp.

He conducted a service for the boys every Thursday evening at seven o"clock. This was difficult as the boot camp was 65 miles from Fort Myers and out in the Everglades. It meant leaving home about 4:30 P.M. and getting home about 10:30 P.M. It meant driving along a lonely unlighted country road. One night while carefully proceeding toward Fort Myers during a heavy rainstorm, he felt the impact of a large egret hitting the windshield of his car. Fortunately, it did not smash the glass. The young men at the boot camp never tried to escape (to run). They said, "We get three good meals here. And where would you go? Out in the swamps with the crocodiles?" The residents remained there from four to six months. Gene was absolutely convinced of the worthwhile effect on the lives of the young men. He was profoundly disappointed when the county commissioners, after four years, refused to finance the project at the boot camp.

He had observed the change in the lives of many of the young men. This was due partly to the militaristic training that the young men received, but it was also due to their exposure to the gospel. One young man was often observed by the guards reading his Bible; and sometime during the early morning or late evening, he would quietly slip aside for a season of prayer. Now he has completed his high school diploma requirements, joined a good church, and is assuming an active role as a good citizen and a sincere Christian.

Salvation Army

Almost everybody is familiar with the work of this organization. Gene volunteered to assist in the rehabilitation of alcoholics and drug addicts, only one small part of the schedule of the Salvation Army of Fort Myers. He began with one day (Friday) each week. He soon found that his work consisted mostly of sitting at a desk in the secretary's office as a guard. It seemed that she had told her superior that she was going to leave--that she was afraid of the people who were being rehabilitated. Gene eventually decided to leave. He had no part in speaking to the residents about Christ. Soon after he left, the secretary resigned.

Habitat for Humanity

The idea behind this organization is commendable. It is to make available affordable low-cost houses for people who needed help. At that time, the construction cost of the standard home offered by Habitat was about $65,000. This could be covered by a mortgage with a low interest rate. To make these homes available, the HFH depended on donations of material and labor. One construction superintendent supervised all the projects, although he relied on a knowledgeable construction carpenter to remain at each construction site all the time. The superintendent was paid but everyone else received no remuneration. During the hot summer, only a few workers were available, but they were experienced construction people. The work proceeded smoothly at a decent pace and was well done. But in the winter, the vacationers (snowbirds) sometimes got tired of loafing so they came over to help. This included old men, women, and children. Gene sometimes felt that he could not vouch for the finished product. After two years, two or three full days per week and working on twelve houses and a storage building for HFH, Gene left permanently.

Masterserve

Hurricane Andrew smashed into southern Florida at Homestead about 20 miles south of Miami. The devastation was hard to imagine. Houses, churches, office buildings, stores, small industrial buildings, etc.--all suffered extensive damage. Gene Sitter had a prosperous business in Illinois and he decided to help rebuild the Homestead area. He organized a nonprofit engineering and construction company and established an office in Fort Lauderdale, a few miles north of Miami. The company office was staffed by five or six persons including Gene Sitter. They had about ten construction superintendents and several persons running a supply yard in Homestead. Sitter concentrated on repairing churches first. The churches usually had adequate insurance. A construction superintendent would inspect the damaged building. By careful use of Christian volunteers and donated material, Masterserve was able to finish the repairs and have some money remaining. This money was then used to pay for repairs to the homes of some of the church members. The motto of Masterserve was SERVING GOD, HELPING MAN.

A friend of Gene Dotter suggested that he question Gene Sitter about the need for a volunteer structural engineer. Gene Sitter thought that it would be very helpful so Gene Dotter left home early every Monday morning. The trip was about 150 miles so his work day started about 9 A.M. At lunch time he ate some free food provided by churches, then usually a late supper after a cold water shower from the garden hose of another church. Finally a night's sleep on the floor of some church that had a dry, clean floor. He spent three days inspecting houses and churches, suggesting repairs and sometimes doing the manual labor with the other Christian volunteer workers. Then he returned home to Fort Myers late Wednesday evening. This schedule continued for two years.

The Homestead area began to look normal again. Sitter expanded the efforts of Masterserve by including additions to churches and Christian schools; in fact, a major project was a new building and an addition to a campus where an organization was helping to rehabilitate alcoholics. But church work remained the major part of Masterserve's work. Quite often this encompassed working with foreign immigrants like Haitians, Mexicans, etc. Gene Dotter's schedule changed. He would remain there for a few days until his part of the project was completed, then return home. He continued this schedule for eight years but it was terminated when his wife, Betty, was diagnosed with Alzheimer's Disease. Gene felt that Betty needed his help continually.

Evangelism Explosion

Dr. D. James Kennedy, Senior Pastor of the Coral Ridge Presbyterian Church in Fort Lauderdale, Florida, conceived a new plan of visitation for the people of the church. In his own words, Dr. Kennedy says in his textbook, "Up to 700 people have gone out weekly to share the Good News of Christ with others. God's gracious working through this effort has been exciting to observe. The church had grown from 17 to 6,500 members in 1983 and from one minister to twelve. The top attendance on a Sunday morning was more than 10,000. About 120 families have left the church to go into full-time Christian service."

The outline of the gospel presentation by a church member:

I. The introduction:

  A. Their secular life.

  B. Their church background.

  C. Our church.

  D. Testimony: personal and/or church.

  E. Two diagnostic questions:

    1. Have you come to a place in your spiritual life where you know for certain that, if you were to die today, you would go to heaven?

    2. Suppose that you were to die tonight and stand before God and He were to say to you, "Why should I let you into my heaven?" What would you say?

II. The Gospel:

  A. Grace.

    1. Heaven is a free gift.

    2. It is not earned or deserved.

  B. Man.

1. Is a sinner.

2. Cannot save himself.

C. God.

1. Is merciful--therefor doesn't want to punish us.

2. Is just--therefor must punish sin.

D. Christ.

1. Who he is--the infinite God-man.

2. What he did--he paid for our sins and a place in heaven for us which he offers as a gift.

E. Faith.

1. What it is not--mere intellectual assent or temporal faith.

2. What it is--trusting in Jesus Christ alone for our salvation.

III. The commitment:

A. The qualifying question, "Does this make sense to you?"

B. The commitment question, "Would you like to receive the gift of eternal life?"

C. The clarification of commitment.

D. The prayer of commitment.

E. The assurance of salvation.

IV. The immediate follow-up:

A. Bible (seven-day call back appointment).

B. Prayer.

C. Worship.

D. Fellowship.

E. Witness.

When Gene was a member of the Union Gospel Church, he organized a small group of four persons for visitation, using the Evangelism Explosion approach. Two three-month periods (Spring and Fall) were scheduled. All visits were "cold"; that is, the visitors from the church were strangers to the residents. This program was continued for five years. It was not very productive, if the number of new church members was the criteria; but many good conversations were available, and some people did receive the gift of eternal life but remained in other churches.

An interesting variation occurred when Gene and Betty met a painting contractor working in the church parsonage. They went through the E.E. presentation with him and he invited them to come to his home that evening. At that time both he and his wife accepted Christ as their Saviour. The next Sunday they were in church with their new baby girl.

Another variation took place when Gene and Betty were members of the Allegheny Center Christian and Missionary Alliance Church. This was a much larger church but only eight persons took part in the E.E. approach. Adjacent to the church was a city park. It was a welcome green area in the crowded buildings and streets. Unfortunately, near the park was an overnight flop house for alcoholics, drug addicts, and the indigent. During the day these people wasted their time sitting or sleeping on the park benches. But it gave the church's E.E. group an opportunity to have a conversation with these poor people. Some professed to accepting Christ but very few managed to live for Christ.

In the evening, these homeless people went to the building where they could get a cot for the night. First they had to take a shower and attend a church service before getting something to eat. Then sleep from 10 P.M. to 6 A.M. Gene often gave a Bible message to these people. Some were open to the gospel. Most just wanted a meal and a place to sleep. One evening Gene was sitting on the platform when his friend next to him said, "Look at that man at the right end of the third row. That is my brother! I have spent many years trying to get him to accept Christ but he never does. He comes home with me for a few days and then he is back here again, dead drunk!"

Betty often played the piano during the song time. One evening after the service she hurried over to a filthy, ragged man struggling to get to his feet. With tears in her eyes, she said, "I know you. You graduated from the University of Pittsburgh the same year that I did! What happened to you?" He hurried past her and she saw the whiskey bottle in his hand. After a few minutes to regain her composure, she told Gene that the man she spoke to had been chosen as the outstanding student of the year when he graduated. His name had been chiseled into the concrete walk leading to the entrance to the Pitt Tower of Learning (a 42-story classroom building).

Another man had come to the piano after an evening service. He courteously told Betty to move over on the piano bench so that he could sit next to her. She reluctantly moved for he was filthy and she really did not want him near her. He explained to her that he thought that a hymn that they had sung would have been more effective if she would have changed it. Then he added that he would show her how to do it. To her amazement, he played like a classical symphonic pianist. She exclaimed, "How did you ever learn to play like that?" He shrugged his shoulders. As he shuffled away, he said, "I graduated from Julliard as one of their outstanding prospects. All I ever became was a filthy drunk!"

Foreign Missions

The place was in southern Gabon, Africa. The sun was setting, the sky was growing dark, and a haze was covering the darkening forest. Gene stood on the rear veranda of the missionary residence high above the Luitzi River. In the quiet stillness came the sound of a drumbeat far off in the distance. Suddenly Gene thought of that great missionary, David Livingston. This is the place where Livingston had come out of the jungle to face the Atlantic Ocean.

David Livingston had come down to South Africa to help the missionary, Robert Moffet. He had finished his studies in Scotland and was now acting as a medical missionary. He married a daughter of Moffet and seemed happy with his growing family. But always he could hear the drumbeat in the distance and see the "thousands of ribbons of smoke rising from the tribal campfires." Finally, he felt the overwhelming desire to visit the lost tribes and bring the gospel of Jesus to them. He and his porters went up the east coast to the middle of Mozambique, then plunged into the jungle on a northwest course. Slowly they made their way through the countries, as we know them today--Zambia, Democratic Republic of Congo, Angola, Congo, and Gabon. It had taken over two years and he could have gone back to South Africa now in the comparative ease of a sailing vessel, but he had promised them that they would guide them home. This meant over two years more of the difficult journey.

How could an "ordinary person" like Gene be used by God just as He had used Livingston? Then Gene remembered another "ordinary person" who had been used by God at this place in Africa. This man had been an attendant in a Midwest zoo in the U.S.A. He was middle-aged when he heard God calling him as a missionary to a place near Gabon. He applied to several missionary boards but was rejected because of his age and his lack of theological training. He was convinced that he should go. When he reached Gabon, he learned of a tribe of pygmies that had never been reached with the gospel of Jesus Christ. Against all advice, he went into the deep forest where they lived. He was captured and brought before an important chief. His death was ordered. He then signified that he had something to tell the chief. He took the chief into the forest where they saw a wild animal. He called to the animal with voice sounds that he had heard in the zoo. To the amazement of the chief, the animal came peacefully to them. The chief then told him that he could remain with the tribe and tell them about this man Jesus Christ if he would teach them the languages of the animals.

God moves in mysterious ways. Gene and Betty were open to His movement in their lives. It was no surprise when Gene met a former missionary, Paris Reidhead, who told him about his plan for helping foreign native Christians to earn a decent living. He had founded an organization called DAS (Development Assistance Society) and wanted Gene to get involved using his engineering expertise.

Development Assistant Society (DAS)

Paris Reidhead called Gene about a year later (1969) and asked him if he would go to Africa with him. The trip was primarily to Niger, then to Cote d'Ivoire, Ghana, and Nigeria. Gene agreed and met Paris and another man at the JFK Airport in New York. They flew to Paris, France, then went to Niamey, the capital of Nigeria. SIM (Sudan Interior Mission) had been requested by the President of Niger to help provide three thousand homes for government workers (they lived in mud huts then). SIM asked Paris Reidhead to handle the project.

Four countries--Niger, Burkina Faso, Mali, and Ghana--had joined together for mutual help. Each country built a quadrangle with four modern homes with all the necessary conveniences. The presidents met four times each year and resided in these homes during each meeting which rotated in each country by country. Paris and his two companions lived in the Niger president's house for a week or so while their report was being prepared, then they had an audience with the president in the presidential palace. He agreed with their observations; but in a rather offhand manner he said that he wished that they were concerned with water supply for the people rather than houses. These people needed a good source of water! The northern portion of Niger lies in the Sahara Desert. In the southern portion, it rains only one month during the year. During that month all of the vegetation turns green. After that, all plant life turns brown and withers away. Swarms of locusts, mosquitoes, etc. fill the air. The Hermana comes--a sand storm that wreaks havoc with machinery. Missionary Air Flights suspends operation. The motors would last only a few days if they did not. Because of the water pollution (and almost everything else) Gene soon developed a painful stomach and diarrhea. That, with the unusual Muslim toilet customs, made life difficult.

The next stop was Cote d'Ivoire for one afternoon and evening at the Christian Guest House in Abidjan. Then on to Ghana for dinner with the Christian Chief of Police in Accra, the capital of Ghana. The next day Gene went on to Lagos, the capital of Nigeria, while Paris and his friend went to the interior of Ghana where Paris (DAS) had established a chicken farm for the Christian believers. Paris then met with two men from the U.S.A. who wanted to organize two businesses with DAS guidance. The first business was to grow lettuce, pack it in refrigerated boxes, and ship it to Europe. The second business was to raise a variety of vegetables, cook them, make several kinds of soup to be canned for distribution.

Gene's Missionary Projects

Organization	Country	Projects	Visits
MTT	Ecuador	2	1
MTT	Alaska	2	0
MTT	USA	15	5
MTT	Mexico	5	4
OMS,EMI	Haiti	6	9
EMI	Dominican Republic	1	1
EMI	Guatemala	2	1
OMS	Colombia	6	3
EMI	Surinam	1	1
OMS	Venezuela	1	1
EMI	Brazil	1	1
EMI	Bolivia	1	1
EMI	Spain	1	1
DAS	Niger	1	1
CAMA	Mali	1	1
JAAR,DAS	Nigeria	3	2
DAS	Cote d'Ivoire	1	1
DAS	Ghana	1	1
MTT	Togo	1	0
CAMA	Gabon	2	1
MTT	Ethiopia	1	0
EMI	Iraq	1	0
EMI	Thailand	1	1
MTT	Japan	1	0
	24	58	37

MTT - Missionary Tech Team

EMI - Engineering Ministries International

DAS - Development Assistance Society

CAMA- Christian and Missionary Alliance

JAAR- Jungle Aviation and Radio

Gene went to a guest house run by the Southern Baptists in Lagos. He was told that he was not to go outside the compound at night. The Nigerian people were antagonistic toward white strangers, especially Americans from the U.S.A. Gene had noticed that nobody at the airport would speak to him. Fortunately, he had the telephone number of the Guest House and a missionary came over to rescue him. Later Gene found out that the Nigerians had been involved in a very bloody civil war a few years before. Unfortunately, the U.S.A. decided to support one of the two belligerents and they chose the group that lost the war.

The reason for Gene's being in Nigeria was that he had agreed to help the Wycliffe Bible Translators to establish a base hangar for a JAAR airplane in Kano in northern Nigeria. He found that it was a difficult task to reach Wycliffe personnel in Kano. For two days he tried the telephone but was unable to make a connection. He was unable to contact the railroad line. Finally he obtained a ticket for a flight by air to Kaduna about 75 miles north of Lagos. On the plane, he started a conversation with the man sitting next to him. This man was a Canadian teaching at a school in Kaduna. He told Gene that the best way to get to Kano, 25 miles further north, was to hitchhike. Go to the only hotel in Kaduna and stand outside at the entrance. Ask all the people leaving the hotel if they were going to Kano. If they were, ask for a ride to Kano. When the plane landed, he started to leave, then he turned to Gene and said, "Come with me. I will get my car and take you to Kano. I have some business there and I might as well do it today."

At the Wycliffe Bible Translators Center Gene was surprised to meet a young man that he had known in Pittsburgh. This man had been studying electrical engineering at Carnegie Institute of Technology. When he graduated, he felt that God was leading him to missionary work. He joined Wycliffe and was sent to a distant part of Chad. He had been there only three years when this Center requested him to come to the Center. He had great ability with languages and dialects. This combined with his electrical engineering background made him an outstanding translator.

Gene remained at the Center for three days gathering information for his hangar design. The airline had lost his luggage. It was hot and humid during the day and even at night. So Gene was glad to leave. His acquaintance from Pittsburgh offered to take him back to Kaduna in a borrowed car. They went about fifteen miles when the motor stopped and they rolled to a halt. Gene asked what was wrong and his friend said, "I don't know. I'm a translator, not a car mechanic." They sat there in the heat and the quiet for ten minutes. Gene began to feel that he would miss his plane reservation. Then a little VW came chugging along with a Nigerian man and his wife. To Gene's surprise, the car stopped and the man asked a question in some dialect. Gene's friend knew the dialect and he explained their dilemma. The man laughed and indicated for them to squeeze into the rear seat. First, Gene's friend went into the forest to a mud hut near the road. When he returned, he told Gene that he had hired a local "guard" to watch the car or they would never see the car again.

At the airport, Gene wondered where the ticket counter was. His friend told him that it was different in Nigeria. When you hear the plane arrive, quickly go to the tarmac where the plane is. Get in line, give your ticket only to a man in uniform, and get on the plane. It will take you back to Lagos. Ask a missionary at the Guest House to look for your lost luggage (it was recovered and Gene met Paris and his friend at the Guest House.) The next day Paris was talking about the future of DAS when he asked Gene if he would join DAS and be his assistant. Gene said that he had no intention of ever coming back to Africa. To this, Paris replied,"When a person gets the dust of Africa on his shoes, he always returns." Gene bent down, took his handkerchief out, and carefully dusted off his shoes. He had another severe case of diarrhea. He said in a very definite tone, "I will never be back." He was wrong!

When Gene returned to Pittsburgh he asked an architect if he would help to provide housing for a needy group of people in Niger, Africa. The architect was interested so he, John Schurko, and Gene spent many hours arriving at a solution to the problem. They sent a set of drawings and a written report to Paris. After several months of waiting, Gene tracked Paris down and asked what had been done. Paris told him that he had approached the U.S.A.I.D. for funding. They were negative. Niger was worthless to the U.S.A. It was landlocked, it was poor, it had no natural resources, and it was not being sought by Russia. If Russia did not want it, the U.S.A. wouldn't waste any time or money helping it. Paris then contacted Germany and Switzerland for help. But both refused so Paris gave up on the project. Gene was very much annoyed. Both he and the architect had spent many hours. Paris could at least have told them what had happened and thanked them for their efforts.

Oriental Missionary Society

The organization was founded by Mr. and Mrs. Charles E. Cowman. It operated in Japan, China, and Korea. At first they spent five years with one hundred workers when they placed the Word of God in 10,300,000 homes in the villages of Japan. Then for twenty years they served in the Bible Training Institute in Japan, China, and Korea.

Mr. Cowman had a stroke and they were forced to return to California. For six pain-filled years he lingered, then slipped away. One day, the Holy Spirit spoke to lonely, bereft Mrs. Cowman about her writing a helpful book to encourage others. She had read a poem one day:

> The way was long, and the shadows spread far as they could see.

I stretched my hands to a human Christ, who walked through the night with me.

Out of the darkness we came at last, our feet on the dawn-warm sod,

And I knew by the light in His wondrous eye, that I walked with the Son of God.

Mrs. Cowman wrote a devotional book, Streams in the Desert, that has been distributed around the world. The profits from the sales of all of Mrs. Cowman's books have been used in worldwide missionary work. It was this income that was used to build the OMS Theological Seminary in Medellin, Colombia, South America.

One day Gene read a request by Charles Cook in the OMS magazine for a structural engineer to come to Medellin. Several buildings at the seminary compound were moving enough to cause cracks in the walls. Gene accepted the invitation and went to Colombia.

He stopped in Bogota to renew his friendship with Howard and Jan Biddulph, missionaries for OMS. Their problem was that they had started a church in their home but soon found that it was too small. They rented another two-story house and wanted to remove some of the walls on the first floor but they were worried that this would weaken the second floor. Gene gave them some structural advice, stayed with them for the night, then went on to Medellin.

At the seminary he found that the entire compound was built on the side of a hill. Each building was situated so that it was acting as a retaining wall. The front of the building was level with the low elevation of the hill. The rear of the building retained a full story of soil. The soil was very slowing sliding down the hill, probably on the inclined rock strata below. This soil was exerting pressure on the building. It was almost imperceptible but after many years it was causing the walls to show cracks. Gene told "Chuck" Cook that he should excavate some of the soil at the rear to relieve the pressure. This had to be done carefully because removing too much soil at the toe of a hill could cause a landslide.

About two years later, Chuck asked Gene if he would design a second story for a girls' dormitory in Magangay about 150 miles northeast of Medellin. Chuck sent the necessary dimensions and Gene produced the structural concrete detail drawings. Ten men from a church in North Carolina volunteered to spend two weeks in Magangay doing the construction. Gene decided to join them for at least one week to explain the drawings. Chuck went to the site to get the materials and living quarters ready. Twelve men lived in one room about 20 feet by 20 feet. All concrete had to be mixed by hand, and all reinforcing bars had to be cut and bent into the proper shape. It was hot and humid. The work was exhausting. As one young farmer said, "Gene, three days of cutting steel bars with just a hacksaw is my limit! Please give me another job for a few days so I can recuperate!"

The biggest project for OMS was a two-story radio station (4VEH) that was 100 feet by 100 feet. It was built in Cap Haitien, Haiti. The manager of the radio station, Marilyn Shaferly, and another administrative person had prepared a sketch showing the layout of the rooms. Gene went to Haiti to start the structural design of the radio station. He was surprised to find that no architectural plans had been started; in fact, no architect had volunteered to work on this project. He asked Chuck how this would be done. After all, it would be difficult for an engineer to produce structural drawings without coordinating with the architectural drawings. Both Chuck and Mrs. Shaferly suggested that Gene do the architectural design as well as the structural. Gene protested that he was no architect. They replied that he had worked with architects on many projects and should be able to make the architectural drawings. Besides, nobody needed a professional license in Haiti. It probably was the poorest country in the world. Still Gene was reluctant to make the architectural drawings. He depended on the cross-check between the architect and the engineer to help eliminate any possible errors.

After all, it took only one mistake to cause a portion of the building to collapse and injure or kill some unsuspecting person.

Finally Gene agreed to do both sets of drawings. He kept in close contact with David Shaferly who was acting as the construction superintendent. Then he went to the site to check if the volunteer workers were following the drawings closely. To his surprise, he noticed that there were more columns in the building than he had called for on the drawings. Shaferly

Radio Station 4VEH in Haiti

told him that some of the volunteers thought that some beams did not look strong enough so they had added extra columns. Actually they had weakened the structure! In the U.S.A. Gene would have insisted that the contractor tear out the concrete columns and beams that had been changed. In this case Gene did not require any expensive renovations. Gene had many years of experience with volunteer workers (and these poor countries) so he had designed the structure to be adequate even if it was changed by some amateur engineers.

The OMS missionaries are happy with the new radio station. They insist that it is the most outstanding building in Haiti. And the cost was far lower than expected. In the U.S.A. the finished building would have cost over one million dollars. Here, because of donated materials and volunteer workers, the cost was kept below $350,000.

Missionary Tech Team (MTT)

Missionary Tech Team was a nonprofit, nondenominational Christian service ministry dedicated to helping like-minded Christian organizations by providing various technical services which enable many different ministries to be more effective and fruitful in their outreach. Most missionaries have the necessary Bible training and experience for evangelism and discipleship; however, they frequently lack the training needed to perform many of the technical functions required in today's mission community.

In 1969 Missionary Tech Team began its ministry of providing technical assistance know-how and support services to mission organizations around the world. MTT's headquarters was in Longview, Texas. It was founded by Birne Whiley, a professor at LeTourneau University nearby. Dotter Engineering, Inc., was often involved in volunteer work with MTT. Very little travel was involved as the headquarters group in Longview obtained all the necessary information and supplied this information and technical advice to the volunteers. MTT and its missionaries were faithfully supported by the prayers and gifts of God's people. Client ministries contributed a small fee for service rendered. The balance of day-to-day operating costs was met by gifts from churches, individuals, and other interested organizations.

The Communication Services of MTT provided graphic design services for literature, displays, and overhead transparencies, including literature production, design, layout, illustrations, typography, portable tabletop and floor display construction, signage, and photography. The Facilities Planning Services arranged for planning, design, and construction services for ministry projects. These services included feasibility and relocation studies, long-range planning, engineering consultation, building design, surveying and drafting, and construction management. The Computer Services provided expertise and guidance in selecting, installing, operating, and maintaining computer systems and networks. The Mechanical Services provided furlough vehicles, automotive repairs, and vehicle purchases for missionaries, ministry workers, missions, and other Christian ministries.

The Facilities Planning Services was the core around which MTT was founded. It arranged for all necessary professional and technical assistance in planning, building design, construction, and landscaping including civil/environmental, structural, mechanical and electrical engineering.

Examples of MTT projects:

- Expanding schools that are too small to hold all the students eager to learn God's Word.

- Developing airstrips to reach remote tribes.

- Planning, designing, and building a new, expanded, or upgraded mission facility.

- Developing a remote electric plant to supply power for gospel broadcasting.

MTT stood ready with technical skills to help every ministry thus helping others "to know Christ and to make Him known." Their Statement of Belief was, "We believe in the verbal inspiration of both the Old and New Testaments; personal salvation made possible because of the virgin birth, the death, burial, and resurrection of the Lord Jesus; that our lives are to be separated unto Him; and in the personal and soon return of our Lord and Savior, Jesus Christ."

Gene was glad to become acquainted with an organization so steadfast in serving the Lord. Between 1980 and 1990, he completed 27 projects for MTT. This required only ten visits to the projects; the remaining seventeen projects were completed from information furnished by the headquarters in Longview. Also, Gene made two trips to headquarters to discuss structural design methods and materials. From the 27 projects, the following projects show very well the variety of structural work that was part of the projects of MTT:

Hospital for Wycliffe Bible Translators,

Ecuador, South America

The Andes Mountains stretch along the entire west coast of South America. They are the world's longest chain of mountains above sea level starting in Panama and Venezuela in the north and proceeding through Colombia, Ecuador, Peru, Bolivia, and ending in the south at Chile and Argentina for a distance of 4,500 miles. Many Andean peaks rise over 20,000 feet. They may be divided into three natural regions: northern, central, and southern. The central Andes form the broadest part of the mountain system. Two ranges running northwest and southeast make up this section. Between these ranges lie the wide, high plains or plateaus of Peru and western Bolivia at the elevation of about 13,000 feet. Farther north, the two ranges draw closer together. The central Andes include the highest peaks with Pissis being the highest at 22,241 feet. Ecuador is located between the northern and central regions where none of the ranges rises as high as the mountains farther south. The highest peak is Cristobal Colon at 18,947 feet in Colombia. Many of the high mountains are volcanoes, some of which are active. The most famous of these volcanoes are Cotopaxi, Tungurahuo, and Sangay in Ecuador. Earthquakes are common in the Andes. Many towns have been wiped out by them. Cities that have been greatly damaged by earthquakes include Quito, Ecuador.

The passes of the Andes Mountains are narrow, steep, and winding. The mountains are so high and rise so sharply from low plains that they divide the continent into Pacific South America and Atlantic South America. Actually, the mainland of Ecuador has three regions: (1) the Coastal Lowland, (2) The Andes Highland, and (3) the Eastern Lowland. The Coastal Lowland is a flat plain along Ecuador's Pacific Coast. It ranges from twelve to 100 miles wide and covers about a fourth of the country. The Andes Highland, often called the Sierra, also makes up about a fourth of Ecuador. Two parallel ridges of the Andes Mountains extend the length of the country. A series of high plateaus lie between the mountain ridges. The Eastern Lowland, often called the Oriente, covers almost one-half the country. It is a region of thick tropical forests in the eastern foothills of the Andes and in part of the Amazon River Basin. Little of this region has been developed and its people travel mostly by boat on the streams and rivers. Pioneer work among the small jungle tribes attracted worldwide attention in 1956 when one person from Missionary Air Flights (MAF), one person from Association of Indian Evangelical Churches (GMU), and three Brethren missionaries were killed by the primitive Waorani (Auca). Nearly all of these tribes now have churches and the Scriptures.

The MTT project was in two parts: (1) the Hospital for Wycliffe Bible Translators and (2) an addition to an office building for HCJB. The hospital was near one of the many rivers that originate in the Andes Mountains. They flow eastward and contribute to the Amazon River, a river that flows to the Atlantic Ocean about 2,800 miles away from the Andes Mountains. In simple terms the Amazon could stretch from New York City to past San Francisco in California. The hospital was built with funds donated by the oil companies located in the Ecuador Eastern Lowlands. This area has rich oil fields, but unequal distribution of oil wealth has widened the gap between the rich and the poor. Income per person is about $1,000 per year (about 5 percent of USA). Failure to curb inflation, natural disasters, and high birth rate, combined with declining revenues from oil, bananas, and coffee have lowered living standards for the majority.

The hospital is of very simple construction. The exterior walls and the interior partitions are concrete block. The floors are poured concrete with small reinforcing bars. The roof framing was light wood trusses supporting wood purlins and tile roof surfaces.

The addition to the existing office building was in the capital city of Quito. It had a population of well over a million persons and a better variety of building materials was available; therefore, the structural framing, both columns and beams, were made with steel. The building was three stories high so it was necessary to consider lateral (horizontal) forces as well as the gravity (vertical) forces. The lateral forces that were considered were forces due to wind and earthquake.

Wind: the design wind pressure for each building was determined in accordance with the following formula:

$$P = C_e C_q Q_s I_w$$

$$= (0.84)(0{,}80+0{,}50)(43.3)(1.00)$$

$$= 47.3 \text{ PSF}$$

Earthquake: the purposes of the earthquake design forces was primarily to safeguard against major structural failures and loss of life, not to limit damage or maintain function. Structures were designed and constructed to resist the effects of seismic ground motions. When the code-prescribed wind design produces greater effects, the wind design shall govern. The building in Quito depended for stability upon moment-resisting frames in which the members and joints are capable of resisting horizontal forces primarily by flexure. The hospital building depended for stability on concrete block shear walls where the shear wall was a wall designed to resist lateral forces parallel to the plane of the wall. The procedures and the limitations for the design of structures shall be determined considering seismic zoning, site characteristics, occupancy, configuration, structural system, and height. The total design base shear in a given direction was determined from the following formula for an earthquake:

$$V = \frac{C_n IW}{R\,T}$$

$$= \frac{(0.51)(1.00)(380)}{(4.50)(0,54)}$$

$$= 80K/FRAME$$

The lateral force per frame for wind is:

$$V = h_n l$$

$$= (47,3)(25 \times 39)$$

$$= 46K/FRAME$$

Therefore, the lateral force due to a possible earthquake was the governing force in the design (80/FRAME) as expected.

Multi-Purpose Building

Indian Mission, Cortez, Colorado

It was a gray, snowy day in Pittsburgh when Gene received a telephone call from MTT. It was Lowell Jensen, Volunteer Contact Leader for MTT, who explained that he had just received a call from Colorado concerning the multi-purpose building at Cortez. On the map this was the place called Four Corners because four states--Colorado, Utah, New Mexico, and Arizona--met in a single point common to the four states. Near this spot the Indian Mission had erected a building on an Indian reservation primarily so the Indians could play basketball inside during the cold winter days and nights. It was a simple building with the side walls of 8-inch concrete block about 16 feet in height. To span the 120 feet from side wall to side wall were wood trusses at 2 feet spacing. The bottom of the trusses formed a segment of a circle, so that they started at a height of 16 feet at each wall and rose to 22 feet at the center. The top of the truss started at a height of 18 feet at each wall and rose to 30 feet at the center. This would produce a truss 2 feet in height at the side walls and 8 feet in height at the center.

Lowell explained that it was snowing in Colorado and about 2 feet of snow had fallen on the roof. Somebody had noticed that the top of the side walls had moved about 3 inches outward. The administrator at the reservation had asked some Indians to shovel the snow off the roof and then he tried to move the walls back at the top with a bulldozer but they would not budge. He was afraid that the walls would collapse and the roof would fall to the floor so he called MTT. In turn, Lowell suggested that Gene go to the site and decide what to do.

Early the next day Gene flew to Denver, Colorado, and then to Cortez. He was immediately taken to the building in difficulty and was relieved to see that the roof had been cleared of snow. He was informed that this building had been erected by a group of volunteer construction men without benefit of a state registered architect and structural engineer. After a few hours of intensive examination, Gene told the administrator that the trusses did not possess adequate strength to support the snow loading; in fact, they were functioning as arch ribs instead of trusses. The difference was important as a truss did not move the end supports outward but an arch rib deflected under load and moved the end supports outward. Two solutions were available. The first solution was to connect the two ends together with a tie wire so that the tops of the walls could not move outward. The second solution was to perform a structural analysis of the truss and reinforce the existing members so that it behaved as a truss.

Both men agreed that the first solution was not feasible as the tie wires would interfere with basketball (the ceiling would be at 16 feet instead of the recommended 20 to 24 feet). So it was decided to adopt the second solution. Gene would provide the structural drawings showing how the trusses could be reinforced in place.

In a week, the drawings were sent. Shortly after, the administrator arranged for a group of volunteers to reinforce the trusses. The building has now stood for thirty years although the administrator gets faint-hearted and sends men to clean the roof from accumulating snow.

Retreat Center, National Presbyterian Church,

San Louis de Potosi, Mexico

The site of the retreat center at San Louis de Potosi is about a hundred miles northwest of Mexico City. This city was the location of a theological seminary built by this denomination for the Mexican pastors and workers. It has been closed now although it can still be used for special occasions. When Gene went to Mexico to examine the site for a church at the new Retreat Center, he used one of the rooms as a bedroom. It was very quiet and lonely at night. One reason for this is that no foreign missionaries are officially permitted even though Mexico is a secular state with freedom of conscience and practice of religion. The 130-year break between the Mexican government and the Vatican ended with official relations being restored in 1992 and the Catholic Church reasserting its position of dominance; however, constitutional changes in 1992 also granted fairer treatment for religious minorities.

Exploitation of oil and development of industry have benefitted the top third of the population, but the poverty of the poorer two-thirds has increased. Massive national debt, inflation, and a deepening economic crisis forced the government to face up to the protectionism, unwise investment policies, entrenched sectional interests, unfairness of existing economic structures, rapid population growth, archaic land-tenure systems, and blatant corruption. Mexico's economic turn-around has been spectacular since the end of the 80's.

The missionary for the National Presbyterian Church picked up Gene at the airport in Mexico City and took him to San Louis de Potosi. During the drive, one noted the gentle hills with sparse vegetation and almost no trees. Scattered widely around on the hillsides were small adobe houses. Everything looked so poor and barren that Gene asked the missionary, "Why build a retreat center? Who will use it?" The missionary replied, "There are more Christians than what is apparent. They keep a low profile because of the persecution by the Catholics. A retreat center will encourage them to be more active." The next day the missionary took Gene to a small town about ten miles away. He pointed out the prominent Catholic church and then pointed to a large tree about 300 feet away. He said in a hushed voice, "That is where a large group of residents were incited by the Catholic priest to kill a Christian man about a week ago!"

The site of the retreat center was about one-half mile from the former theological seminary along a road bordered by homes. It was convenient to use both facilities for an event scheduled by the local Christian churches. Gene was already familiar with the project. He had designed the structural framing for the dining hall and for a large concrete water storage tank elevated on a pedestal about 30 feet high. In addition, the adjacent ground had been graded for use as a soccer field or other activities. Now he envisioned a church seating about five hundred persons where religious messages and seminars could be offered. A site for the church was conveniently available so Gene took some measurements and elevation readings. Then he explored the foundation bearing situation by having some test holes dug. He made some sketches and headed back to Mexico City and Pittsburgh, Pennsylvania.

Gene suggested a concrete structural frame to Dan Smith, the architect at MTT. Dan responded with a very attractive building, and soon a set of architectural and structural drawings were completed. Shortly after, the mechanical and electrical drawings were added. Gene made another trip to check the construction progress and was gratified so see how well the project was moving along.

Power Generating Station for Evangelical Baptist Church,

Bassar, Togo, Africa

The small country of Togo is in northwest Africa where it is wedged between Ghana and Benin. It is about 325 miles long from north to south. The southern end is at the Atlantic Ocean and the coastline is only about 34 miles long. The population is about 250,000 persons and is made up by 78 ethnic groups in two major language groups, the Kwa and the Gur, with smaller groups of Fula, Bisa, and Hausa. Only five languages have a Bible translation, and only four more have a New Testament translation. The country became independent from France in 1960 but political crises have brought anarchy and violence to the country.

The government of Togo has not been able to furnish a reliable source of electricity, especially in the outlying districts of the country. The Evangelical Baptist Church has tried to augment the power supply by providing a generator to furnish electricity when the national supply fails. This is not always reliable either because of the scarcity of fuel. So MTT was requested to design another means of electrical supply that would be more reliable.

A volunteer engineer for MTT had a great deal of experience with the design of dams for power generation in various countries of South America. He went to Togo to see if this was feasible and he chose one church as a prototype. He found that a stream flowed from a range of mountains which furnished the necessary amount of water. He noticed a plateau about 900 to 1,000 feet above the church at a distance of about one-half of a mile. He suggested that a dam be built on the plateau and a sluiceway conduct the falling water to a generating plant near the church at elevation zero. Gene was asked to furnish the structural design drawings from this man's notes.

Gene designed an earth dam on the plateau to collect the water. The earth was used for stability and a concrete apron was used for impermeability. From the dam downward, conveying the water to the generator, was a concrete sluiceway. The generating plant was a simple building with concrete block walls and corrugated galvanized steel roofing. The floor was a concrete slab reinforced with welded wire fabric. The walls extended below the ground surface to adequate bearing. The final problem was to conduct the effluent to the original stream bed to be used for irrigation purposes. The dam expert handled the choice and procurement of the generating equipment.

Engineering Ministries International (EMI)

In 1981, the island of Saipan was hit by a typhoon. Michael Orsillo was able to provide structural engineering advice in restoring a damaged building at the mission compound during a short-term missionary trip. Shortly after this, he left his engineering job to begin EMI, involving design professionals in serving around the world. The organization had grown until in the year 2000 it involved one thousand design professionals. EMI is a nonprofit organization and all permanent personnel are supported by freewill offerings of churches. Much of the work was done by volunteers who paid all of their own expenses.

When a missionary organization requested help from EMI, the case was considered by the headquarters in Colorado Springs, Colorado. The missionary organization must be in need financially and must depend on EMI to furnish the technical help in order to provide the design drawings and construction information to complete the project. A team was formed. The leader was usually an architect chosen from the staff at headquarters. The architect arranged and shaped spaces functionally and aesthetically to house the missionary program. He may assist in program analysis and site selection; prepare schematics, design proposals and construction documents, and monitor construction. Although the architect was well qualified to solve the design problems, he must have the assistance of a consultant team to render the specialized help needed to complete the project. This included a landscape architect, a structural engineer, a mechanical engineer, and an electrical engineer. This team visited the site of the proposed project and prepared a preliminary solution to the problem.

The team's report was submitted to headquarters where a project folder was prepared for the use of the professional work group. An example of this document is as follows:

1.0 Introduction

1.1 Ministry overview

Description of the ministry being helped.

1.2 Team overview

Team members' names and fields of expertise.

1.3 Project overview

Description of team objectives and project goals.

1.4 Scope of work

Specific intention of report and drawings; i.e., master plan, construction documents, feasibility study.

2.0 Site Evaluation

2.1 Survey

Description of the site--size, topography, type of survey, boundary, fence line, legal description, contours, document utilities, existing buildings, bench marks, trees, percolation test holes.

2.2 Geotechnical Report

Soils information and source. Soil type, percolation rate, determination of bearing capacity.

2.3 Drainage

During wet season and dry season.

3.0 Transportation

3.1 People Movement

To and from the site. By vehicle or on foot.

3.2 Parking Requirements

Type of vehicles and number of seats for each parking space.

3.3 Airstrips, roads, bridges, boats, fords

4.0 Architectural Facilities Design

4.1 Overall Program

A detailed list of all spaces (rooms, corridors, stairs, etc.) and the necessary square footage.

4.2 Aesthetic Consideration

Type of adjacent buildings. Application of slogan, "Form follows function." General appearance. Cost. Sun shade. Wind.

4.3 Program Design

List of buildings. Need for various uses.

4.4 Architectural Materials

Exterior and interior walls (brick, block, stucco, metal, stone). Types of windows. Ventilation.

4.5 Landscape Treatment

Drainage (trenches, pipes, swales). Bushes, trees, gardens, walks, roads.

5.0 Structural Design

5.1 Local Structural Design

Commonly used types. Application of new types. Bearing walls, beam and column, trusses, rigid frames.

5.2 Local Design Criteria

Gravity, dead, live loads. Lateral wind and seismic loads. Floods.

5.3 Local Available Materials

Strength of concrete and reinforcing. Types of structural steel shapes and strengths. Strength of brick, concrete block, proprietary systems.

5.4 Local Available Work Force

Degree of proficiency for constructing, choosing, installing. Labor costs.

5.5 Destructive Agents

Wind, water, termites.

6.0 Mechanical Design

6.1 Water Resources

Potable drinking water, source and distribution. Rain water collection, surface, municipal. Well type and depth, rainfall date, streams, rivers, dams. Treatment facilities. Piping.

6.2 Sewage Disposal

Municipal arrangement. Private treatment. Type and ultimate disposal. Piping. Septic tank.

6.3 Air-conditioning

Power source. Size of installation. Number of units. Length of use.

7.0 Electrical Design

7.1 Location of source, hours of service. Sizes of transformers. Guidelines for different types of facilities.

7.2 Supplementary Private Supply

Number of units needing service. Number, type, and size of generators. Distribution.

7.3 Future Needs.

Growth in size and number of buildings. Upgrading of equipment and conveniences. Population increase.

7.4 Design Drawings

Workmen proficiency at interpretation and installation.

8.0 Cost Estimation

8.1 Previous Construction

Local contractors for records. Consult missionaries.

8.2 Material Costs

Often materials are only available by transporting them from other areas of the country or from abroad. Transportation may be more expensive than the materials.

8.3 Labor Costs

Balance low wages against poor workmanship. Use volunteer labor whenever possible.

8.4 Substitutions

Change design drawings in order to lower cost and to expedite construction methods and procedures.

9.0 Contractor and Surveyor Participation

9.1 Experience

Residents in other lands can be helpful. Seek advice. Offer suggestions.

The next task was to produce a set of construction documents. Although the projects were in undeveloped countries and it was often felt that a preliminary set of drawings was sufficient, it was important that a complete set of calculations, working drawings, and specifications were made.

Gene participated in eleven projects. Of these, only four will be discussed. They are as follows:

Church for Project Amazon (PAZ) at Santarem, Brazil

A. General Criteria.

The PAZ vision was that they believed in a big God with big plans for the people of the Amazon River Basin, the world's largest fresh-water system. Seventeen million persons lived in an unexplored frontier covering 2.3 million square miles of rain forest, lakes, and hundreds of tributaries. Few accessible roads existed for vehicles to reach people because of flooding and dense jungle growth. Consequently, many of the Portuguese-speaking residents living in remote villages had never heard the gospel of Jesus Christ. PAZ's vision was to plant 100,000 churches focusing on the Amazon Basin and then to use these Christians to extend around the world. Luke Huber, the mission's founder, envisioned at least one church in each of the Amazon's estimated 80,000 villages. To reach these river people, PAZ built boats and manned them with trained nationals. The task was so huge that PAZ divided the Basin into fifteen strategic areas, each with a proposed base of operations.

The people had staggering needs, and PAZ sought to minister to the whole person: spirit, mind, and body. PAZ trained its church members to serve God by preaching the gospel, every new church starting a sister church, helping the poor, street children, and recovering addicts. They began an educational ministry where, under local church supervision, Christian elementary schools were started and teachers were trained for the schools and for other literacy work. PAZ's medical boats helped river people with health care, food, clothing, and other forms of social assistance. The Christians learned basic dentistry and hygiene, how to dispense medications, and do vaccinations. Contaminated drinking water caused a variety of intestinal diseases. The construction of wells was a way PAZ served whole communities.

PAZ has established eight "base stations" in the Amazon River Basin: Manaus, Porto Veldo, Parantins, Santarem, Xingu, Macaa, Belem, and Sao Luiz. The ministry headquarters was at Santarem which was the location of the largest church. It was known as the Central Church and had about two thousand members. PAZ had asked EMI to assist them in the design of an 8,500-seat church facility to replace the existing Central Church building. The new facility was to be built on a site of 3.2 acres in the center of Santarem. In addition to accommodating 8,500 persons for Sunday services, this facility was to include administrative offices, classrooms for a Christian school and seminary, and storage rooms for food, medical, and clothing distribution programs.

B. Structural Design.

The first suggestion from Gene was to consider the use of a Geodesic Dome for the structural framing. He contacted a firm in California which specialized in the design and construction of long-span buildings. They responded with a preliminary design of a round building with a diameter of 325 feet. The cost of the design and construction of this building in Santarem would be about $9,000,000. This concept was immediately abandoned for the site could not accommodate the diameter of 325 feet and the cost of $9,000,000 was too great for PAZ.

Two alternative building systems were then considered:

1. **Steel Rigid Frames.**

   The rigid frames span about 177 feet and are spaced at 22 feet on centers. Each frame could be built in six sections at the boat shop and taken to the site where they would be connected together. The frames would be composed of four angles, one at each corner of a rectangular member which would be about two feet wide and four to seven feet deep. Each face would be fabricated with top and bottom chords connected by angle diagonals similar to trusses. The roof system should be steel purlins and steel roof decking. This system provides column-free space and is the recommended system.

2. **Cable Suspended Fabric.**

   This system requires a sophisticated layout of cables spanning from the exterior columns. The columns could be steel sections and could be stabilized laterally with shear walls or tie cables from the top of each column to a deadman support at the ground level. Special care must be exercised to insure stability against horizontal wind forces and suction wind forces acting in a vertical direction. This system requires highly skilled workers and specialized equipment so it is not recommended.

Soil bearing capacity is low, probably 2,000 to 3,000 pounds per square foot. The column footings can be estimated at 7 feet by 7 feet by 2 feet deep.

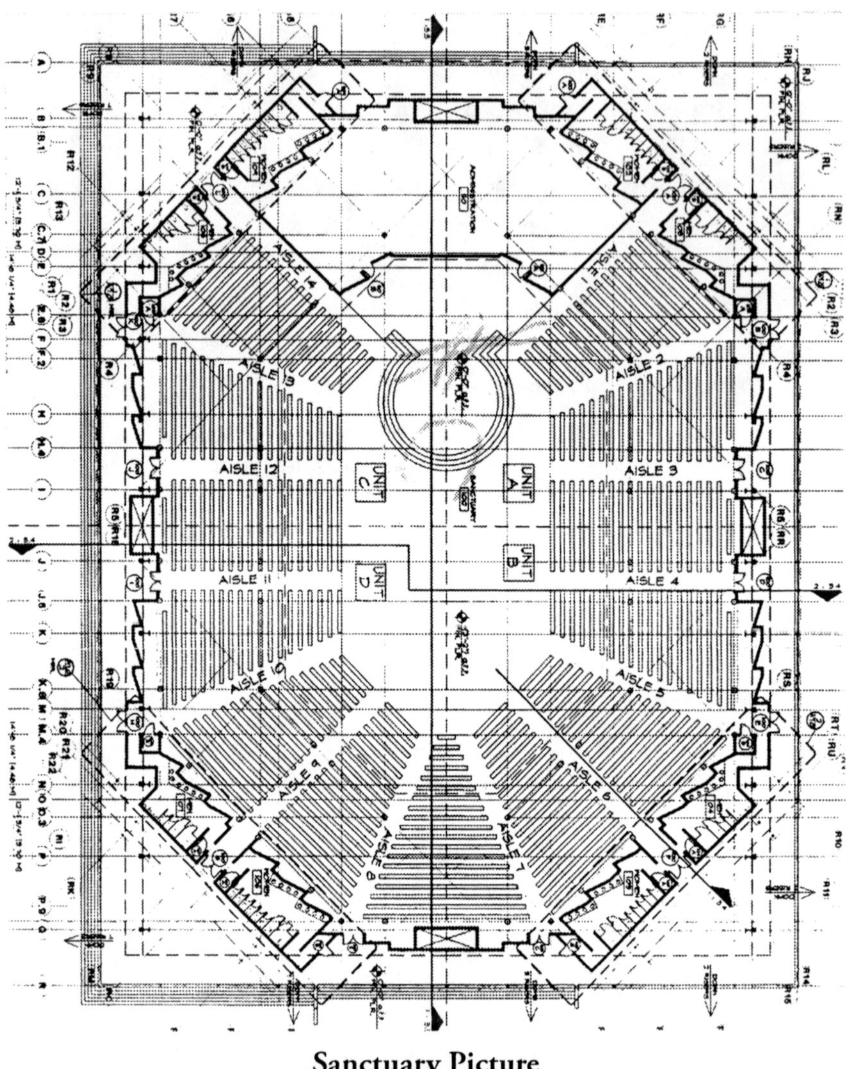

Sanctuary Picture

The estimated construction cost using Alternative No. 1 (steel rigid frames) was $3,500,000. This was higher than PAZ anticipated so they postponed embarking at this time on such an ambitious project. At this point Gene felt that by filling in the floor area at the front of the platform with movable chairs would have added 750 prime seats. Then lengthening the columns supporting the front of the balcony to support the roof also would have reduced the cost of the roof considerably because the roof members would have had a much smaller span.

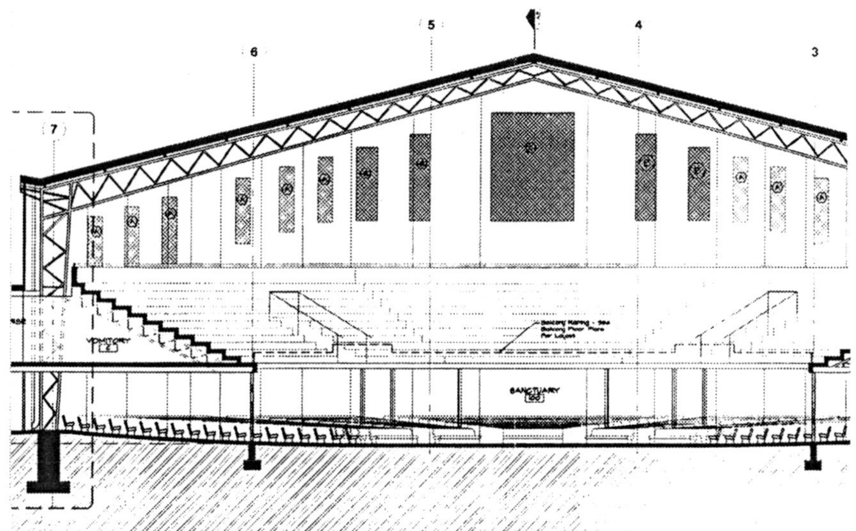

Sanctuary Picture

One of the tasks for our groups of architects and engineers was to visit a typical small village in Amazonia, the area extending about 2,400 miles along the Amazon River and about 1,000 miles wide. The village was about 40 miles west of our headquarters in Santarem. The mission furnished a boat about 30 feet long. The group included three Brazilian men as crew, two Brazilian women as cooks, eleven technical people, and two PAZ (Project Amazon) men.

We boarded the boat at noon. The motor refused to start. The PAZ mechanic came, and three hours later it came to life. Off we went at 5 to 10 miles per hour up the river. At 6 P.M. the sun went down and it was as black as pitch. The river was several miles wide but had many shallow areas so one Brazilian had to sound the depth with a pole as we chugged along forward, backward, and to the side. Finally the pilot indicated that we had reached the village. Not one light in sight. Suddenly a Brazilian in a dugout canoe appeared. A short conversation and then he disappeared. The message was that the pastor of the new village church had misunderstood the plan and had left for another village. So our pilot turned around and started back. Kind of a disappointment as we were expecting to establish plans for a typical village church to be duplicated many times.

So we ate dinner. In about an hour, the pilot again went close to shore. Suddenly, a Brazilian in a canoe appeared. One of the PAZ missionaries jumped into the canoe and disappeared. Another hour or two of chugging along, then the pilot stopped the boat, threw over the anchor, and ordered the hammocks to be strung. With a sigh of relief, Gene climbed into a hammock and tried to sleep with his back hitting the steel deck every time the boat rolled. After a few hours of agony he awoke to a terrific blast of horns. For about an hour, one thousand bullfrogs serenaded us. Finally the pilot pulled up the anchor and took off. The sun came up. So did the wind and the waves. Man the pump, bail the water out. Another hour and the motor sputtered, the pilot couldn't keep the boat facing into the waves, so he headed for the nearest island and beached the boat on the sand. About 100 yards away was another boat that had been beached in the past and was now a deserted wreck.

Gene thought of the Apostle Paul telling everyone on the ship to jump into the water and make it to the beach. He looked for a life preserver but the pilot told all to relax while he fixed the motor. Sure enough, a few hours later, he asked several men to jump into the river to free the boat from the sand. Gene remembered George Constance's telling him that the piranhas could strip the flesh from a person in five minutes. While he was thinking about the warning about alligators and sting rays, some of the more energetic fellows got the boat loose and off they went. A few hours of rolling, pumping, and praying and they were back. Disappointed but thankful.

The Life and Truth School, Cup of Cold Water Ministries,

Caranavi, Bolivia, South America

This school was founded in 1987 by the Cup of Cold Water Ministries (CCWM), a Christian ministry based in Caranavi. The school was prompted by concerned parents who wanted their children's education to be founded upon solid Christian teaching. The foremost goal of the staff and the school director, John Donhowe, was that each child have the opportunity to come to a knowledge of salvation through Jesus. The majority of the students lived in Caranavi. Most of the people live on an extremely low income; and for those families who were not able to afford tuition, CCWM provided scholarship through the means of donors in the United States. The tuition cost for enrollment per student was under ten dollars a month, which covered only a portion of the school's expenses. The remaining expenses were paid by a subsidy from CCWM.

When the school began in 1987, there were twelve children in the kindergarten and first grade. With each consecutive year the school had to add an additional grade, causing the school to expand and meet in various places. Currently, in 2005, the school extends from kindergarten through high school with an approximate enrollment of six hundred students. The school continues to grow and needs a campus of its own. Three acres of property were purchased and EMI was requested to furnish a master plan. Plans were completed but before construction began John Donhowe decided to build a three-story school building in town, then concentrate on the campus outside the town on the side of a nearby mountain. That is when Gene with a group of other professional engineers and architects went to Caranavi to plan the school.

Administration Building

Gene left Fort Myers, Florida, on a hot afternoon with the temperature around 95 degrees and at elevation zero. He went to Miami to board a plane in the evening and arrived at the capital city of Bolivia, La Paz, at 5 A.M. He walked from the plane to the airport administration building in light clothing with the temperature at 50 degrees because of the elevation of 13,000 feet. The team was taken to the missionary's apartment for breakfast. Gene could not eat, he was "sick as a dog." The missionary, John Donhowe, immediately had Gene lie down all morning with a tank of oxygen. Gene would gladly have stayed on the bed all day but he was given a sandwich and a small bottle of Coca Cola for lunch and told to pick up his belongings and head for the bus station. He was squeezed into a rickety old bus with Bolivians and animals inside and on the roof. Then began a long, slow ascent up the Andes Mountains, up to an elevation of about 19,000 feet on a one-lane dirt road. Gene looked out the window and all he could see was a sheer drop of 3,000 or 4,000 feet straight down. He mumbled to the missionary, "What happens when we meet a vehicle going down the mountain?" His answer was not very comforting: "The vehicle going down has the right-of-way. The vehicle going up (like ours) must back down to a place where the road is wide enough to allow the downward vehicle to pass, then proceed happily (?) on the way upward!" Everybody seemed quiet and content so Gene closed his eyes, pretended to be asleep, and prayed.

Finally, after eight hours (100 miles horizontally), the bus descended to the valley where the town of Caranavi is. Dinner, a short organizational meeting, and off to bed. It is a well known fact that working in Third World countries means "to bed by nine and up at six." The electricity is not very reliable. Or, as many children were taught, "Early to bed and early to rise, makes a person healthy, wealthy, and wise."

The structural framing for the school building was constructed of reinforced concrete. That included the columns, beams, footings, and floors. All walls and partitions were made of concrete block. Under the able direction of the architect, Pat Morgan, the investigation proceeded quickly. The school director, John Donhowe, received the preliminary drawings gladly. The team returned to the U.S.A. and completed the final Construction Documents. The site was graded and actual construction began using a local contractor with John Donhowe as clerk of the work. The project had been placed in the hands of the staff architect, Gary MacPhee, at EMI. Almost immediately he received criticism from Donhowe about the structural design. Donhowe had been convinced by the contractor that the design had used too much reinforcing. He would have liked to eliminate about 50 percent of the bars. It appeared to Gene that the local contractors had not considered the lateral forces of wind and earthquakes. The wind design was based on a wind velocity of 70 miles per hour. The seismic zone for this area was Zone 3. Of the two, the forces due to earthquake governed and resulted in the use of more reinforcing than the local contractors were accustomed to. It reminded Gene of the Master Buildings of the Middle Ages constructing the cathedrals. The building knowledge was handed down from generation to generation. Often, however, if the latest Master Builder felt that the information was too conservative, he would eliminate some of the masonry. If the cathedral remained standing, he was hailed as a great builder. If it collapsed, the Master Builder would have to run for his life. Gene told Gary that he refused to change his drawings. Gary had the responsibility of telling Donhowe to make any changes that he was comfortable with. But to remember that an earthquake could cause a building collapse with possible loss of life if Donhowe allowed the contractor to remove some reinforcing bars. This matter was never discussed again.

Recently Gene enrolled at Florida Gulf Coast University (FGCU) for a course entitled, "Faces of Culture." One of the lessons was "Alejandro Mamani: A Case Study in Psychological Anthropology."

An Indian Farmer

See page 252

Alejandro Mamani was an old man living in Vitocota, a small village near Lake Titicaca, 12,000 feet above sea level. He was an Aymara Indian living in the Bolivian Andes where he was a peasant farmer relying on his land where he planted primarily potatoes and raises chickens, goats, and sheep. By Aymara standards, Mamani was a wealthy man. Not only did he have enough land and animals to make a living, but he secured title to his land for his children despite bureaucratic obstruction.

On the way home from a funeral where he became drunk, Mamani went to sleep at a place where the evil spirits took possession of his body while he was asleep. Since then, he could not sleep at night, as he had nightmares with the spirits appearing as man and woman, one of them his dead wife. Curers proposed to treat him by transferring his illness to several animals. It did not work. He tried to fumigate the spirits with sulphur. They left only temporarily. He considered a medical doctor but the doctor could not help.

When his family tired of having to pay for his cures, Mamani called them together and transferred his property to them. He then slipped away early in the morning and commited suicide by jumping from a high cliff to his death. Although suicide is disapproved of in Aymara culture, Mamani is remembered with respect and his action was considered logical in view of his affliction.

Explanation for this occurrence by the authors of the textbook was closely attached to the framework of modern psychiatry. When the team passed through Vitocota on their way to Ayata at an elevation of 18,000 feet, Gene was impressed by the thought that the answer to Mamani's problem was not found in modern psychiatry but in Jesus Christ. This sad tale of Alejandro Mamani is the reason for the Cup of Cold Water Ministries constructing the Life and Truth School for the Aymara Indian children so that they have the opportunity to come to a knowledge of salvation through Jesus.

Pastor Training Center - Frontier Laborers for Christ,

Chiang Mai, Thailand

Frontier Laborers for Christ (FLC) is based in Chiang Mai, the second largest city in Thailand, and known as the "pearl" of the north. Their ministry extends to the hill tribe people throughout northern Thailand, Laos, and Burma (Myanmar). FLC founders are Daniel and Beverly Kalnin. Daniel is originally from the Rawang hill tribe in Burma and has a great heart for the tribal people who live within this "Golden Triangle" of northern Thailand, Laos, and Burma.

FLC's ministry consists of a network of pastors and evangelists throughout the Golden Triangle and the mission's central staff in Chiang Mai. The evangelists hike into the mountains to non-Christian villages to preach the gospel. Buddhism is the state religion and numbers about 93.4 percent of the people. Muslims comprise 4.0 percent, Chinese religions about 1.6 percent, and Christians about 1.0 percent. The land is in bondage to the complex web of culture, spirit appeasement, occult practices, and Buddhism, with a social cohesiveness out of which few dare to leave. The rottenness at the core of Thai society can only be fully excised and changed through a turning to God. Corrupt leaders have protected the large sex industry, drug networks, crime syndicates, and ecological degradation of the country. The growth of the Church has been disappointing. After four centuries of Catholic and 160 years of Protestant work, Thai Christians are only 1.0 percent of the population.

FLC has a Barefoot Doctors Program for the evangelists to learn how to diagnose and treat common diseases. These evangelists are sent with medicine into villages that would not otherwise receive outsiders, but are grateful for the medical help. The team of architects and engineers from EMI visited a Christian village by driving 50 miles south of Chiang Mai and hiking 8 miles east into the forest. They were surprised to find a village of about 250 persons, with an attractive, spacious, bamboo church, bamboo homes on bamboo stilts, a large water storage tank, sanitary facilities, and adequate piping. The people had cleared the forest for farmland and raised coffee, rice, tea, and fruit.

An interesting story was told about the founding of this village. The people had originally lived in a village of 650 persons about thirty miles away. The mayor of the village was a witch doctor who was very strict with the people and he allowed no outsiders to enter the village. One day, a man went to Chiang Mai to appease his curiosity about how these people lived. After several months he was exposed to Christian beliefs. In a short time he accepted the teaching of the gospel and became a believer in Christ. He decided that he must tell the good news to the people of his village. He returned and quietly preached to small groups until he had converted about two hundred persons. Then the witch doctor learned about the Christian minority in his village. He was furious. They would recant or be punished severely. The "preacher" knew Daniel Kalnin and he sought his advice. Daniel knew of this site and advised the Christian believers to slip away and start a new Christian village. The witch doctor threatened death to all who left his village, but for some reason he never did anything drastic.

The witch doctor had a teen-age son whom he loved very much. The son became sick unto death. The witch doctor's evil potions failed to help, and he felt that he had no way to turn for help. In God's mercy, one of the Christian evangelists found his way into the village. He administered some medicine and prayed for the witch doctor's son. Immediately the son began to recover and in a few days was back to normal health. The witch doctor gave up his evil practices and announced that he had become a Christian and his village was now a Christian village. He then went to his former villagers and apologized for his behavior in the past.

FLC's expanding ministry was now outgrowing its building in Chiang Mai, and Daniel Kalnin had received a vision to expand the ministry into a Pastor Training School. Consequently, FLC purchased thirteen acres of land for the new Pastor Training School. All present uses of the Center Building in Chiang Mai would be moved to the new site.

The EMI team visited the site and completed the following:

1. Boundary and topography survey.

2. Interviews with FLC staff to determine the scope and program of the project.

3. Utilities research and planning.

4. Research of available construction materials and techniques.

5. Preliminary building design.

6. Conceptual Master Plan and preliminary building architecture.

7. Cost estimation research.

The Master Plan includes 22 buildings but only four buildings will be built during Phase 1: a medical clinic, a dining hall, a men's dormitory, and a central training building. The clinic and dining hall buildings maintained the same uses through all phases of design and construction. Once the main dormitories were built, the Phase 1 men's dorm would become the marketing showroom building (baked goods; handcraft ministry of Yao, Lisu, Lahu, and Ahka women; embroidery, weaving, and applique). The training center would house the offices, library, classrooms, and the women's dorm during Phase 1, but eventually would be used as the administration building.

The architecture of Chiang Mai was rather sophisticated so the architectural treatment of the proposed buildings was more sophisticated than that of most Third World projects. The architect realized this and gave this project more time and effort than usual. Finally, after months of waiting, Gene received the architectural drawings for the four buildings in Phase 1. He knew that the structural design would be simple. Seismic lateral forces were not considered as Thailand was in Seismic Zone 0. Wind forces were moderate and hardly important with the wind velocity of 70 miles per hour; in fact, lateral forces could be discounted with the buildings of one story height. The crux of the structural problem was for an engineer with experience to lay out the roof framing with the light steel members available at Chiang Mai. Gene designed the members and laid out the arrangement of the beams, purlins, and supports. This information was sent to another volunteer structural engineer who prepared the final structural drawings and sent them back to Gene for a final check. It was obvious that the drawings were incomplete. Gene marked them up as necessary and returned them to the other volunteer who, for some unknown reason, took them to EMI headquarters in Colorado Springs. Gene was never informed what had happened to the drawings or the project.

The EMI team had interviewed the local building inspector who was the person to review buildings built on the FLC site. He signified that he would approve the drawings if the buildings were strong, durable, and of good materials. The signature of a licensed Thai engineer was not required. There were no official inspections required during construction once he had approved the drawings. There were no guidelines more than his being willing to approve the drawings. He would need two sets of blueprints but no calculations were required. The drawings would be in English and Daniel Kalnin could translate anything required. The service charge was minimal.

Orphanage School for Christian Orphanages, Inc.,

Paramaribo, Suriname, South America

The country of Suriname became independent from Netherlands in 1975. The post-independence experience has been disastrous. All the people were given the choice of staying in Suriname or going to Netherlands where they were accepted as citizens and helped to find acceptable jobs. Most of the educated people and experienced workers left Suriname. It was surprising to the EMI team to see many construction projects partially completed with forms rotting away and concrete disintegrating after years of idleness because they had been abandoned when the design professionals and construction workers left for Netherlands.

Actually, the economy had good potential but ruinous policies of the military regime caused widespread decline through government controls, neglect of infrastructure, mismanagement, and cutting off of Western aid. The main exports were rice, bauxite, aluminum, and forest products. Due to the constant war between the government military and the rebels, it had been difficult to obtain forest projects because they were found mainly in the north where the country was controlled by the rebels. This was true to some extent for bauxite and aluminum also where the dams and refineries of Alcoa in the north were.

EMI was requested by Christian Orphanages, Inc., mainly to determine if the school could be increased in size by adding a second floor above the existing school. The existing building was 180 feet long and only 28 feet wide. The arrangement was a string of classrooms only one wide and six in one line. The question posed by the administrator was to use the present columns and footings as existing and extend the columns to support a new floor above the existing roof, then add a new roof, walls and outrigger walkway with a stairway at the end of the building.

Gene dug the soil away from several column footings so that he could examine the soil type and the size of the footings. From experience he was able to assign a safe soil bearing capacity. Then he measured the column size and calculated the allowable load that the column could support. He could report that the existing structural framing would safely support an additional floor and roof for classrooms. He prepared a preliminary drawing for the architect who included it on his architectural drawings. Later, electrical and mechanical drawings were added at the EMI headquarters in Colorado Springs. Gene never heard if construction was started. He doubted anything had been done because of the condition of the country.

THE FUTURE

In 1941 Gene was awarded the degree of B.S. in Civil Engineering with a major field of study in Structural Engineering from the Newark College of Engineering (now known as the New Jersey Institute of Technology). That means that Gene has been active in this professional field for almost 65 years. He loved his work and received a thrill of excitement and anticipation whenever he approached another project. He was never too weary of the energy expended. Some nights when all his neighbors were fast asleep, the lights were still burning brightly in Gene's den, perhaps to well after midnight. He no longer requires a fee. All work now is as a volunteer and practically all projects are in Third World countries. At the age of 85, Gene looks forward to using his expertise in the

An Indian Farmer

year 2006 for missionary work. Both MTT and EMI have contacted him for the future.

* * *

In order to finalize the answer to the question, "What is truth?" Gene refers to the Expository Dictionary of New Testament Words by W. E.

Vine. Three words are examined: TRUE, TRULY, AND TRUTH as they are used in the text of the Bible.

A. Adjective.

ALETHINOS which denotes true in the sense of real, ideal, and genuine: it is used (a) of God, John 17:3, "And this is eternal life, that they may know You, the only true God, and Jesus Christ whom You have sent," which declares that God fulfills the meaning of His name, He is "very God" in distinction from all other gods, fake gods. (b) of Christ, John 1:9: "That was the true Light which lighteth every man that cometh into the world." (c) God's words, Revelation 21:5b, "...And he said unto me, Write: for these words are true and faithful." (d) His ways, Rev. 15:3b, "...Great and marvellous are thy works, Lord God Almighty; just and true are thy ways, thou King of saints." (e) His judgments, Rev. 16:7b, "...Even so, Lord God Almighty, true and righteous are thy judgments." (f) His riches, Luke 16:11, "If therefore ye have not been faithful in the unrighteous mammon, who will commit to your trust the truc riches?" (g) His worshippers, John 4:23, "But the hour cometh, and now is, when the true worshippers shall worship the Father in spirit and in truth: for the Father seeketh such to worship Him."

B. Verb.

ALETHEUO signifying to deal faithful or truly with anyone, Ephesians 4:15, "But speaking the truth in love, may grow up into Him in all things, which is the head, even Christ."

C. Noun.

ALETHEIA, truth is used (a) objectively, signifying "the reality lying at the basis of an appearance; the manifested veritable essence of a matter," II Corinthians 11:10, "As the truth of Christ is in me, no man shall stop me of this boasting in the regions of Achaia"; the meaning not merely ethical truth, but truth in all of its fullness and scope, as embodied in Him; He was the perfect expression of the truth; (b) subjectively, truthfulness, truth, not merely verbal, but sincerity and integrity of character, III John 3, "For I rejoiced greatly, when the brethren came and testified of the truth that is in thee, even as thou walkest in the truth."

D. Adverb.

1. ALETHOS, truly, surely, as rendered "of a truth," Matthew 14:33, "Then they that were in the ship came and worshipped Him, saying, Of a truth, thou art the Son of God."

2. GNESIOS, sincerely, honorably is rendered "truly," "genuinely," and "naturally," Philippians 2:20, "For I [Paul] have no man like-minded, who will naturally care for your state."

Surely Gene could have answered the plaintive cry of Pilate, "What is truth?" The words of Paul the Apostle as quoted above from the Bible, "As the truth of Christ is in me, no man shall stop me of boasting in Christ...." Not merely ethical truth but truth in all of its fullness and scope, as embodied in Him. He was the perfect expression of the truth.

* * *

V. PART FIVE

Reflections of a Christian Engineer

1. Luke Huber.

A young man graduated from a Bible school in Indiana. He felt that God was calling him to become a missionary to Brazil so he, and his wife with their baby son, went to Sao Paulo, a major city of Brazil. After a year of learning the Portuguese language, he bought an old truck, packed it with all their belongings, and made the tortuous journey to Santarem, a city of 300,000 persons, on the Amazon River about 500 miles west of the Atlantic Ocean. He did not belong to any denomination or missionary organization so they were alone without a place to live. They used the truck for a home until Luke could build a shed with several rooms. Then they lived in the shed while Luke built a home for a residence and a place to conduct religious meetings. While the work of evangelization proceeded, he built two more homes for anticipated missionary helpers, and then a large guest house.

His vision was to evangelize the entire 2,400 miles of the Amazon River. The means of transportation had to be by boat. To build boats he needed a large machine shop where he could fabricate 30-foot boats from sheet steel. So he built the shop and then used it where he cut the sheet of steel to the proper size, bent the sheets to the design that he required, and then welded the pieces to form the hull of a boat. He and several helpers constructed two large storage buildings for administrative people and to gather supplies to take in the boats--literature, clothing, medicine, etc. He built a church for 500 members and then a school for children's education and a school for adult education. In 20 years the church was enlarged four times to seat the 2,500 members and seekers. The fleet of boats numbered ten for evangelization and two for medical work. One thousand churches had been founded in remote river villages and each church had begun at least one sister church at the next village farther away from the river. All the village people accepting Christ were given a basic education and enlisted in the work of spreading the gospel in the Amazon River Basin or even in other parts of Brazil. Luke's vision was to send these Amazonians around the world! And he wished to build a church seating 8,500 persons in each of eight central cities.

Luke labored without pausing, either constructing buildings, boats, or preaching the Word. Whenever possible he went in a boat to found a village church. But he chafed at the slow speed of the boats. Finally, he decided to use airplane transportation. He purchased the plans for building a "light weight" airplane. In a short time the plane was ready for use. Luke was exuberant when he was able to visit many more village churches or perspective sites. But God had other plans for Luke. After several years of increased activity, at the age of 47, Luke was called home to be with the Lord. While flying over the Amazon River, he ran into a vicious wind and rain storm. The plane was sent tumbling into the river and Luke was drowned.

Luke was a real hero of the faith.

2. The expert.

Gene once heard the definition of the difference between an "expert" and a "general practitioner." It was said in a joking way about an engineer but it could refer to an attorney as well. An expert is a person who knows more and more about less and less, until he knows everything about nothing. A general practitioner knows less and less about more and more until he knows nothing about everything. Seriously, Gene had often observed that an expert engineer or attorney had desperately tried to convince the jury that his testimony was the one to accept even though he knew that he was perverting the truth to make a point. It was really ludicrous when an engineer or attorney made a forceful statement and then had the opposition "expert" say exactly the opposite.

In some cases, it may not be an outright lie but a careful manipulation of the truth. An example of this procedure happened to Gene during a court case. He was explaining to the jury how the weather analyst predicts the wind velocity and pressure. The attorney for the opposition repeatedly asked for more information about minute details. The jury gave a decision in favor of the opposition. The opposition attorney spoke to Gene after the trial and laughingly said that he knew that Gene was right and should have won the case, but that he also knew that this jury of lower-than-average mentality would soon get tired of Gene's detailed explanations and in exasperation render a verdict for the opposition.

3. "Simplicity" and "Honesty."

Life is full of decisions to be made. Often a structural engineer finds that a project has many variables; facets that may or may not affect the final solution in a tangible way. Gene had adopted the procedure of carefully examining all aspects of the project, then eliminating all of the extraneous factors so that the problem can be analyzed objectively. Then expressing or involving the use of facts without distortion by personal feelings or prejudices. To simplify was to reduce to base essentials, to diminish in scope or complexity, to streamline, to make more intelligible, and to clarify. Directness of expression and freedom from pretense or guile is essential.

This simplified gathering of facts must now be treated with honesty; adherence to the facts; fairness and straightforwardness of conduct; sincerity and integrity. To sum up the engineer's attitude, he must be a person with uprightness of character and action.

As an expert in structural design and in construction of buildings for the American Arbitration Association, Gene was asked to arbitrate a controversy between the owner of a large super-market, the building contractor, the supplier of the roof joists, and the consulting structural engineer. He met with these men and gathered some statements from the participants:

a. The roof columns were spaced at 60 feet by 60 feet with the open-web steel roof joists spaced at 5 feet on centers.

b. The joists supported metal roof deck, insulation board, and 3-ply roofing material.

c. The roof joists in the three central bays had collapsed.

d. The owner accused the contractor of using faulty materials.

e. The contractor accused the supplier of providing faulty joists.

f. The supplier accused the consulting engineer of choosing the wrong type of joists.

g. The owner said that it had snowed off and on for four days and had accumulated to the depth of two feet.

h. The contractor said that it had accumulated to a depth of four feet.

i. The consulting engineer said that four feet of snow weighed about 30 pounds per square foot and that did not exceed the City of Pittsburgh code as it only required a live load (snow) of 30 pounds per square foot for roof design.

j. The owner insisted that he had measured the two feet himself when he noticed that the joists were deflecting excessively--about 4 inches at the center of the span.

k. Gene checked his copy of the City of Pittsburgh Building Code.

l. Gene checked his copy of the supplier's joists tables.

m. Gene checked with the Weather Bureau about the actual accumulation of snow.

In a short period of time, Gene announced his opinions:

The snow had fallen for a day and night and measured 2.5 feet. The owner had measured the depth of the snow at that time. During the next day the sun shone brightly and melted at least one foot or more of snow. This water trickled down through the snow and froze into two inches or more of ice as soon as it reached the roofing. That night it snowed again until it reached 4.2 feet. And again during the day the sun melted another foot of snow. The weight of snow and ice was now about 55 to 60 pounds per square foot. Quite a bit higher than 30 pounds per foot!

The examination of the Pittsburgh Building Code showed that the consulting engineer had used the required loads and the logical materials, so he was not at fault.

The examination of the supplier's joists table showed that the joists were adequate for the code requirements.

The examination of the building had shown that the contractor had erected the materials properly.

It was the responsibility of the owner to clean the roof of snow (and ice) when he examined the roof during the snowfalls.

4. Miracles.

A miracle is an extraordinary event manifesting divine intervention in human affairs. Viewed as mere wonderful events for man's astonishment, miracles are highly improbable occurrences, but considered as signs of moral and religious revelation, and witnesses of evidences of the commission of Christians to instruct and inform mankind. They are no longer improbable, but are signs of the presence of God in action. The miracles of Jesus were a necessary part of his mission and formed an integral part of his teaching, and were therefor more than mere signs or specimens of the presence of God, and more than mere proofs of a divine commission. The mission of Christ was to teach and redeem mankind; to tell them what to believe and how to be saved, and to be himself the author of their salvation. Christ was God in the flesh, and Christianity is God in action, made known, or communicated to man. A miracle for the Christian must be a vehicle to teach or instruct others in some facet of Christianity that will be a help for them in reaching out to more people.

An example of a miracle by Jesus is found in John 5:1-15. A great multitude of sick people lay at the pool of Bethesda waiting for a miracle of healing. Jesus spoke to a man who had been sick for 38 years. Jesus said to him, "Rise, take up your bed and walk." Immediately the man was made well, took up his bed and walked. He did not know who had healed him for Jesus had withdrawn because of the multitude. Jesus had healed him physically but it was necessary for the healed man to be well spiritually. So afterwards Jesus found him in the temple and said to him, "See, you have been made well. Sin no more lest a worse thing come upon you." The man departed and told the Jews that it was Jesus who had made him well. This man was healed physically and spiritually and then he witnessed to others about the miracles by Jesus.

In the next chapter in John 6:1-14, there is recorded another miracle by Jesus. Jesus went up on a mountain and sat with his disciples. A great multitude came to Jesus. At dinner time, Jesus tested Philip by asking him, "Where shall we buy bread, that these may eat?" Philip could only offer a practically useless answer. But Andrew mentioned that there was a lad with a lunch of five barley loaves and two small fishes. And then showed his lack of faith in Jesus by saying, "but what is that among so many?" Immediately Jesus performed a miracle by feeding the five thousand men (and probably five thousand women and five thousand children). When the people were filled, Jesus said to his disciples, "Gather up the fragments that remain, so that nothing is lost." The disciples filled twelve baskets with the fragments of the five barley loaves which were left over by those who had eaten. That was the physical miracle performed by Jesus. But it was used by Jesus to teach the people a spiritual lesson. In verse 14 it says, "Then those men, when they had seen the miracle [sign] that Jesus did, said, This is of a truth that prophet that should come into the world." In other words, Jesus is the Son of God, the Messiah, the Saviour who will redeem the lost.

The miracles of the ages since the Christian Church was established are different from those recorded in the Scriptures. Even today we hear of miracles reported by contemporary Christians. Gene tells of an incident that he feels was a certain miracle. He had left Fort Myers at midnight in order to reach the airport at West Palm Beach at six o'clock in the morning. He had a reservation on an airplane operated by a Christian airline and used as a convenience for the missionaries in Haiti. A few minutes after reaching Highway 80 he encountered a very heavy wind and rainfall. It caused him to slow the car practically to a crawl. After traveling for three hours he had covered only 60 miles--about the midpoint of his trip. But here at Lake Okochobee he lost his way and began traveling south on Highway 27 toward Miami. After 10 miles he realized he was lost so he turned around and retraced his journey to Highway 80. In the darkness and rain, he began traveling west back to Fort Myers.

About one mile west, he was relieved to see a lighted service station. He quickly entered the station and drove up to the building. To his amazement, the station was locked and without any attendants. Suddenly, he noticed a young woman standing in the pouring rain. She indicated that she would like a ride. Gene indicated that he would not pick her up. Instead he drove about 50 feet to a light over a gasoline pump and began to study his map. Then came a tap on his window, and there she was! He opened the window partially and asked her to explain why she was standing in a rainstorm about three o'clock in the morning. She replied, "I lost my bicycle and please give me a ride home!" Gene was exasperated. He told her that it was imperative that he get to West Palm Beach in less than two hours. He absolutely could not afford to miss the plane. People were relying on him to be there. She smiled and said, "Please, I need to get home!" Gene relented and allowed her to get in the car. Off they went, one mile east, two miles south. It was raining heavily and absolutely pitch black in a wooded area. He slowed and asked her to tell him when to stop. "Oh, just three miles farther at the end of the road." Sure enough after three miles, he slowed the car. And she said, "Turn left and go one mile." At that point she asked for his map and his pen. She carefully pointed out, one mile farther, five miles left, and you will be back at Lake Okochobee. Then pass nine traffic lights and turn right on Highway 455, that will take you to the airline at the airport. She smiled, said thank you, and walked off in the rain and total darkness into the woods.

Gene followed her instructions and found her to be absolutely correct. He arrived at the Christian airline about 15 minutes before 6 A.M. He is convinced that God had sent an angel to guide him when he was lost, and it was a miracle to allow him to complete the missionary project in Cap-Haitien, Haiti.

5. Christian Witnessing.

Gene has had experience in how to reach the lost for Christ. But often he has felt that he has failed to make a positive impact for Christ. One day he read a small pamphlet, "How Can I Break the Silence?" by Herb Vander Lugt of RBC Ministries which helped him to be more effective in evangelism. He stressed knowing the basics. If you want to have the joy of leading a person to faith in Christ, you need to know a few basic truths--and you need to know them well. These truths can be stated in different ways, but they boil down to the following four points:

(1) Every person is by nature a sinner who stands guilty and condemned before God.

(2) Every person is helpless to save himself by his own effort.

(3) In love, God provided salvation for sinners through Jesus Christ, who became a member of the human family, lived sinlessly, and then died on the cross to pay for our sins.

(4) Salvation is an individual matter and requires a personal response on the part of anyone who wants to be saved. Because God accepted Jesus' sacrifice by raising Him from death, all who acknowledge their sin and place their trust in Christ are adopted as God's children.

Then Herb Vander Lugt went on to give four ways to explain the gospel:

(1) The ABC's of Salvation.

a. Admit that you are a sinner, "All have sinned and fall short of the glory of God" (Romans 3:23).

b. Believe on Christ, "Believe on the Lord Jesus Christ, and you will be saved" (Acts 16:31).

c. Confess your faith, "If you confess with your mouth the Lord Jesus and believe in your heart that God has raised Him from the dead, you will be saved. For with the heart one believes to righteousness, and with the mouth confession is made to salvation" (Romans 10:9, 10).

(2) The Roman Road.

a. Romans 3:23: "All have sinned and fall short of the glory of God." MAN'S NEED.

b. Romans 6:23: "The wages of sin is death; but the gift of God is eternal life through Christ Jesus our Lord." SIN'S PENALTY.

c. Romans 5:8: "God demonstrates His own love toward us, in that while we were still sinners, Christ died for us." GOD'S PROVISION.

d. Romans 10:9, 10: "If you confess with your mouth the Lord Jesus and believe in your heart that God has raised Him from the dead you shall be saved. For with the heart one believes to righteousness, and with the mouth confession is made to salvation." MAN'S RESPONSE.

3. Four Things That God Wants You to Know.

a. Your need as God sees it. (Isaiah 64:6, Jeremiah 17:9, John 3:3, Romans 3:10, Romans 11:23)

b. Your own helplessness. (Proverbs 14:12, John 14:6, Acts 4:12, Galatians 2:16, James 2:10)

c. God's provision for your need. (Isaiah 53:6, John 3:16, 2 Corinthians 5:21, 1 Peter 3:18).

d. God's promise to meet your need. (John 10:28, Philippians 1:6, Hebrews 7:25, Jude 24)

Therefore, change your attitude toward sin (Acts 3:19). Put your trust in Jesus Christ (Acts 16:31). Make your decision today (Romans 10:9, 10).

4. <u>The Bridge to Eternal Life</u>.

Because all of us have sinned (Romans 3:23), we are not only destined to die physically (Romans 6:23), but we are presently in a state of spiritual death or separation from God (Ephesians 2:1-4).

When Jesus died on the cross, He took our condemnation and paid the price for our sins (Romans 4:25, 1 Corinthians 15:3). By suffering and dying as our substitute, Jesus provided a righteousness that God can credit to our account (2 Corinthians 5:21) and made reconciliation possible between sinners and a Holy God (1 John 2:1,2).

How did Gene break the spiritual sound barrier with a non-Christian? Consider the case of the architects and draftsman that he visited periodically as clients, or they visited him. When time permitted, he spent time talking about common interests. He built relationships. He showed that he was a real person with many interests, not only an excellent structural engineering foundation. But sooner or later he began asking questions that related to things that they had been talking about. The answers he got often led to an opportunity to share the gospel. Examples were subjects like moral issues, bad circumstances, or family problems.

Formal preaching is still an important way to communicate the gospel. The problem, though, is that relatively few unsaved people will go to church, attend evangelistic mass meetings, or change the channel on the TV to listen to a preacher. We must be more effective in using small gatherings in the homes. And we must get back to talking about Jesus wherever we are.

6. Excel.

To excel is to be superior to; to surpass in accomplishment or achievement. Gene often spoke to the young men at the Detention Center from the Book of Proverbs: "To know wisdom and instruction; to perceive the words of understanding. To receive the instruction of wisdom, justice, judgment, and equity. To give subtlety to the simple, to the young man knowledge and discretion. A wise man will hear and will increase learning and a man of understanding shall attain unto wise counsels." He felt that knowledge was the accumulation of facts and teaching, but wisdom was the application of knowledge. God has given everyone a special gift to use to help others. We must develop it with all our strength.

In 1 Corinthians 12:27, 28: "Now we are the body of Christ, and members in particular. And God hath set some in the church, first apostles, secondarily prophets, thirdly teachers, after that miracles, then gifts of healing, helps, governments, and diversities of tongues." These are spiritual gifts to be desired although Paul goes on to say that there is a more excellent way. All gifts, however good as they are, are nothing without charity (love).

During his entire professional life of 65 years, Gene always studied, listened, and learned more about his field of structural engineering but he never allowed the things that did not count for eternity to be the most important in his life. Fame and fortune would soon fade away but what we did for Christ would last.

In some cases God surprises us by bringing out at the appropriate time latent talents that we never realized that we had. For instance, Gene grew up during the Depression in the poorest areas of the city--and with the least desirable of boyhood companions. After he accepted Christ as his Saviour, his area of service for the Lord was with adults. Then he retired and he went to a new place to live. He was led to Prison Fellowship to volunteer for prison work. To his surprise, he was soon engrossed in reaching boys and young men for Christ. He seemed to excel in this work. Then he realized that God had prepared him for this work during his youth. Now he could understand from experience how these undisciplined young men actually felt.

7. A Sacrificial Life.

Many years ago William Borden graduated from Yale University. He completed his theological seminary education and, to the surprise of his family, he applied for a missionary appointment. Because of the immense wealth of his parents, it was assumed that he would receive an attractive position in a denominational office. Instead he felt that he had been called to Northwest Africa. At this time the area was known as the "White Man's Grave"; in fact, some missionary appointees took a coffin with them to prepare for an early death. William Borden went to Africa and served God for three years before he passed away.

To make a sacrifice is to give up, to renounce for an ideal, belief, or end. The act of offering to deity something precious. In the case of William Borden, it was his life. In some cases we would rarely hear of the life sacrificed for God. In New York City a single woman lived in the basement apartment of a dilapidated tenement house, in the middle of abject poverty. A person once asked her why she continued to live there year after year. She replied that the people around her recognize her as a true Christian, living where they live, and witnessing for Christ. Many gave their hearts to Christ because she was there when needed.

Mr. LeTourneau invented and built huge earth-moving machines. He grew immensely wealthy and founded a Christian university in Texas. He would speak at groups of men who invited their non-Christian friends and he would give an outspoken testimony for salvation in Christ. Sometimes he would travel several thousand miles for a speaking engagement, in his own plane which was equipped with a drafting table and drawing instruments, etc. He was challenged because of his wealth. His answer was that he gave over 90 per cent of his income to the Lord's work. He and his wife lived in a modest home at LeTourneau University and were known as Mom and Pop to the students.

Gene and Betty have lived a sacrificial life for Christ. All of their time and money belongs to the Lord. A pastor once said that he did not want to "wear out" or "rust out" for the Lord. Instead he wanted to achieve a happy medium. Gene feels very strongly that he wants to "wear out" for Christ!

* * *

Until we meet again, may the wind be at your back, and God hold you in the hollow of His hand.

COPYRIGHT NOTES

1. The four maps (pages 67, 70, 80, and 81) were used with the permission of Hammond World Atlas Corporation, Union, New Jersey 07083.

2. The picture of Fallingwater (page 158) appears in the book, Three Centuries of Notable American Architects, edited by Joseph J. Thorndike, Jr., and published by American Heritage Publishing Co., Inc., New York (1981). Permission to use this picture was sought by the author, Eugene Victor Dotter, but not obtained. His research showed that the publisher is no longer in business and the editor is deceased.

3. The picture of St. Andrew's Church, Park Ridge, Illinois (pages 175 and 189) appears in the book, Religious Buildings for Today, edited by John Knox Shear and published by F. W. Dodge Corporation (1957). Permission to use these pictures was sought by the author, Eugene Victor Dotter, but not obtained. His research showed that the publisher is no longer in business and the editor is deceased.

4. All other pictures in this book, My Son - The Engineer, are the personal property of the author, Eugene Victor Dotter. They are included in the copyright and must not be reproduced without the written permission of the publisher, Author House, Bloomington, Indiana 47403.

* * *

A grateful expression of thankfulness to Jewel Hall, former missionary to Thailand and first secretary to the Foreign Secretary of The Christian and Missionary Alliance, New York, for her careful typing of this manuscript and for her many appropriate suggestions.

ABOUT THE AUTHOR

Eugene V. Dotter attended three prestigious universities: New Jersey Institute of Technology, Massachusetts Institute of Technology, and the University of Pittsburgh. He majored in Civil Engineering with emphasis on Structural Engineering and is the recipient of four academic degrees.

He has spent 65 years in the practice of engineering. The more than four thousand projects have been in the United States of America as well as 25 other countries of the world. Often these projects required a written report analyzing the design and construction of the buildings. These buildings have ranged from one-story residences to seventy-story skyscrapers.

His experiences in writing these reports have developed a succinct style which adds interest to the particular narrative. The many examples of buildings have been described in down-to-earth terms that can be understood by readers who are not experienced in engineering.

But Eugene Dotter is a born-again Christian who always testifies to the presence of his Saviour, the Lord Jesus Christ. The gospel, the good news of Jesus Christ, appears in his writing as well as his everyday life.

* * *

Printed in the United States
116371LV00003B/118-141/A

9 781425 941093